THE SOURCEBOOK
OF ARCHITECTURAL
& INTERIOR ART 19

THE SOURCEBOOK
OF ARCHITECTURAL
& INTERIOR ART 19

GUILD Sourcebooks
Madison, Wisconsin
USA

THE SOURCEBOOK OF ARCHITECTURAL & INTERIOR ART 19

GUILD Sourcebooks
An imprint of GUILD, LLC
931 East Main Street
Madison, Wisconsin 53703-2955
TEL 608-257-2590 • TEL 877-284-8453

ADMINISTRATION
Toni Sikes, CEO and Founder
Michael Baum, President
Carla Dillman, Director of Sourcebooks
Marcia Kraus, Director of Trade Relations

DESIGN, PRODUCTION AND EDITORIAL
Georgene Pomplun, Art Director
Sue Englund, Project Designer / Production Artist
Jill Schaefer, Director of Editorial and Production, Writer
Rachel Rasmussen, Writer
Kristine Buie, Administrative Assistant / Copy Editor
Melita Schuessler, Proofreader
Mary Jo Abell, Image Specialist

ARTIST CONSULTANTS
Nicole Carroll • Amy Lambright
Laura Marth • Paul Murphy

Copyright ©2004 GUILD, LLC
ISBN (hardcover) 1-880140-55-1 • ISBN (softcover) 1-880140-54-3

Printed in China

COVER ART: Hank Kaminsky, *World Peace Prayer Fountain* (detail), see page 87.
PAGE 1: Hank Kaminsky, *World Peace Prayer Fountain*. Photographs: Jim Bailey.
PAGE 5: Dillon Forge, French rail, see page 60. Photograph: Max Birnkammer.
FACING PAGE: Susan Venable, *Mysterioso*, see page 211.

■

GUILD.com is the Internet's leading retailer of original art and fine craft.
Visit www.guild.com.

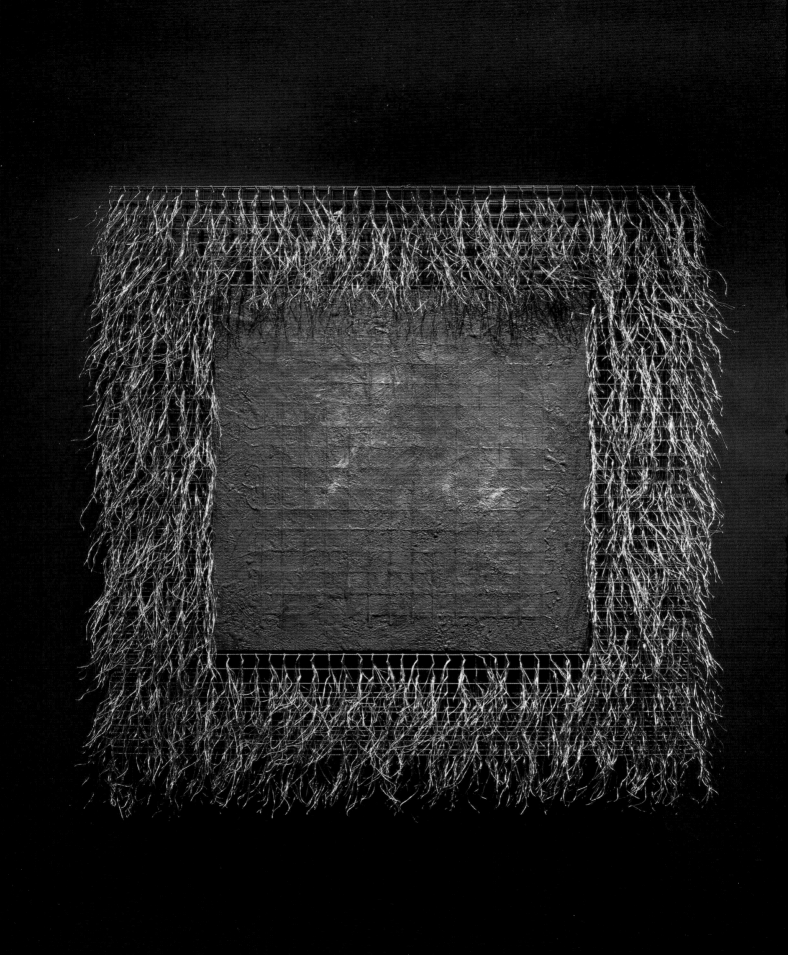

NOTHING LESS

As THE GUILD closes its second decade of playing matchmaker to artists and those who work with them, we dedicate this 19th edition of our sourcebook to the people who help us accomplish our mission. Even with the difficult economic climate of the past few years, determined trade professionals have continued to include commissioned art in their projects and budgets.

We know who you are, and you are our heroes.

Here at THE GUILD, we work very hard to put this bounty of artistic talent and other related resources under one cover. But our efforts would be for naught if it weren't for you. Our mission is only accomplished when someone calls an artist for more information, or takes this book along to a client meeting, or even sits with it, flipping through the pages and dreaming of all the possibilities.

Interspersed throughout these pages are stories of trade professionals and artists who worked together to transform spaces with original artwork, with marvelous results.

We salute the people who play such an important role in bringing commissioned art into the places where we live and work. You show us, time and again, that it is possible to make buildings and community spaces worthy of the public's interest and delight.

And, I think, nothing less will do.

Toni Sikes
Publisher

9

Opposite: Yoshi Hayashi, *Mountain Moon*, see page 177.

TABLE OF CONTENTS

TABLE OF CONTENTS

The Sourcebook of Architectural & Interior Art shows artwork of enduring value; we think you'll refer to it for years to come.
If, at any time, you're unable to reach an artist through contact information included in this book, call THE GUILD at 1-877-284-8453.
We keep track of updated phone numbers and the like, and are glad to share our most current information.

Using the Sourcebook

The GUILD Sourcebook is designed specifically for individuals and trade professionals seeking artists to create large- or small-scale commissioned artwork. In addition to each artist's display of images, listings in the back of the book describe the artist's range of work, commissions and recent projects. These listings are organized in alphabetical order by the heading on each artist's page. They contain all the information necessary to contact the artist about your project, thus making the sourcebook a unique direct-call resource.

PRODUCT SEARCH

If you already know what type of work your project calls for, a search by section will help you find results quickly. Artists in the sourcebook are arranged in sections covering work as varied as large-scale glass in the Architectural Glass section to art quilts and tapestries in Art for the Wall: Fiber. Check the Table of Contents for a list of sections.

When paging through a particular section, keep in mind that the photos presented on each of the artists' pages are representative of the work that they do, not the full extent of their capabilities. If you like an artist's style but are interested in having him or her take on a different type of project than the ones pictured, contact the artist and see if it's a good fit. Likewise, you can broaden your searches to several different sections to find an even wider variety of choices. If you are searching for freestanding sculpture, for example, you might want to look through not only the Representational Sculpture and Non-Representational Sculpture sections, but the Public Art section as well.

ARTIST SEARCH

If you know the name of the artist you want to work with, you can easily search using the Artist Statements section or the Index of Artists & Companies, both found in the gray pages at the back of the sourcebook. The Artist Statements section provides a wealth of detail about each artist, including the materials and techniques they use, examples of their commissions and collections, and publications that feature photographs of their artwork (including previous GUILD sourcebooks). Both the Artist Statements section and the Index of Artists & Companies include page references so you can easily locate the artist's full-color page in the book.

Want to know more about an artist's work? Don't hesitate to call the artist directly for more information.

LOCATION SEARCH

Looking for an artist in your area or another specific region? Turn to the Location Index. Located in the back of the book, this index can help you find artists from across the United States, Canada and abroad.

INSPIRATIONAL BROWSING

Even if you don't have a specific project in mind, the Sourcebook will prove an invaluable tool. It can be taken to client meetings to show a world of possibilities, browsed through for future inspiration and used to see the newest projects of artists you've collaborated with in the past.

Opposite: Ellen Mandelbaum, *Ark Doors*, see page 22. Photograph: Kenneth Wyner.

The Commission Process

The nearly 180 artists featured in *The Sourcebook of Architectural & Interior Art 19* represent a remarkable spectrum of artistic talent and vision. Whether you're looking for a large-scale public sculpture or a residential accessory, this book can put you directly in touch with highly qualified artists throughout North America. Any one of these artists can be commissioned to create a unique work of art—but with so many exceptional artists to choose from, finding the right one for your specific project can be a challenge. Once the artist has been selected, careful planning and communication can help ensure a great outcome.

Having watched art commissions unfold since the first GUILD sourcebook was published in 1986, we can suggest steps to ensure successful partnerships between artists and trade professionals. We especially want to reassure those who have been reluctant to try such a collaboration because of questions about how the process works.

This article is a how-to guide to the art commissioning process. It suggests strategies to help selection and hiring go smoothly. It also describes steps that can help set common (and realistic) expectations on the part of artists and clients, and explains advantages of including the artist in the design team early in the planning process.

FINDING THE ARTIST

By far the most important step in a successful commission is choosing the right artist for your particular project and budget. This choice is the decision from which all others will flow, so it's worth investing time and energy in the selection process and seasoning the search with both wild artistic hopes and hard-nosed realism. The right choices at this early stage will make things go more smoothly later on.

Some clients will want to help select and work with the artist. Others will want only minimal involvement, leaving most of the decision-making to the design team. No matter who makes the decisions, there are several ways to find the right artist. Obviously, we recommend browsing through *The Sourcebook of Architectural & Interior Art 19*. Every artist featured on these pages is actively seeking commission projects; that's why they're included in the book. Many of these artists have already established strong track records working with designers, architects and art consultants; you will gain from their professionalism and experience. Others are newer in their field; their determination to prove themselves can fuel an exciting and successful collaboration.

Above: Warren Carther, *Sea of Time*, see page 40. Photograph: Gerry Kopelow.

NARROWING THE FIELD

Once your "A-list" is narrowed down to two or three names, it's time to schedule meetings, either face-to-face or by phone. As you talk, try to determine the artist's interest in your project, and pay attention to your own comfort level with the artist. Try to find out if the chemistry is right—whether you have the basis to build a working relationship. This is also the time to confirm that the artist has the necessary skills to undertake your project. Be thorough and specific when asking questions. Is the artist excited about the project? What does he or she see as the most important issues or considerations? Will your needs be a major or minor concern? Evaluate the artist's style, approach and personality.

If it feels like you might have trouble working together, take heed. But if all goes well and it feels like a good fit, ask for a list of references. These are important calls; don't neglect to make them! Ask about the artist's work habits, communication style and, of course, the success of the artwork. You should also ask whether the project was delivered on time and within budget. If you like what you hear, you'll be one important step closer to hiring your artist.

EXPECT PROFESSIONALISM

If this is an expensive or complicated project, you may want to request preliminary designs. Since most artists charge a design fee whether or not they're ultimately hired for the project, start by asking for sketches from your top candidate. If you're unhappy with the designs submitted, you can go to your second choice. But if the design is what you'd hoped for, it's time to finalize your working agreement with this artist.

As you discuss contract details, be resolved that silence is not golden and ignorance is not bliss! Be frank. Discuss the budget and timetable, and tell the artist what you expect. Now is the time for possible misunderstandings to be brought up and resolved—not later, after the work is half done and deadlines loom.

WORKING WITH AN ART CONSULTANT

As your project gains definition, you'll need to pay attention to its technical aspects, including building codes, lighting specifications, and details related to zoning and installation. Most designers find the artist's knowledge and understanding of materials, code, safety and engineering complete and reassuring. However, complex projects may warrant hiring an art consultant to help with these details, as well as the initial selection of art and artists. Just as you would when hiring any other professional, call references to be sure the consultant you hire is sophisticated and experienced enough to provide real guidance with your project. This means the ability to help negotiate the technical aspects of a very specific contract, including issues like installation, insurance, storage, transportation and engineering costs.

PUTTING IT IN WRITING

It is a truism in any kind of business that it is much cheaper to get the lawyers involved at the beginning of a process rather than after something goes wrong. A signed contract or letter of agreement commits the artist to completing his or her work on time and to specifications. It also assures the artist that he or she will get paid the right amount at the right time.

Contracts should be specific to the job. Customarily, artists are responsible for design, production, shipping and installation. If someone else will install the artwork, be sure you specify who will coordinate and pay for the installation; if not the artist, it's usually the client. With a large project, it's helpful to identify the tasks that, if delayed for any reason, would set back completion of the project. These should be discussed up front to ensure that both parties agree on requirements and expectations.

Most trade professionals recognize that adequate compensation for artists ensures the level of service needed to fulfill the client's expectations. The more complex the project, the more you should budget for the artist's work and services.

PAYMENT SCHEDULE

Payments are usually tied to specific milestones in the process. These serve as checkpoints and assure that work is progressing in a satisfactory manner, on time and on budget. Payment is customarily made in three stages, although this certainly depends on the circumstances, scope and complexity of the project.

The first payment is usually made when the contract is signed. It covers the artist's time and creativity in developing a detailed design specific to your needs. You can expect to go through several rounds of trial and error in the design process, but at the end of this stage you will have detailed drawings (and, for three-dimensional work, a maquette, or model) that everyone agrees upon. The cost of the maquette and the design time are usually factored into the artist's fee.

The second payment is generally set for a point midway through the project and is for work completed to date. If the materials are expensive, the client may be asked to advance money at this stage to cover costs. If the commission is canceled during this period, the artist keeps the money already paid for work performed.

Final payment is usually due when the work is installed. If the piece is finished on time but the building or project is delayed, the artist is customarily paid on delivery, but still has the obligation to oversee installation.

You will find that most artists keep tabs on the project budget. Be sure that the project scope does not deviate from what was agreed upon at the outset. If the scope changes, amend the agreement to reflect the changes.

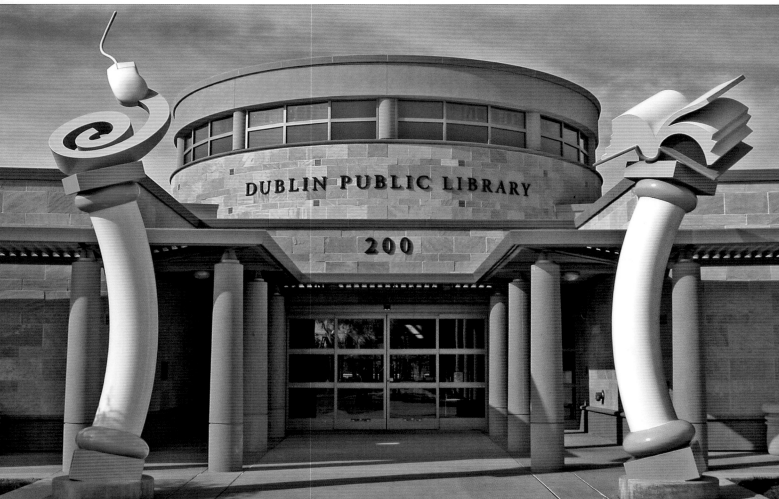

The Artist as Designer

Not every artist charges a design fee; some consider preliminary sketches a part of their marketing effort. But it's more common for an artist to require a design fee of 5% to 10% of the final project budget. In some cases, especially when the artist has a strong reputation in a specialized area, the design fee may be as high as 25% of the project budget; this is most common when an artist is asked for specific solutions to complicated architectural problems.

A few points about design are worth highlighting here:

1. Design Ideas Are the Artist's Property

It should go without saying that it is highly unethical, as well as possibly illegal, to take an artist's designs—even very preliminary or non-site-specific sketches—and use them without the artist's permission. Some artists may include specific language about ownership of ideas, models, sketches, etc., in their contracts or letters of agreement. Even if an artist does not use a written agreement, be sure you are clear at the outset about what you are paying for and what rights the artist retains.

2. Respect the Artist's Ideas and Vision

When you hire a doctor, you want a thoughtful, intelligent diagnosis, not just a course of treatment. The same should be true when you hire an artist to work with a design team. Most GUILD artists have become successful through many years of experience, and because of their excellence in both technique and aesthetic imagination. Take advantage of that expertise by bringing the artist into the project early, and by asking him or her for ideas.

3. Consider a Separate Design Budget for Your Project

A design budget is particularly helpful when you:
- want to get lots of ideas from an artist;
- need site-specific ideas that involve significant research;
- require a formal presentation with finished drawings, blueprints or maquettes.

To evaluate designs for a project from several artists, consider a competition with a small design fee for each artist.

4. Keep the Artist Informed of Changes

Tell the artist about changes—even seemingly minor details —which may have a significant impact on the project design. If the artist is working as a member of the design team, it's easier to include him or her in the ongoing dialog about the overall project.

It comes down to an issue of professionalism. Artists have the technical skills to do wonderful and amazing things with simple materials. But they also have sophisticated conceptual and design talents. By paying for these talents, trade professionals add vision and variety to their creative products. In such a partnership, both parties gain, and the ultimate result is a client who is delighted by the outcome of the collaboration.

17

A COLLABORATIVE ATMOSPHERE

With most commission projects, it's best to bring the artist into the process at about the same time you hire a general contractor. By involving the artist at this early stage, the space will be designed with the art in mind, and the art will be designed to enhance the space. As a result, there will be no unpleasant surprises about size or suitability of artwork. Furthermore, when art is planned for early on and is a line item in the budget, it's far less likely to be cut at the end of the project, when money is running low.

Early inclusion of the artist also helps ensure that the collaborative effort will flow smoothly throughout all phases of the project. If the artist is respected as part of the team, his or her work can benefit the project's overall design.

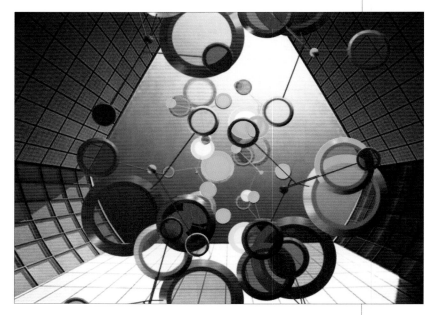

Naturally, the scope of the project will determine the number of players to be involved with the artist. How will decisions be made? Who is the artist's primary liaison? Will a single person sign off on designs and recommendations? Are committees necessary? It's important that all individuals understand both their own responsibilities and the responsibilities of their collaborators.

SEEK TWO-WAY UNDERSTANDING

Be sure the artist understands the technical requirements of the job, including traffic flow, intended use of space, building structure, maintenance, lighting and environmental concerns. By fully explaining these details, you'll ensure that the artist's knowledge, experience and skills inform the project.

Keep the artist apprised of any changes that will affect the work in progress. Did you find a specified material unavailable and replace it with something else? Did the available space become bigger or smaller? These changes could have a profound impact on an artist's planning.

At the same time, the artist should let you know of any special requirements that his or her work will place on the space. Is it especially heavy? Does it need to be mounted in a specific way? Must it be protected from theft or vandalism? What kind of lighting is best? You may need to budget funds for these kinds of installation or maintenance expenses.

Most artists experienced with commissioned projects factor the expense of a continuing design dialog into their fee. There is an unfortunate belief harbored by some trade professionals (and yes, artists too) that a willingness to develop and adapt a design based on discussions with the client or design team somehow indicates a lack of commitment or creativity. On the contrary. The ability to modify design or execution without compromising artistic quality is a mark of professionalism. We recommend looking for this quality in the artist you choose, and then respecting it by treating the artist as a partner in any decisions that will affect his or her work.

Of course, part of working together is making clear who is responsible for what. Since few designers and architects (and even fewer contractors) are used to working with artists, the relationship is ripe for misunderstanding. Without constant communication, things can easily fall through the cracks.

FORGING A PARTNERSHIP

The partnership between artists and trade professionals is an old and honorable one. Many venerable blueprints indicate, for example, an architect's detail for a ceiling with the scrawled note: "Finish ceiling in this manner." The assumption, of course, is that the artisan working on the ceiling has both the technical mastery and the aesthetic skill to create a whole expanse of space based on a detail sketched by the architect's pen.

The artists whose work fills these pages—and with whom we work every day at GUILD—are capable of interactive relationships like those described here. We're delighted to see increasing numbers of trade professionals include artists on their design teams. After seeing the arts separated from architectural and interior design for too many years, we're happy to be part of a renewed interest in collaboration.

COMMISSION GUIDELINES

- Bring the artist into the project as early as possible.

- Be as specific as possible about the scope and range of the project, even in early meetings before the artist is selected.

- Be honest and realistic when discussing deadlines, responsibilities and specific project requirements—and expect the same from the artist. Don't avoid discussing the areas where there seem to be questions.

- For larger projects, use specific milestones to assure continuing consensus on project scope and budget. It may also be necessary to make adjustments at these points.

- Choose an artist based on a solid portfolio of previous work and excellent references. And remember that it's less risky to use an artist who has worked on projects of similar size and scope, who can handle the demands of your specific job.

- Consider hiring an art consultant if the commission is particularly large or complex. The consultant should help with complicated contract arrangements, and should make certain that communication between artists and support staff (including sub-contractors and engineers) is thoroughly understood.

- Trust your instincts when choosing an artist. Like selecting an advertising agency or an architect, choosing an artist is based partly on chemistry. You need to like the work and respect the artist, and you also need to be able to work together comfortably.

Architectural Glass

ELLEN MANDELBAUM GLASS ART

ELLEN MANDELBAUM ▨ 39-49 46TH STREET ▨ LONG ISLAND CITY, NY 11104-1407
TEL/FAX 718-361-8154 ▨ E-MAIL EMGA@IX.NETCOM.COM ▨ WWW.EMGLASSART.COM

22

Left: *Mystic Rose Window*, 2001, Chapel at Marian Woods Convent, Hartsdale, NY, leaded glass and glass painting, 34" x 69". Photograph: Stephen Ostrow.
Top right: *Wind of the Spirit Transom*, 2001, Chapel at Marian Woods Convent, Hartsdale, NY, leaded glass, 6' x 4.75'. Photograph: Stephen Ostrow.
Bottom right: *Martinique*, independent panel, *plein air* painting on glass and leaded antique glass, 18" x 21".

ARTHUR STERN

ARTHUR STERN STUDIOS ▨ 1075 JACKSON STREET ▨ BENICIA, CA 94510
TEL/FAX 707-745-8480 ▨ E-MAIL ARTHUR@ARTHURSTERN.COM ▨ WWW.ARTHURSTERN.COM

Prairie Quilt, (detail), atrium window at St. Catherine Hospital, Garden City, KS, 35'W x 10.5'H, laminated hand-blown and plate glass with beveled glass prisms. Inset: *Prarie Quilt,* (detail).

AANRAKU STAINED GLASS

2323 SOUTH EL CAMINO REAL ▦ SAN MATEO, CA 94403 ▦ TEL 650-372-0527 ▦ FAX 650-372-0566
E-MAIL AANRAKU@ABASG.COM ▦ WWW.BAYAREASTAINEDGLASS.COM

24

Top: Entryway, San Mateo, CA, 15' × 8'.
Bottom left: Bathroom, private residence, Hillsborough, CA, 36" × 38". Bottom right: Entryway, private residence, San Francisco, CA, 48" × 72".

Printed in China © 2004 GUILD LLC: The Sourcebook of Architectural & Interior Art

LARRY ZGODA

LARRY ZGODA STUDIO ▨ 2117 WEST IRVING PARK ROAD ▨ CHICAGO, IL 60618 ▨ TEL 773-463-3970
E-MAIL LZ@LARRYZGODASTUDIO.COM ▨ WWW.LARRYZGODASTUDIO.COM

25

Main entry, Sacred Heart of Jesus Chapel, 2002, Our Lady of Victory Convent, Lemont, IL, stained and leaded glass.
Inset: Main entry, Sacred Heart of Jesus Chapel (detail). Photographs: Richard Bruck.

DAVID WILSON DESIGN

DAVID WILSON ▨ 202 DARBY ROAD ▨ SOUTH NEW BERLIN, NY 13843-2212 ▨ TEL 607-334-3015 ▨ FAX 607-334-7065
E-MAIL MAIL@DAVIDWILSONDESIGN.COM ▨ WWW.DAVIDWILSONDESIGN.COM

26

Glass windows, 1998, Robert C. Byrd U.S. Courthouse, Charleston, WV. Photograph: Richard Walker.

PAUL HOUSBERG

GLASS PROJECT, INC. ▨ 875 NORTH MAIN ROAD ▨ JAMESTOWN, RI 02835
TEL 401-560-0880 ▨ E-MAIL INFO@GLASSPROJECT.COM ▨ WWW.GLASSPROJECT.COM

Fused/cast glass features, 2003, ballroom and pre-function areas, Le Meridien Hotel, Minneapolis, MN.
Interior Design: Yabu Pushelberg, Toronto, ON. Photographs: Dana Wheelock Photography.

ARCHITECTURAL GLASS ART, INC.

KENNETH F. vonROENN, JR. ▨ 815 WEST MARKET STREET ▨ LOUISVILLE, KY 40202
TEL 800-795-9429 ▨ FAX 502-585-2808 ▨ E-MAIL INFO@AGAINC.COM ▨ WWW.AGAINC.COM

28

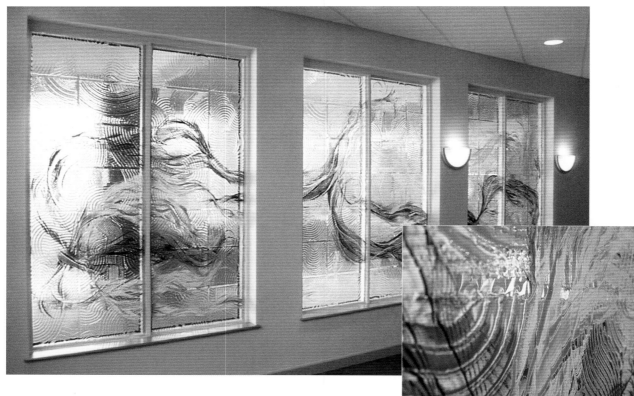

Top left: Kentucky Museum of Arts & Design, Louisville, KY, laminated beveled glass with blown glass elements, 1,200 square feet.
Top right: Kentucky Museum of Arts & Design (detail). Bottom: *Home of the Innocents,* Louisville, KY,
cast glass with frit, 4 windows, 5' x 7'. Inset: *Home of the Innocents* (detail). Photographs: David Harpe.

KERSEY'S GLASS WORKS

STEPHEN KERSEY ■ MARY KERSEY ■ 23960 CLAWITER ROAD ■ HAYWARD, CA 94545
TEL 510-782-7813 ■ FAX 510-782-2062 ■ E-MAIL MKERSEY@KERSEYGLASS.COM ■ WWW.KERSEYGLASS.COM

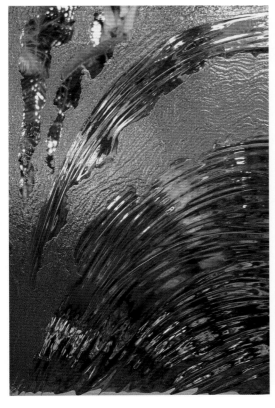

Top: *Quartz*, 1998, corporate office, Concord, CA, carved and glue-chipped glass, 9' × 5'. Bottom left: *Splash*, 1998, Maui, HI, carved, glue-chipped and polished glass, 46" × 70". Photograph: Kay Lloyd. Bottom right: *Ark*, 2003, Temple Isaiah, Lafayette, CA, frosted and fire-polished glass, 8' × 12' × 3'. Design by Peter Stackpole. Background art glass by Mark Adams.

ORKA ARCHITECTURAL ART GLASS

SHARON ROADCAP-QUINLIVAN ▨ LORRI ROADCAP-CLOWER ▨ JEREMY ROADCAP ▨ 1181 JENSEN DRIVE
VIRGINIA BEACH, VA 23451 ▨ TEL 757-428-6752 ▨ FAX 757-428-6750 ▨ E-MAIL LROADCAP@ORKA.COM ▨ WWW.ORKA.COM

Top: *Scales*, 2004, Virginia Beach Visitors Center, Virginia Beach, VA, three .5" clear annealed pattern cut and carved panels.
Inset: *Scales* (detail). Photographs: Keith Lanpher. Bottom: *Tapestry of Life*, 1998, Jean and Mack Henderson Women's Center/Wellstar Kennestone Hospital,
Marietta, GA, custom carved laminated glass, five panels: 7'H x 5'W x 1.5". Inset: *Tapestry of Life* (detail). Photographs: Tom Ewasko.

ORKA ARCHITECTURAL ART GLASS

SHARON ROADCAP-QUINLIVAN ▨ LORRI ROADCAP-CLOWER ▨ JEREMY ROADCAP ▨ 1181 JENSEN DRIVE
VIRGINIA BEACH, VA 23451 ▨ TEL 757-428-6752 ▨ FAX 757-428-6750 ▨ E-MAIL LROADCAP@ORKA.COM ▨ WWW.ORKA.COM

Top: *World Map* (detail). Bottom left: *World Map*, 2001, (formerly Enron Center South), Houston, TX, custom carved laminated glass, 20,000-lb. suspended 16'Dia. cylindrical sculpture, each panel: 18'H x 2'W x 1.5". Bottom right: *World Map* (detail). Photographs: Rob Narracci. Sculpture design by Gregg Jones, Cesar Pelli & Associates, New Haven, CT.

ANDREW CARY YOUNG

PEARL RIVER GLASS STUDIO, INC. ▦ 142 MILLSAPS AVENUE ▦ JACKSON, MS 39202
TEL 601-353-2497 ▦ FAX 601-969-9315 ▦ E-MAIL PRGS@NETDOOR.COM ▦ WWW.PRGS.COM

32

Top: St. Dominic's Hospital, Jackson, MS, slumped art glass, silver leaf and gold leaf. Bottom left: St. Dominic's Hospital (detail).
Bottom right: *Maters*, lead, hand-blown glass and glass paint, 30" x 40".

INDIANA ART GLASS

GREGORY R. THOMPSON ■ 6400 BROOKVILLE ROAD ■ INDIANAPOLIS, IN 46219
TEL 317-353-6369 ■ FAX 317-359-9630 ■ E-MAIL GREG@INDIANAARTGLASS.COM ■ WWW.INDIANAARTGLASS.COM

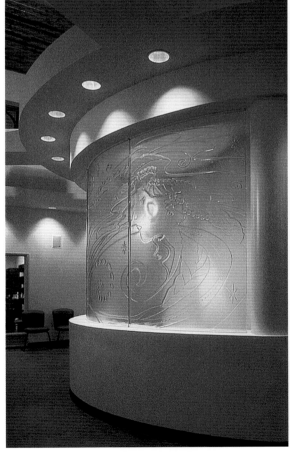

Top: *Firefighter Historical Mural*, 2003, Firefighters Credit Union, Indianapolis, IN, etched glass panel, 97" x 45". Photograph: Steve Richardson Photography.
Bottom left: *Face of Beauty*, 2003, Honors Beauty College, Indianapolis, IN, bent and tempered cast glass, 156" x 72". Photograph: Steve Richardson Photography.
Bottom right: Three-story hanging cast glass water feature, 2003, St. Vincent Hospital, Carmel, IN. Photograph: Wayne Terrebonne.

ART GLASS ENSEMBLES

CHRISTIE A. WOOD ▨ 208 WEST OAK STREET ▨ DENTON, TX 76201
TEL 940-591-3002 ▨ FAX 940-591-7853 ▨ E-MAIL ENSEMBLES@COMPUSERVE.COM

34

Top: *Willow Tree,* 2001, North Wales, PA, stained glass, 9'W × 7'H. Bottom: *Austin Oak,* 2003, Austin, TX, stained glass, 69"W × 60"H.

DEANNE SABECK STUDIOS

DEANNE SABECK ▨ JEFFERY LAUDENSLAGER ▨ 574 ARDEN DRIVE ▨ ENCINITAS, CA 92024 ▨ TEL/FAX 760-943-0988
E-MAIL DEANNE@DEANNESABECK.COM ▨ WWW.DEANNESABECK.COM ▨ WWW.LAUDENSLAGERSCULPTURE.COM

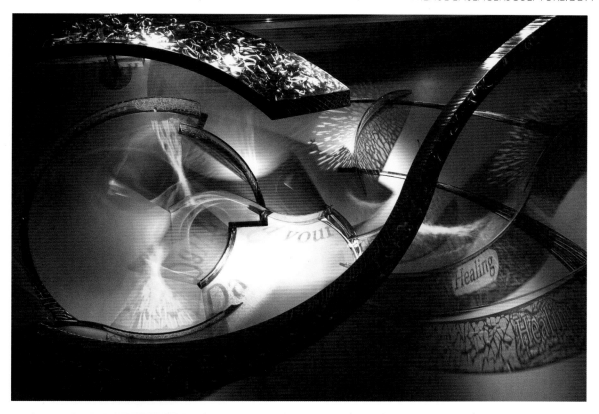

Top: *Light, Dawn, Healing* (detail).
Bottom: *Light, Dawn, Healing,* Florida Hospital Waterman, 2003, glass, light, text and steel, 24'W × 12'H × 2'D.

GAYA GLASS

DAN KING-LEHMAN ◼ EVE KING-LEHMAN ◼ 4742 NORTH STREET ◼ SOMIS, CA 93066
TEL 805-386-4069 ◼ E-MAIL ART@GAYAGLASS.COM ◼ WWW.GAYAGLASS.COM

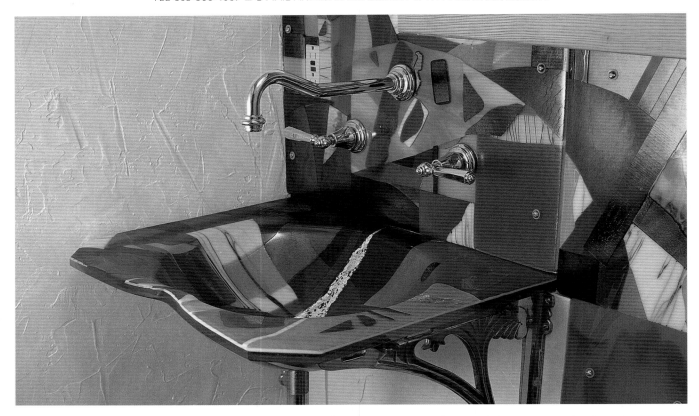

36

Top: *Whimsical*, 2003, abstract glass sink and backsplash. Photograph: Maureen Donaldson.
Bottom: Iridized sink inspired by the surrounding marble, 2003. Photograph: George Post.

BJ KATZ

MELTDOWN GLASS ART & DESIGN ▦ 3225 NORTH WASHINGTON STREET ▦ CHANDLER, AZ 85225
TEL 480-633-3366 ▦ FAX 480-633-3344 ▦ E-MAIL BJKATZ@MELTDOWNGLASS.COM ▦ WWW.MELTDOWNGLASS.COM

Top: *The Big Bang*, 2002, water wall and stage backdrop, cast glass with dichroic, Desert Ridge Marketplace, Phoenix, AZ, 11'H x 15'W.
Bottom left: *The Big Bang* (night photo). Bottom right: *The Big Bang* (detail). Photographs: Daniel Braha.

KATHY BRADFORD

NORTH STAR ART GLASS, INC. ▧ 142 WICHITA ▧ LYONS, CO 80540 ▧ TEL/FAX 303-823-6511
E-MAIL KATHYBRADFORD@WEBTV.NET ▧ WWW.KATHYBRADFORD.COM

Top left: *Blessings of Nature*, 2003, Centura Health Parker Hospital, Parker, CO, sandblast carving glass, 3' × 7' × .4".
Top right: *Children First* (detail), 2003, Oak Park Pavilion, St. Louis Park, MN, sandblast combined with dichroic glass 24" × various lengths. Photograph: Jason Leonardson.
Center right: *Children First* (detail). Photograph: Jason Leonardson. Bottom: *Children First* (detail). Photograph: Jason Leonardson.

STUART REID ARCHITECTURAL GLASS

STUART REID ■ 364 ANNETTE STREET ■ TORONTO, ON M6P 1R5 ■ CANADA
TEL 416-762-7743 ■ FAX 416-762-8875 ■ E-MAIL STUARTREID@SYMPATICO.CA ■ WWW.STUARTREID.NET

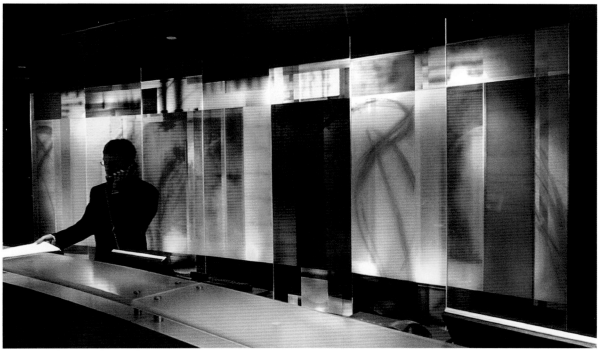

Top: *Liquid Veil*, 2003, Azure bar/restaurant, Intercontinental Toronto Centre, acid-etched antique glass, 9' × 18'.
Bottom: *Urban Ribbon*, hotel reception, Intercontinental Toronto Centre, enamel laminated float glass, 8.5' × 20'. Photographs: M. Hudson.

WARREN CARTHER

CARTHER STUDIO INC. ■ 80 GEORGE AVENUE ■ WINNIPEG, MB R3B 0K1 ■ CANADA
TEL 204-956-1615 ■ FAX 204-942-1434 ■ E-MAIL WARREN@CARTHERSTUDIO.COM ■ WWW.CARTHERSTUDIO.COM

40

Ponce's Crystal Sphere, (detail), 2003, Orange County Convention Center, Orlando, FL, reflective carved glass panels,
mirrored glass with dichroic glass and carved glass laminations, 27' x 15'. Inset: *Ponce's Crystal Sphere*.

GALVIN GLASS WORKS LTD.

ANDREW GALVIN ■ 339 EAST AVENUE SUITE 400 ■ ROCHESTER, NY 14604 ■ TEL 585-325-6910 ■ FAX 585-546-1394
E-MAIL GGWLTD@AOL.COM ■ WWW.GALVINGLASSWORKS.COM

Top: Cast glass bar top and slump cast glass dividing wall, 2002, Pearl Restaurant, Rochester, NY.
Bottom left: Cast glass bar top (detail). Bottom right: Cast glass bar top (detail), 2002, Pearl Restaurant, 24' × 21" × 2". Photographs: Dan Neuberger.

Architectural Ceramics, Mosaics & Wall Reliefs

KAREN HEYL

1310 PENDLETON STREET, ML#2 ■ CINCINNATI, OH 45202
TEL 513-421-9791/760-489-7106 ■ E-MAIL HEYLSTONE2@AOL.COM ■ WWW.KARENHEYL.COM

44

Top: *Blessings*, Questhaven Retreat Center, San Marcos, CA, limestone, 15.3'L × 4'H.
Bottom: *Come to Me and I Will Refresh You*, St. Elizabeth Medical Center, Edgewood, KY, limestone side panels, each: 7'H × 3'W.

ELIZABETH MACDONALD

BOX 186 ■ BRIDGEWATER, CT 06752 ■ TEL 860-354-0594 ■ FAX 860-350-4052
E-MAIL EPMACD@EARTHLINK.COM ■ WWW.ELIZABETHMACDONALD.COM

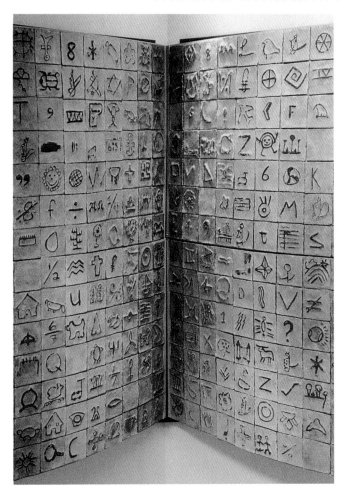

45

Top left: *Book* (detail), 2002, St. Patrick's Episcopal Day School, Washington, DC, ceramic relief, 7' × 16' × 2'. Top right: *Book* (detail). Photographs: Marjory H. Train.
Bottom: *East Rock–Late Spring*, Wilbur Cross High School, New Haven, CT, 6' × 12'. Photograph: Robert Perron.

E. JOSEPH McCARTHY

E. JOSEPH MCCARTHY STUDIO ■ 76 HOPE STREET ■ GREENFIELD, MA 01301
TEL/FAX 413-772-8816 ■ E-MAIL CTS@CROCKER.COM ■ WWW.CROCKER.COM/~CTS/

Top: Savannah Hotel, Barbados, 80 individual tile paintings, 4' x 5' each. Bottom: Savannah Hotel, Barbados (detail). Photographs: Willie Alleyne.

MOTAWI TILEWORKS

NAWAL MOTAWI ■ 170 ENTERPRISE DRIVE ■ ANN ARBOR, MI 48103 ■ TEL 734-213-0017 ■ FAX 734-213-2569
E-MAIL MOTAWI@MOTAWI.COM ■ WWW.MOTAWI.COM

47

Top left: *Boy Reading Mural*, 2001, 5' × 5.5'. Photograph: Steve Kuzma.
Top right: *Ship Mural*, 2002, 34" × 34". Photograph: Steve Kuzma. Bottom: *Pine Landscape Mural*, 18" × 42". Photograph: Jerry Anthony.

HOWDLE STUDIO INC.

BRUCE HOWDLE ■ 225 COMMERCE STREET ■ MINERAL POINT, WI 53565 ■ TEL 608-987-3590
E-MAIL BHOWDLE@CHORUS.NET ■ WWW.BRUCEHOWDLE.COM

Top: *Reaching for New Heights,* 2003, TDS Metrocom Building, Madison, WI, 6' × 15'H. Photograph: Skot Weidemann, Middleton, WI.
Bottom: Brighton police municipal court facility, 2002, Brighton, CO, 9' × 27'. Photograph: Frank Ooms.

MARY LOU ALBERETTI

ALBERETTI STUDIOS ◼ 16 POSSUM DRIVE ◼ NEW FAIRFIELD, CT 06812 ◼ TEL 203-746-1321
E-MAIL MLALB@AOL.COM ◼ WWW.SOUTHERNCT.EDU/~ALBERETT/

Top: *Morena*, 2003, ceramic relief, 15" × 21.5" × 2". Photograph: Bill Quinnell. Bottom left: *Janus*, 2003, ceramic relief, 12.5" × 10" × 2". Photograph: Bill Quinnell.
Bottom right: *CUFIC*, 2003, ceramic relief, 16" × 12" × 1.75".

MERRYWOMAN STUDIOS

CHRISTINE MERRIMAN ■ 7076 US ROUTE 4 ■ PO BOX 153 ■ BRIDGEWATER, VT 05034
TEL 802-672-2230 ■ E-MAIL MERRYWOMAN@VERMONTEL.NET ■ WWW.VERMONTEL.NET/~MERRYWOMAN

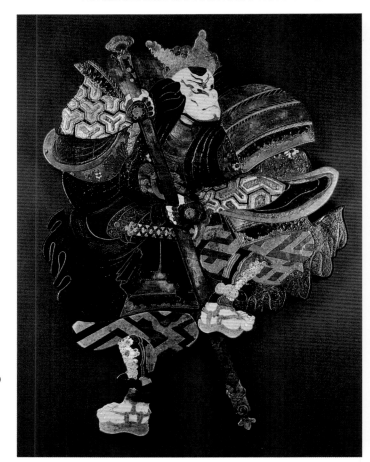

50

Top left: *Raging Samurai*, 2003, raku tile art, 54"H × 48"W × 1.5"–2"D. Top right: *My Meiko/Young Geisha*, 2004, 48"H × 30"W.
Bottom: *Koi Pond Drama*, 2003, clay raku, 30"H × 72"W × 2-4"D. Photographs: Don Ross.

ROBERT SUNDAY

240 LOVESEE ROAD ■ ROSCOE, IL 61073 ■ TEL 815-623-7487
E-MAIL ROBERTSUNDAY@AOL.COM

Top: *Graduation*, 2002, Giovanni's Ballroom, Rockford, IL, raku-fired ceramic tiles, 80" x 120". Inset: Raku-fired ceramic tile installation, 2001, Rockford, IL, 30" x 48".

JACQUES LIEBERMAN

484 BROOME STREET ▦ NEW YORK, NY 10013 ▦ TEL 646-613-7302 ▦ FAX 646-613-7305
E-MAIL JACQUESLIEBERMAN@MAC.COM ▦ HTTP://HOMEPAGE.MAC.COM/JACQUESLIEBERMAN

52

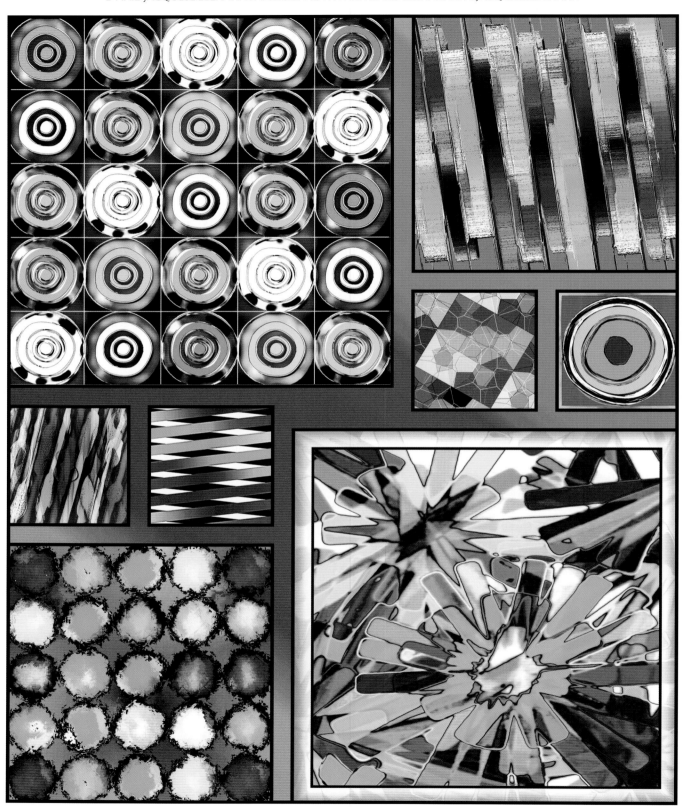

Various works. Any image created by me can be applied to ceramic tiles, murals, textiles, edition prints, furniture and furnishings, and more.

PRECISION CUT TECHNOLOGIES, INC.

STEVAN R. BRONNER ▧ 361 WEST MORLEY DRIVE ▧ SAGINAW, MI 48601 ▧ TEL 866-754-3555 ▧ FAX 989-752-3444
E-MAIL SBRONNER@PRECUTTECH.COM ▧ WWW.PRECUTTECH.COM

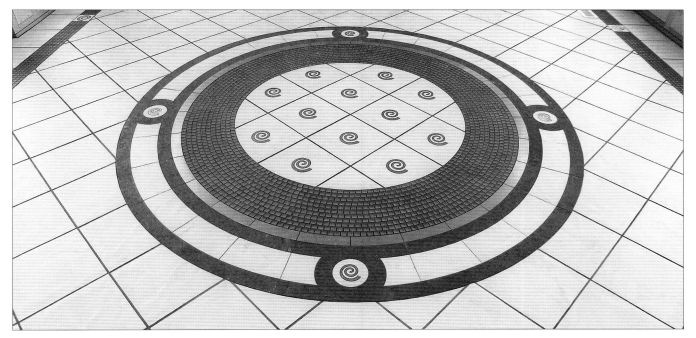

Top: Custom medallion, 2003, Saginaw Art Museum, Saginaw, MI, glass mosaics, stainless steel and porcelain, 7'Dia.
Bottom: *Anchor Medallion*, 2003, New Anchor Bay High School, New Baltimore, MI, porcelain tile and mosaics, 48'Dia. Photographs: Thomas Kaekel.

SUSAN AHREND

COTTONWOOD DESIGN ▨ 321 SAINT JOSEPH AVENUE ▨ LONG BEACH, CA 90814
TEL 562-438-5230 ▨ WWW.COTTONWOODTILE.COM

54

Top: *Josephine's Amaryllis*, 2003, private collection, ceramic tile, 2'H × 3.5'W.
Bottom left: *Koi Pond*, 2003, private collection, ceramic tile, 20"H × 20"W.
Bottom right: *Blue Iris*, 2001, private collection, ceramic tile, 20"H × 16"W. Photographs: Jay Ahrend.

JOAN ROTHCHILD HARDIN

JOAN ROTHCHILD HARDIN CERAMICS ▧ 393 WEST BROADWAY #4 ▧ NEW YORK, NY 10012
TEL 212-966-9433 ▧ FAX 212-431-9196 ▧ E-MAIL JOAN@HARDINTILES.COM ▧ WWW.HARDINTILES.COM

Top: *Dragon,* 2003, hand-painted ceramic art tiles, each: 6" × 6". Center: *Frogs,* 2003, hand-painted ceramic art tiles, each: 6" × 6".
Bottom: *Dragon Flies,* 2003, hand-painted ceramic art tiles, each: 6" × 6". Photographs: D. James Dee.

SUSAN BEERE

PO BOX 70 ▧ DEL MAR, CA 92014 ▧ TEL 760-942-9302 ▧ FAX 760-942-1702
E-MAIL SUSAN@SUSANBEERE.COM ▧ WWW.SUSANBEERE.COM

Top: *Egret's View*, private collection, freeform high-relief tile mural, 3' × 5'. Bottom: *Morning in Kapaa,* private collection, Hawaii, free-hanging tile mural, 2' × 3'.

ROBERT VOGLAND

VOGLAND.COM ▪ PO BOX 6288 ▪ KANEOHE, HI 96744 ▪ TEL 808-262-8479
E-MAIL VOGLANDR001@HAWAII.RR.COM ▪ WWW.VOGLAND.COM

57

Top: *Dream Ride (John Pretending to be Pulled)*, hand-sculpted ceramic tile mural. Bottom: *Three Hula Girl Hibiscus and Floating Beach Ball*, hand-sculpted ceramic tile mural.

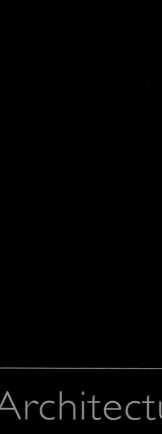

Architectu

DILLON FORGE

MICHAEL DILLON ■ 14250 BIRMINGHAM HIGHWAY ■ ALPHARETTA, GA 30004 ■ TEL 770-649-8012 ■ FAX 678-366-0542
E-MAIL DILLONFORGE@MINDSPRING.COM ■ WWW.DILLONFORGE.COM

60

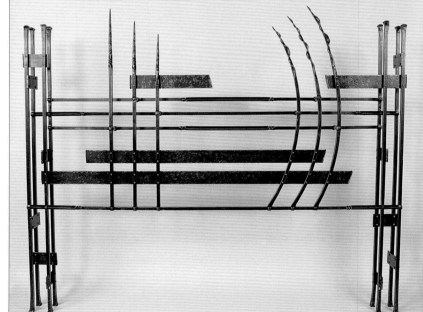

Top left: French rail, 2000, private residence, iron, 47' × 36"H. Top right: Gate, 2000, private residence, iron, 13'H × 16'W × 3". Bottom left: Mortis & tennon headboard, 2000, private residence, iron, 74"H × 74"W × 4". Bottom right: End iron, 2002, private residence, iron and bronze, 24"H × 16"W × 10". Photographs: Max Birnkammer.

STEVE FONTANINI

STEVE FONTANINI ARCHITECTURAL & ORNAMENTAL BLACKSMITHING ▨ PO BOX 2298 ▨ 11400 SOUTH HOBACK JUNCTION RD.
JACKSON, WY 83001 ▨ TEL 307-733-7668 ▨ 307-734-8816 ▨ E-MAIL SFONTANI@WYOMING.COM ▨ WWW.STEVEFONTANINIBLACKSMITH.COM

61

Left: Classic European-style forged railing, traditional joinery (no electrical wielding). Design by JLF and Associates, Livingston, MT.
Right: Contemporary style railing and staircase with forged joinery, Parks residence, Teton County, WY.
Design by Tom Ward, Ward-Blake Architects, Jackson, WY.

Building Artful Relationships: Tony Spolar & Sandy Bosetti

Jeff Salzer Photography

ARTIST
Tony Spolar

TITLE
Floating sculpted mural, 2003

COMMISSIONED FOR
Master Lock Entry Atrium,
Milwaukee, WI

TIMELINE: 4 months

DIMENSIONS: 40'W × 16'H

TRADE PROFESSIONAL
Sandy Bosetti,
Marketing Services
& Brand Specialist,
Master Lock Company

Tony Spolar is a collaborative artist. Within his Milwaukee-based firm, nine employees are credited with making Spolar Studio wall murals and finishes come to life. In working with the Master Lock Company, he extended his collaboration to include an independent design firm, as well as officials from Master Lock. ▪ "Master Lock wanted to take the ordinary-looking lock to an artistic level in their new building," Spolar reports. "Mary Jo Krüger [from marketing/design firm Haack Whelan Krüger] had done some advertising work for Master Lock and referred them to our studio." ▪ Sandy Bosetti of Master Lock was introduced to Spolar soon afterward and began working directly with the art team. "We wanted to create a showcase of Master Lock's heritage that would be dramatic and interesting to visitors and employees. We had many terrific archived images that no one had ever seen, but we needed to display them in a contemporary building décor."

▪ Spolar's solution was to scan the historic images and print them on archival paper, which was then mounted to a durable but lightweight PVC foam. The mounted images were then carved and cut before being hung slightly away from the wall, at various angles, with metal brackets. When the project was complete, Spolar Studios had created six of these "floating" sculpted murals and nearly 70 single images. ▪ Bosetti agrees that teamwork was key to the project. "This was a collaborative effort with a very tight timeline. We all worked extremely well together and enjoyed seeing the project unfold. Having the right people with the right talents will help any project run smoothly." ▪ Today the pieces are a point of pride for Master Lock. "The artwork definitely enhances the building," Bosetti reports. "It's great to see a visitor touring the various artworks; it really gives them a sense of Master Lock. Most people are truly impressed and enjoy viewing all the pieces."

VALERIE EGLAND

ECLIPSE ART ■ 870 SCHOOL ROAD ■ SAN JUAN BAUTISTA, CA 95045 ■ TEL 831-623-2664 ■ FAX 831-623-1719
E-MAIL VEGLAND@HOLLINET.COM ■ WWW.VALERIEEGLAND.COM

Top: Back bar, oak motif, 2003, Santa Lucia Preserve golf clubhouse, Carmel, CA, carved redwood, 10' × 5' × 14".
Bottom: Crowning ornaments with the client's historic motifs, 1992-2003, private residence, carved and tinted wood, 5-6' × 18-20" × 2". Photographs: Charles Harris.

CARVINGS BY C.B. MARTIN

CAROL B. MARTIN ▦ 1155 INDUSTRIAL AVENUE ▦ ESCONDIDO, CA 92029
TEL/FAX 760-746-5896 ▦ E-MAIL CBCBM@SAN.RR.COM

Top left: *Torrey Pines Blowing in the Wind,* doors, carved mahogany, 8' × 6' × 3".
Right: *Springtime in the Garden,* refrigerator doors, carved alder, 68" × 48". Bottom left: *Iris Trio,* wall sculpture, carved butternut, 22" × 14" × 4".

SAR FURNITURE, LLC

SCOTT A. REITMAN ▩ 1420 EAST 36TH STREET, 6TH FLOOR ▩ CLEVELAND, OH 44114
TEL 216-426-9990 ▩ FAX 216-426-9991 ▩ E-MAIL SCOTT@SARFURNITURE.COM ▩ WWW.SARFURNITURE.COM

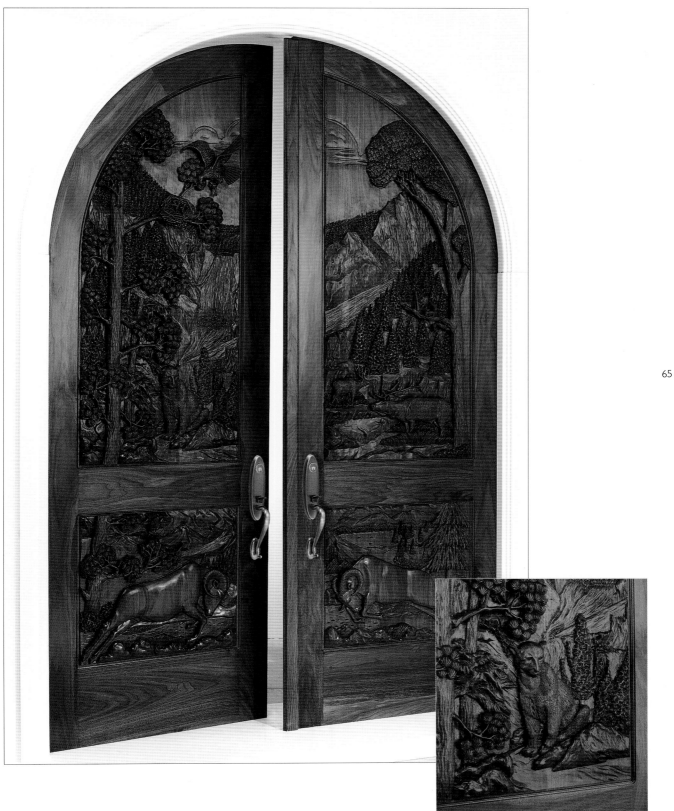

The Spirit of Yellowstone, 9'H × 6'W. Inset: *The Spirit of Yellowstone* (detail).

Atrium Sculpture

MYRON WASSERMAN

WASSERMAN STUDIOS ▦ 1817 NORTH FIFTH STREET ▦ PHILADELPHIA, PA 19122 ▦ TEL 215-739-5558 ▦ FAX 215-739-5448
E-MAIL MYRONWASSERMAN@EARTHLINK.NET ▦ WWW.WASSERMANSTUDIOS.COM

68

Left: Multi-axis kinetic mobile, 2004, Liberty Ridge Corporate Center, Malvern, PA, mixed metals, patinas and clear coat, 35'L × 13'W. Right: Stabile, fixed kinetic sculpture, 2003, Astra Zeneca Inc., U.S. Business Center, Wilmington, DE, mixed metals and paint on concrete base, 12'H × 55"W. Photographs: Fred Kenner.

RALF GSCHWEND

RALFONSO.COM ▨ 301 CLEMATIS STREET, #3000 ▨ WEST PALM BEACH, FL 33401
TEL 561-655-2745 ▨ FAX 561-655-4158 ▨ RALFONSO@RALFONSO.COM ▨ WWW.RALFONSO.COM

Top left: *ExoCentric Spirits*, 2003, fiberglass, 70-disc assembly with colored lenses mobile design. Top right: *Moving on UP*, 2003, fiberglass and aluminum kinetic wind sculpture. Bottom: *Infinity 1*, 2004, anodized aluminum kinetic motor-driven sculpture design.

JUDY DIOSZEGI

JUDY DIOSZEGI, DESIGNER ▪ 1295 MARGATE LANE ▪ GREEN OAKS, IL 60048
TEL 847-367-8395 ▪ FAX 847-367-8395 *51 ▪ E-MAIL JDIOX2@AOL.COM ▪ WWW.JDIOSZEGI.COM

Top: *Tropical Reigns–Children's Pool*, 2002, Elgin Recreation Centre, 100% nylon flag cloth, birds: 7', streamers: 30"W × 45'L.
Bottom: *Tropical Reigns–Adult Lap Pool*, 2002, Elgin Recreation Centre, 100% nylon flag cloth, triangles: 7', streamers: 16"-24"W × 24'-34'L. Photographs: John Dioszegi.

JILL CASTY

JILL CASTY DESIGN ▦ 494 ALVARDO STREET ▦ MONTEREY, CA 93940 ▦ TEL 831-649-0923 ▦ FAX 831-649-0713
E-MAIL JILLCDESIGN@HOTMAIL.COM ▦ WWW.JILLCASTYDESIGN.COM

71

Top: One of four mobiles in Center Court of Country Club Plaza, Sacramento, CA, painted aluminum and Plexiglas, 17'W x 12'H.
Bottom left: One of four mobiles in another corridor of Country Club Plaza, painted aluminum and Plexiglas, 17'W x 5.75'H.
Bottom right: One of four mobiles in a corridor of Country Club Plaza, powder-coated and painted aluminum, 17'W x 7'H. Photograph: Robb Hallock.

AIRWORKS, INC.

GEORGE PETERS & MELANIE WALKER ▓ 815 SPRUCE STREET ▓ BOULDER, CO 80302 ▓ TEL/FAX 303-442-9025
E-MAIL AIRWORKS@CONCENTRIC.NET ▓ WWW.AIRWORKS-STUDIO.COM

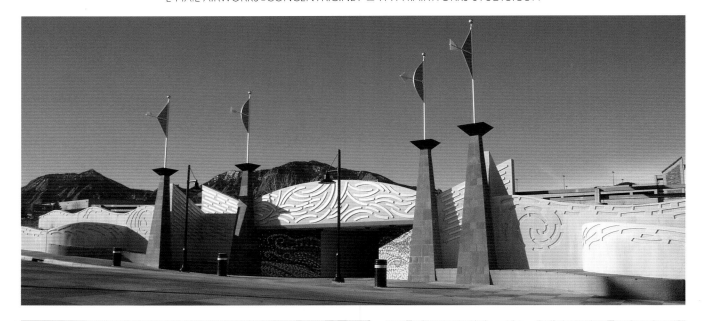

Top: *Wind Tunnel* , 2003, bike and pedestrian underpass, Boulder, CO, concrete, concrete stain, sandstone, aluminum and porcelain tile, 275'W × 35'D × 32'H.
Bottom left: *Turning Leaves,* 2003, McGraw/Hill Companies, London, U.K., fiberglass bar & rod, mylar, prismatic film and polyester sunscreen, 6'W × 5'H × 40'L, ten units.
Bottom right: *Balance Act,* 2002, Public Safety Center, Westminster, CO, aluminum, fiberglass, carbon/graphite rod and prismatic mylar, 60'L × 10'W × 8'H.

IE CREATIVE ARTWORKS

1399 RAILSPUR ALLEY, GRANVILLE ISLAND ▩ VANCOUVER, BC V6H 4G9 ▩ CANADA
TEL 604-254-4374 ▩ FAX 604-683-4343 ▩ E-MAIL STUDIO@IECREATIVE.CA ▩ WWW.IECREATIVE.CA

73

Left: *Enchanted Constellation*, 2003, BC Children's Hospital, Vancouver, BC, glass, metal and wood, 80' x 15' x 15'.
Top right: *Enchanted Constellation* (detail). Bottom right: *Enchanted Constellation* (detail). Photographs: Derek Lepper.

DANIEL GOLDSTEIN

224 GUERRERO STREET ■ SAN FRANCISCO, CA 94103
TEL 415-621-5761 ■ FAX 415-643-8369 ■ E-MAIL DANIELJGOLDSTEIN@YAHOO.COM

74

Top: *Transport,* 2001, Norcal Waste Inc., San Francisco, CA, glass and stainless steel, 54" × 96" × 12".   Bottom left: *Light Rain,* 2002, Astra Zeneca, Wilmington, DE, painted aluminum and stainless steel, 40' × 30' × 20'.   Bottom right: *Wings,* 1993, Synoptics, Santa Clara, CA, expanded aluminum, 12' × 12' × 12'.

Printed in China © 2004 GUILD LLC: *The Sourcebook of Architectural & Interior Art*

ROB FISHER

228 NORTH ALLEGHENY STREET ■ BELLEFONTE, PA 16823 ■ TEL 814-355-1458 ■ FAX 814-353-9060
E-MAIL GLENUNION@AOL.COM ■ WWW.ROBFISHERAMERICANDREAM.COM

Slice of Life, 2002, AstraZeneca Pharmaceuticals Visitor Center, Wilmington, DE,
powder-coated perforated aluminum and stainless steel, 35' × 85' × 35'. Top photograph: Marcus Gardega.

Building Artful Relationships: Karen Heyl & Bruce Olson

Bruce Olson

ARTIST
Karen Heyl

TITLE
Ecological Tapestry, 2002

COMMISSIONED FOR
Orange County Convention Center,
Orlando, FL

TIMELINE: 2 years

DIMENSIONS: 30'H x 11'W;
Each panel: 3.5'W x 5'H

TRADE PROFESSIONAL
Bruce Olson,
Art Consultant,
L'Idee, Corporate Art Concepts, Inc.

When Karen Heyl was chosen to create a sculpture for a west entrance of the Orange County Convention Center (OCCC) in Orlando, she needed a little help. Not with the sculpture itself, as under her chisel, limestone is transformed into intricate stories in great detail. But, because she couldn't build directly into the wall of the building, she turned to art consultant Bruce Olson for guidance. ■ "She had to build something to hold her work since it couldn't be incorporated into the wall. So she told me what she wanted to do, and we decided to put it into a freestanding easel," explains Olson, who is an accomplished artist himself. "I designed and drew up the shop drawing for the easel, put it out to bid, chose the fabricator and installed the work for Karen." ■ With the logistics settled, Heyl went to work creating a piece of art to turn a large, vacant and unattractive section of the building into a comfortable and inviting space. "I had to pick a motif, and I wanted the work to relate to its environment. One side of the piece relates to Orange County, while the other side represents Florida," she says. ■ Working together, the project was a huge success. "It was a perfect fit," Heyl says about working with Olson. "I have learned that [working with an art consultant] allows me to focus on the project so I don't have to wear so many hats." ■ "Artists may sometimes feel that part of a project is outside their comfort zone," Olson explains. "Consultants need to find a way to circumvent those anxieties and help them make it happen. The OCCC now has a signature piece of monumental art, and the county benefits from the millions of people who attend conventions and are taken in by the art's presence."

CLOWES SCULPTURE

JONATHAN AND EVELYN CLOWES ▨ 98 MARCH HILL ROAD ▨ WALPOLE, NH 03608 ▨ TEL/FAX 603-756-9505
E-MAIL JON@CLOWESSCULPTURE.COM ▨ WWW.CLOWESSCULPTURE.COM

Spring Fire, 2003, cherry veneer, fiberglass, wire and blown glass, 5'H x 3'W. Photograph: Jeff Baird.

Public Art

NICOLE BECK

NICOLE BECK STUDIOS ■ 805 SOUTH OAKLEY BOULEVARD ■ CHICAGO, IL 60612 ■ TEL 312-563-0457
E-MAIL NBECKARTS@AOL.COM ■ WWW.NICOLEBECK.COM

80

Top: *Quasarc*, PierWalk 2001, painted steel and lenses, 10' × 25' × 5'. Photograph: keithbakerphotography.com
Bottom left: *Hand-formed*, 2003, commissioned maquette, forged and fabricated steel, 14" × 14" × 12".
Bottom right: *Quantaloop*, PierWalk 2000, presently at South Bend Airport, IN, steel and lenses, 12' × 12' × 12'. Photograph: Digital Imaging, 3rdeyesite.com.

LUIS TORRUELLA

TENERIFE BUILDING, APARTMENT 1201 ▨ 1507 ASHFORD AVENUE ▨ SAN JUAN, PR 00911
TEL/FAX 787-722-8728 ▪ TEL 787-268-4977 ▪ E-MAIL LUISTORRUELLA@AOL.COM ▪ WWW.LUISTORRUELLA.COM

81

Solazo (detail), 2003, office center, San Juan, PR, painted and brushed aluminum, 48' × 19' × 16'. Inset: *Solazo* (detail). Photographs: Alberto Gratacos.

TED JONSSON

HUMONGOUS ARTS ▨ 805 NE NORTHLAKE WAY ▨ SEATTLE, WA 98105
TEL 206-547-4552 ▨ FAX 206-324-7326 ▨ E-MAIL SCULPTUREWORKS@AAAHAWK.COM

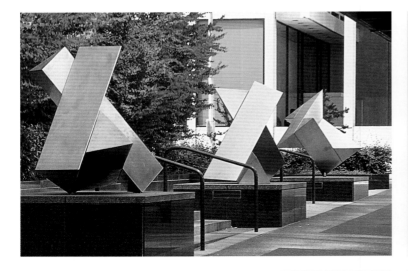

Top left: New plaza sculpture suite, 1991, Federal Reserve Bank of San Francisco, Seattle, WA, stainless steel, 86"H x 864" x 64".
Top right: Fountain, 1975, Seattle Water Control Center, stainless steel, 144"H x 312" x120". Bottom left: *Torque*, 1982, Continental Plaza,
Seattle, WA, stainless steel, 108"H x 72" x 48". Bottom right: Fountain, 1998, S.A.P. Labs, Inc., Palo Alto, CA, stainless steel, 156"H x 96" x 48".

ARISTIDES DEMETRIOS

2694 SYCAMORE CANYON ROAD ▨ SANTA BARBARA, CA 93108 ▨ TEL 805-565-2217 ▨ FAX 805-565-7721
E-MAIL ARISDEMETRIOS@AOL.COM ▨ WWW.DEMETRIOSSCULPTURE.COM

83

Top: *Joyous Resonances,* 2002, Montecito, CA, bronze, 6'H.
Bottom: *Joie de Vivre,* 2003, Montecito, CA, bronze, 7' figures. Photographs: Larry Dale Gordon.

ARCHIE HELD

ARCHIE HELD STUDIO ▨ 5-18TH STREET ▨ RICHMOND, CA 94801 ▨ TEL 510-235-8700 ▨ FAX 510-234-4828
E-MAIL ARCHIEHELDSTUDIO@COMCAST.NET ▨ WWW.ARCHIEHELD.COM

84

Community, 2003, The Village Shopping Center, Corte Madera, CA, bronze and water, 15' x 15' x 12.5'H.

DALE ENOCHS

8635 SOUTH KETCHAM ROAD ▩ BLOOMINGTON, IN 47403 ▩ TEL/FAX 812-824-8181
E-MAIL DENOCHS@BLUEMARBLE.NET ▩ HTTP://HOME.BLUEMARBLE.NET/~DENOCHS

Top left: *Earth Stone, White River Gardens*, Indianapolis, IN, limestone, bronze and water, 12' × 6' × 3'. Photograph: Mike Cavanagh.
Right: *Tree of Life*, Willennar Genealogy Center, Auburn, IN, limestone and gold leaf, 20' × 8' × 4". Photograph: Tim Brumbeloe. Bottom left: In foreground: *Sphere*, DePauw University, Greencastle, IN, limestone and steel, 6' × 5' × 5'. In background: *Ishi Kawa Venus*, limestone and copper, 11' × 2' × 2'. Photograph: Mike Cavanagh.

Building Artful Relationships: Marina Popova & Dean Singer

Claude Simon Langlois

ARTIST
Marina Popova

TITLE
Untitled, 2003

COMMISSIONED FOR
Main ballroom,
Fairmont Queen Elizabeth Hotel,
Montreal, Quebec

TIMELINE: 3 months

DIMENSIONS: 10'H x 18'W

TRADE PROFESSIONAL
Dean Singer
(Former) Design Director
Hirsch Bedner

Dean Singer believes in supporting local artists and art programs. "If my client is willing and has artistic vision, and if it's within the budget of the project, then I always rely on the talents of local artists. It really gives the viewer a flavor of the city and the area artwork," he explains. ■ When it was time to find a work of art that represented the flavor of Montreal for the Fairmont Queen Elizabeth Hotel ballroom, Singer had to look no further than painter Marina Popova. "Dean saw my catalog and really seemed to like my artwork. I visited the space to get a feel for the room—and the designers had a color scheme they wanted me to work within," Popova reports. "Beyond that, the design team really encouraged me to work with my own vision and style on the piece." The final piece is an abstract portrait of Montreal as seen through Popova's eyes. ■ "I'm very pleased with the way the project turned out," say Singer, who now owns his own design company, Design360Unlimited, in Santa Monica. "The bold use of color and subject matter certainly makes the artwork the major focal point of the room. Marina was a real pleasure to work with—she simply took our initial guidelines and really ran with the project." ■ "I think that including an artist from the very beginning of any design project works best because it helps him or her become much more interested the project," Singer adds. "An interested artist shows rich emotion in his or her work—and I think that emotion comes across to the viewer. That's what makes a great piece of artwork."

HANK KAMINSKY

808 SOUTH GOVERNMENT AVENUE ■ FAYETTEVILLE, AR 72701 ■ TEL 479-442-5805 ■ FAX 479-442-3927
E-MAIL SCULPTOR@KAMINSKY.COM ■ WWW.SCULPTOR.KAMINSKY.COM

87

Top: *World Peace Prayer Fountain*, 2002, Fayetteville, AR, bronze, 10'Dia. Bottom left: *Peace Rock*, 1998,
private collection, concrete, 4' × 2' × 3'. Bottom right: *World Peace Prayer Fountain* (detail). Photographs: Jim Bailey.

B.S.K. DEVELOPMENT

STEPHEN GEDDES ■ ROBERT L. MOORE ■ 1453 COVERED BRIDGE ROAD ■ CINCINNATI, OH 45231
TEL 513-231-4309 ■ TEL 513-921-7651 ■ E-MAIL SLGEDDESS@CINCI.RR.COM ■ WWW.BSKDEVELOPMENT.COM

Top: *Reds Relief: Owner's Suite*, 2003, Great American Ballpark, carved wood, 25' x 10'.
Bottom left: *Reds Relief* (detail). Bottom right: *Reds Relief* (detail). Photographs: Roger Rowitz.

ROBERT W. ELLISON

ELLISON STUDIO ▨ 6480 EAGLE RIDGE ROAD ▨ PENNGROVE, CA 94951 ▨ TEL 707-795-9775 ▨ FAX 707-795-4370
E-MAIL ROBERT@ROBERTELLISON.COM ▨ WWW.ROBERTELLISON.COM

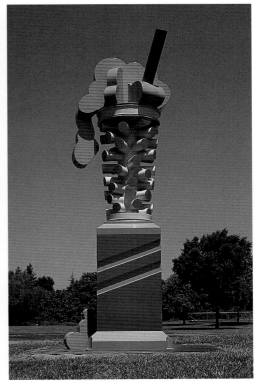

Top: *Know Way*, 2003, Open Book Plaza, Dublin Public Library, Dublin, CA, painted, welded steel, 20' × 22' × 4'. Photograph: Brian Moran.
Bottom left: *Spin*, 2002, Embarcadero Station, Bay Area Rapid Transit, San Francisco, CA, painted, welded steel, 8' × 50' × 3'. Photograph: Brian Moran.
Bottom right: *Cherry Soda*, 2003, Lookout Sculpture Park West, Luchessi Park, Petaluma, CA, painted, welded steel, 19' × 6' × 4.5'.

MAX-CAST

STEVE MAXON ■ DORIS PARK ■ PO BOX 662, 611 B AVENUE ■ KALONA, IA 52247
TEL 319-656-5365 ■ FAX 319-656-3187 ■ E-MAIL MAX-CAST@KCTC.NET ■ WWW.MAX-CAST.COM

Irving B. Weber, Portrait of a Gentleman, 2003, Iowa City, IA, bronze. Photograph: Mark Tade.

STEVEN LIGUORI

LIGUORI DESIGNS ▦ 818 PARK PASEO ▦ LAS VEGAS, NV 89104
TEL 702-525-0506 ▦ E-MAIL SLIGUORI01@AOL.COM

Top left: *Highscaler Monument* (detail), 2000, Hoover Dam, bronze and stone, 22'H. Top right: *Powder Monkeys* (detail), 2000, Hoover Dam, bronze and stone, 10" × 2' × 2'.
Bottom: Veteran's Memorial Monument, 1995, Boulder City, NV, steel and stainless steel, 8'H × 16'L × 8"D. Photographs: Lee McDonald.

MOBERG STUDIO ART GALLERY

2921 INGERSOLL AVENUE ■ DES MOINES, IA 50312 ■ TEL 515-279-9191 ■ FAX 515-279-9292
E-MAIL GALLERYINFO@MOBERGSTUDIO.COM ■ WWW.MOBERGSTUDIO.COM

92

Top left: *By a Nose*, mixed media sculpture, 12' × 14' × 5'. Top right: *Story City Swinging Bridge*, gypsum plaster sculpture, 10' × 14'.
Bottom: *American Gothic*, welded steel painted flat black, 18' × 16' × 6". Photographs: Rodney White.

CANNETO STUDIOS INC.

STEPHEN CANNETO ■ 1450 ROADS END PLACE ■ COLUMBUS, OH 43209 ■ TEL 614-237-9078 ■ FAX 614-237-9059
E-MAIL CANNETO@CANNETOSTUDIOS.COM ■ WWW.CANNETOSTUDIOS.COM

93

Top: *ColorPlay*, 2004, stainless steel, glass, stone and masonery, 20'H x 20'L x 20'W. Bottom left: *Passage*, 2000, stone, bronze and glass, 6'H x 12'L x 1'W. Photograph: Larry Hamill.
Bottom right: *Releve*, 2001, stainless steel, bronze and stone, 24"H x 10"L x 8"W. Photograph: Gregg Goldston.

Building Artful Relationships: Rob Fisher & Marsha Moss

Richard McMullin

ARTIST
Rob Fisher

TITLE
American Dream, 2000–2003

COMMISSIONED FOR
Percent for Art Program,
International Arrivals Hall,
Philadelphia International Airport, PA

TIMELINE: 4 years

DIMENSIONS: Words: 12' × 250' × 6"D;
Railing: 42"H × 90'L

TRADE PROFESSIONAL
Marsha Moss, Public Art Consultant

The Percent for Art Program of Philadelphia was put into place more than 40 years ago to promote artwork that enriches the environment, furthers the public's understanding of the visual arts and resonates with Philadelphia's character and landscape. That's precisely what Rob Fisher captured when he created *American Dream*. ■ *American Dream* is a visionary construct of America as seen through the eyes of an artist whose family, with its immigrant roots, has lived the American dream. Rendered in metal, glass and light, the suite of three artworks that comprise *American Dream* creates a unified work of art from words, signatures and images of the Declaration of Independence. ■ "The Declaration of Independence was prepared in Philadelphia, and even as a child, I was fascinated by the document and its contents. I recognized that the International Arrivals Hall was a gateway, not only to the city, but to the United States," Fisher says of the project. ■ Marsha Moss, public art consultant on the project, couldn't agree more. As a juror on the Percent for Art panel, she was looking for a proposal that would welcome, engage and communicate with the airport's millions of fast-moving visitors in the most dynamic and meaningful way. ■ "*American Dream* has so vastly enhanced the Arrivals Hall that it is impossible to imagine the space existing without it," she says. ■ Working together was key to *American Dream*'s success. "A good working relationship is essential for creating an artwork that resonates with the site," Fisher explains. "Listening is an art, and there are often many useful and exciting ideas that are generated when a group of professionals focus on producing a major project."

SCOTT K. PARSONS

802 SANTA FE DRIVE #4 ■ DENVER, CO 80204 ■ TEL 303-902-0625
E-MAIL SCOTTKPARSONS@YAHOO.COM ■ WWW.SCOTTKPARSONS.COM

Algorithmic Tapestry, 2002, Engineering Centers Building, University of Wisconsin at Madison,
epoxy terrazzo design and fabrication, 11,000 square feet. Photograph: Jim Wildeman.

DOUGLAS CHICK

2541 CHESWICK DRIVE ■ TROY, MI 48084 ■ TEL 248-642-1508 ■ FAX 248-642-4005
E-MAIL DCHICK642@AOL.COM ■ WWW.DOUGCHICKSCULPTURE.COM

96

Top left: *Fabled Flight* (detail). Right: *Fabled Flight*, 2003, West Bloomfield Township Library, MI, bronze, 6.8'H, limited edition of 25, also available in smaller size. Bottom left: *Fabled Flight* (detail).

SCOTT WALLACE

PO BOX 8 ▨ HENDRICKS, MN 56136 ▨ TEL 507-275-3300 ▨ FAX 507-275-3304
E-MAIL SWALLACE@ITCTEL.COM ▨ WWW.WALLACESCULPTURE.COM

97

Left: *Keepsake*, bronze, 11.8'H. Right: *Still Life with Flower*, painted aluminum, 22'H.

Non-Representational Sculpture

JONATHAN COX

COX FINE ART ■ 768 PRIVATE DRIVE 3952 ■ WILLOW WOOD, OH 45696 ■ TEL 740-867-0658 ■ FAX 304-696-6505
E-MAIL COXJ@MARSHALL.EDU ■ WWW.JONATHANCOXSCULPTURE.COM

100

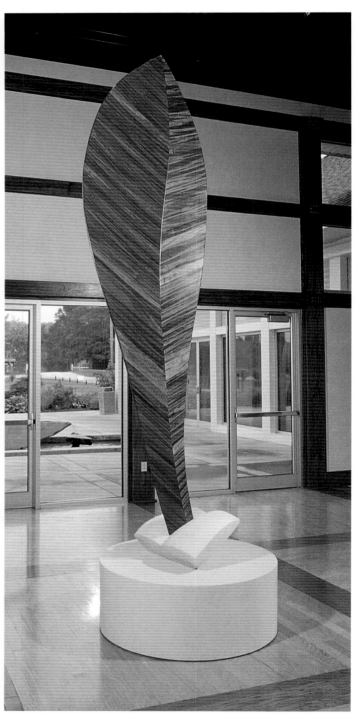

Top left: *The Discovery*, 2000, Huntington Museum of Art, marble and poplar, 14.8' × 5.1' × 2.1'. Right: *The Ascent of Knowledge*, 2001, marble and mahogany, 10.66' × 3.33' × 2.33'. Bottom left: *Icicles in the Snow*, 2002, marble, mahogany and obsidian, 21" × 34.5" × 12.5".

MICHAEL BAUERMEISTER

6560 AUGUSTA BOTTOM ROAD ■ AUGUSTA, MO 63332 ■ TEL/FAX 636-228-4663
E-MAIL MICHAEL@BAUERMEISTER.COM ■ WWW.MICHAELBAUERMEISTER.COM

Left: *Tall Vessels* (from left to right), stained birch, 65" × 19"; linden, 40" × 11"; birch, 73" × 20". Top right: *Tall Vessels* (from left to right), walnut, 38" × 12"; oak, 50" × 14"; painted oak, 26" × 11". Center right: *Sprout Vessels*, various woods, 40"-17" tall. Bottom right: *Two Painted Vessels*, linden with paint, 34" × 14"; right, birch with paint, 56" × 15".

LITA KELMENSON

199 NORTH MARGINAL ROAD ■ JERICHO, NY 11756
TEL 516-822-3219 ■ E-MAIL LITAKEL@YAHOO.COM

 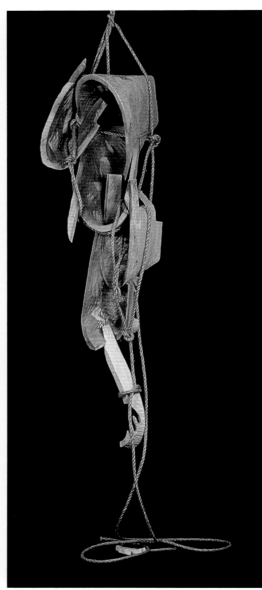

Left: *Forced Migration*, 2001, wood and tailpipes, 36" × 30" × 24".
Right: *Echoes of Fear*, 2000, wood and sisal, 96" × 13" × 21". Photographs: Lawrence J. Chatterton.

DAN RIDER

DAN RIDER SCULPTURE ▓ 133 BRIDGE STREET ▓ ARROYO GRANDE, CA 93420 ▓ TEL 805-474-5959
E-MAIL DAN@DANRIDERSCULPTURE.COM ▓ WWW.DANRIDERSCULPTURE.COM

Top left: *Spirit Marker #14*, copper and concrete, 6' x 30" x 12".
Right: *Spirit Marker #9*, copper and concrete, 8' x 42" x 12". Bottom left: *Spirit Marker #13*, copper and concrete, 6' x 48" x 12".

RUTH BURINK

BURINK SCULPTURE STUDIO ▨ 1550 WOODMOOR DRIVE ▨ MONUMENT, CO 80132
TEL/FAX 719-481-0513 ▨ E-MAIL RUTH@BURINKSCULPTURE.COM ▨ WWW.BURINKSCULPTURE.COM

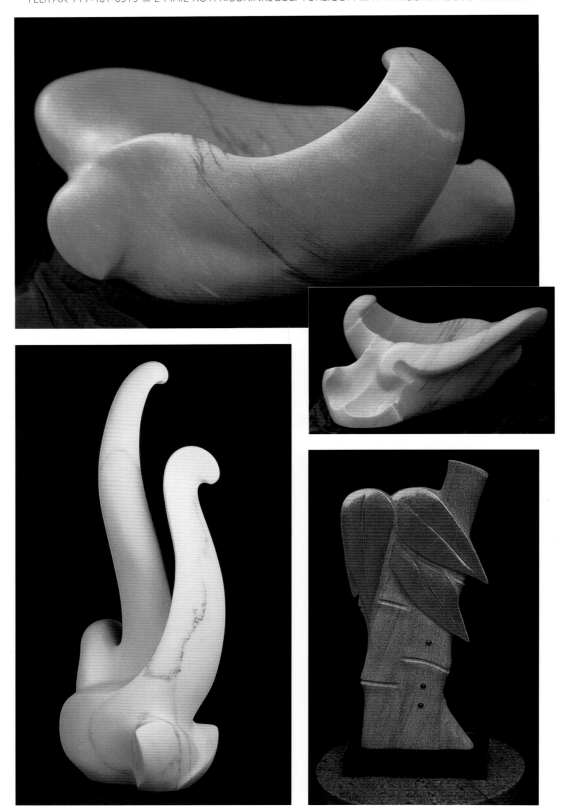

Top: *Gray Dove Basin*, 2003, marble, 12"H × 20"W × 22"D. Inset: *Gray Dove Basin* (back view). Photographs: Casey Chinn.
Bottom left: *Swan, Wings Unfurled*, 2003, marble, 30"H × 8"W × 11"D. Photograph: Casey Chinn. Bottom right: *Bamboo*, 2001, limestone and gold leaf, 18"H × 7"W × 3"D.

MARY BATES NEUBAUER

#3 NORTH BULLMOOSE CIRCLE ▧ CHANDLER, AZ 85224 ▧ TEL 480-821-1611 ▧ FAX 480-821-8218
E-MAIL MARY.NEUBAUER@ASU.EDU ▧ WWW.SCULPTURE-DIGITAL.NET

105

Top: Exhibition view, 2001, Tucson Museum of Art, large-scale bronze sculptures. Photograph: Robin Stancliffe.
Bottom left: *Sonophon,* 2003, bronze, 36" × 36" × 36". Photograph: Damien Johnson. Bottom right: *She Dreams,* 2001, bronze, 20' × 35" × 12". Photograph: Ralph Rippe.

DAVID CODDAIRE

755 EAST 10TH STREET ■ OAKLAND, CA 94606 ■ TEL 510-451-7353 ■ FAX 510-451-7351
E-MAIL TALLIRONVASES@MINDSPRING.COM ■ WWW.TALLIRONVASES.COM

106

Mariner, 1996, steel, 96" x 66" x 80".

DAVID CODDAIRE

755 EAST 10TH STREET ▦ OAKLAND, CA 94606 ▦ TEL 510-451-7353 ▦ FAX 510-451-7351
E-MAIL TALLIRONVASES@MINDSPRING.COM ▦ WWW.TALLIRONVASES.COM

107

Top left: *Security,* 2004, steel, 62" × 28" × 22".
Right: *Clocker,* 1996, steel, 100" × 50" × 60". Bottom left: *Sammy,* 2004, steel, 60" × 32" × 40".

NORMA LEWIS

NORMA LEWIS STUDIOS ▩ 30500 AURORA DEL MAR ▩ CARMEL, CA 93923
TEL 831-625-1046 ▩ FAX 831-625-5733 ▩ E-MAIL NORMAART@DLEWIS.COM

108

Connections, 2004, Library & Technology Center, Monterey Peninsula College, Monterey, CA, 8'H.

RIIS BURWELL

3815 CALISTOGA ROAD ■ SANTA ROSA, CA 95404 ■ TEL 707-538-2676
E-MAIL RIISBURWELL@RIISBURWELL.COM ■ WWW.RIISBURWELL.COM

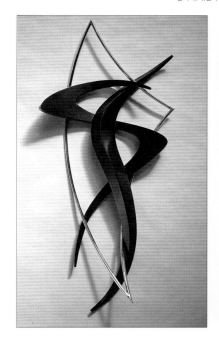

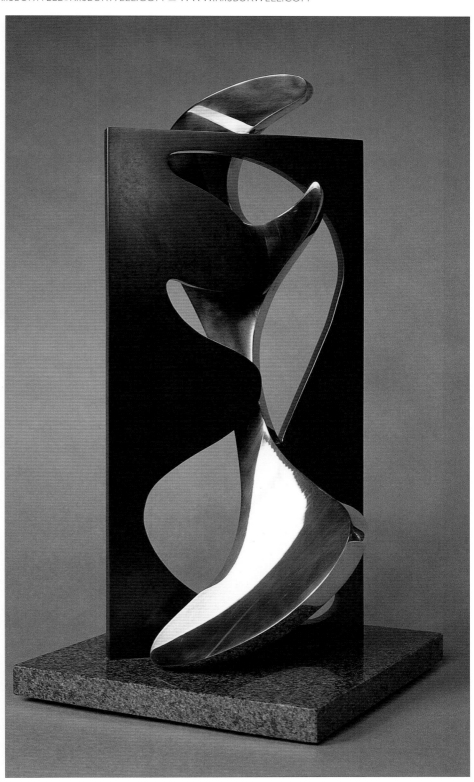

Top left: *Entropy Series #45*, 2003, bronze and stainless steel, 46" × 24" × 8".
Right: *Cloud Form*, 2003, bronze, 30" × 12" × 12". Bottom left: *Synergetic #4*, 2003, bronze, 24" × 8" × 8".

JAMES C. MYFORD

320 CRANBERRY ROAD ■ GROVE CITY, PA 16127
TEL 724-967-1612 ■ TEL/FAX 724-458-9672 ■ E-MAIL JCMYF@ZOOMINTERNET.NET ■ WWW.MYFORDSCULPTURE.COM

110

Left: *Dependence,* 1990, sculptor's residence, aluminum, 86" × 26" × 13". Top right: *Columns,* 2003, sculptor's residence, aluminum, 96" × 56" × 24".
Bottom right: *Triangular Form,* 2002, sculptor's residence, aluminum, 96" × 66" × 24". Photographs: Robert Ruschak.

BRUCE A. NIEMI

NIEMI SCULPTURE GALLERY & GARDEN ▦ 13300 116TH STREET ▦ KENOSHA, WI 53142 ▦ TEL 262-857-3456 ▦ FAX 262-857-4567
E-MAIL SCULPTURE@BRUCENIEMI.COM ▦ WWW.BRUCENIEMI.COM

Top: *Celestial Messenger*, 2003, stainless steel and bronze, 5'H x 7.3'W x 12"D.
Bottom left: *The Last Samurai*, 2003, 9.4'H x 7'W x 3'D. Bottom right: *Let's Dance*, 2003, stainless steel, 8.5' H x 2.7'W x 2.3'D.

RON FOSTER & MICHAEL LINSLEY

KALEIDOSCULPTURE ▥ 2921 PEBBLE DRIVE ▥ CORONA DEL MAR, CA 92625 ▥ TEL 949-650-0662 ▥ FAX 949-650-6890
E-MAIL RON@KALEIDOSCULPTURE.COM ▥ MICHAEL@KALEIDOSCULPTURE.COM ▥ WWW.KALEIDOSCULPTURE.COM

112

Kaleidosculpture, private residence, Corona del Mar, CA, steel and ceramic, 5' × 8'.

MICHAEL BAKER

MICHAEL BAKER STUDIOS ■ 85 GUNTER DRIVE ■ COLBERT, GA 30628 ■ TEL 706-354-4959
E-MAIL SCULPTURE@MICHAELBAKER.COM ■ WWW.MICHAELBAKER.COM

113

Top left: *Stacked Elements #2*, 2003, stainless steel, 42" × 24" × 12".
Right: *Still Life*, 2003, stainless steel, 78" × 63" × 14". Bottom left: *Birth*, 2003, stainless steel, 40" × 16" × 10".

JAMES T. RUSSELL SCULPTURE

JAMES T. RUSSELL ■ 1930 LOMITA BOULEVARD ■ LOMITA, CA 90717 ■ TEL 310-326-0785 ■ FAX 310-326-1470
E-MAIL JAMES@RUSSELLSCULPTURE.COM ■ WWW.RUSSELLSCULPTURE.COM

Top: *Encounter in Flight*, 2003, City of Hope, Duarte, CA, polished stainless steel, 9.6'H. Bottom left: *Springtime*, 2001, Sunset Development, San Ramon, CA, polished stainless steel, 6.6'H. Bottom right: *Eternal Flight*, 2001, private residence, Woodside, CA, polished stainless steel, 5.8'H on a 4' base.

JAMES T. RUSSELL SCULPTURE

JAMES T. RUSSELL ▪ 1930 LOMITA BOULEVARD ▪ LOMITA, CA 90717 ▪ TEL 310-326-0785 ▪ FAX 310-326-1470
E-MAIL JAMES@RUSSELLSCULPTURE.COM ▪ WWW.RUSSELLSCULPTURE.COM

Synergy, 2003, Coast Aluminum, Santa Fe Springs, CA, polished stainless steel, 10'H.

SCHULTE STUDIOS

KAI SCHULTE ▨ 41W020 SEAVEY ROAD ▨ SUGAR GROVE, IL 60554-9573 ▨ TEL 630-406-0404 ▨ FAX 630-406-0505
E-MAIL KAI@SCHULTESTUDIOS.COM ▨ WWW.SCHULTESTUDIOS.COM

116

Left: *Obelisk*, 2003, stainless steel, 9'H, base: 24" × 24". Right: *Crane*, 2002, stainless steel, 5.5'H. Photographs: Steve Jorstad.

KEVIN ROBB

KEVIN ROBB STUDIOS ▓ 7001 WEST 35TH AVENUE ▓ WHEAT RIDGE, CO 80033-6373
TEL 303-431-4758 ▓ FAX 303-425-8802 ▓ E-MAIL 3D@KEVINROBB.COM ▓ WWW.KEVINROBB.COM

Top left: *Flute Dance*, 2002, stainless steel, 100" × 47" × 42". Bottom left: *Flying Paper*, 2002, stainless steel, 36" × 24" × 28".
Right: *Dancing Triangles*, 2002, stainless steel, 117" × 47" × 44" on 12" base.

NICOLA PAN

125 HOLLOW HORN ROAD ▓ ERWINNA, PA 18920 ▓ TEL 610-294-9514
E-MAIL NICOLA@NICOLAPAN.COM ▓ WWW.NICOLAPAN.COM

Left: *Red + Grey*, bronze and stone, 32" x 18" x 7". Right: *Pacea Exelsa*, bronze and stone, 31" x 7" x 7".

NEIL SATER

WATER WONDERS, INC ▓ 3042 INDUSTRIAL PARKWAY ▓ SANTA MARIA, CA 93455
TEL 805-549-1880 ▓ FAX 805-925-3485 ▓ E-MAIL SALES@WATERWONDERS.COM ▓ WWW.WATERWONDERS.COM

 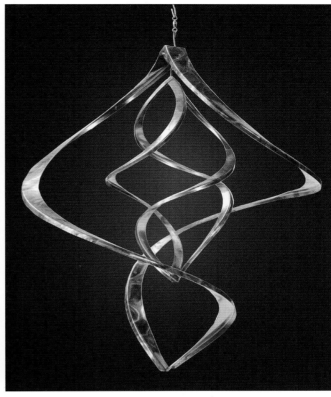

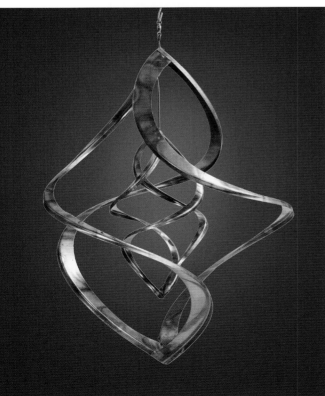 

Top left: *Triple Spirit*, 75" × 6.5" × 64". Top right: *Orbiter*, 23" × 30" × 46".
Bottom left: *Double Infinity*, 33" × 42" × 60". Bottom right: *Haiku Tower*, 28" × 24" × 57".

ROB FISHER

228 NORTH ALLEGHENY STREET ▪ BELLEFONTE, PA 16823 ▪ TEL 814-355-1458 ▪ FAX 814-353-9060
E-MAIL GLENUNION@AOL.COM ▪ WWW.ROBFISHERAMERICANDREAM.COM

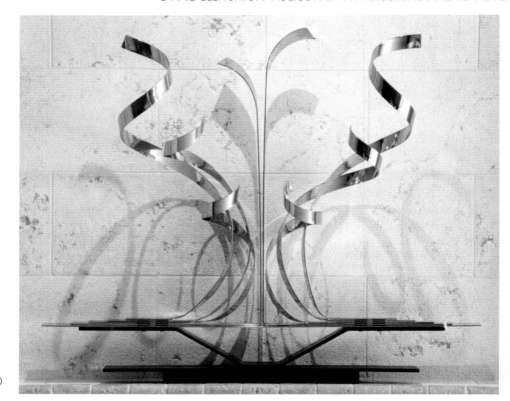

120

Top left: *Menorah*, 1998, Temple Beth Or, Hohokus, NJ, brass and painted steel, 4.5'W × 4'H × 1.5'D.
Top right: *Brother Fire*, 2002, Capuchin Monastery, Detroit, MI, stainless steel, powder coated, 8'H × 24"Dia. Bottom: *Muse*, 2003, stainless steel, powder coated, 39"W × 32"H × 24"D.

ELLIE RILEY

PO BOX 491417 ■ LOS ANGELES, CA 90049 ■ TEL 310-560-5003
E-MAIL BERTY222@AOL.COM ■ WWW.ELLIERILEY.COM

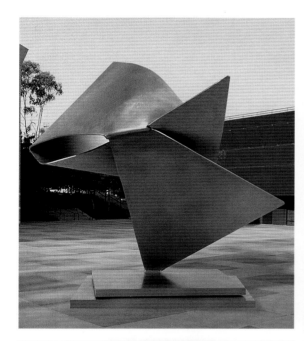

121

Top left: *Beacon,* 2002, brushed aluminum, 20" × 19" × 16". Right: *Natural Curve,* 2002, painted aluminum, 20" × 14" × 10".
Bottom left: *Let's Talk,* 2001, painted aluminum, 19" × 20" × 21". Photographs: Randall Michelson.

BANDHU DUNHAM

SALUSA GLASSWORKS, INC. ▧ PO BOX 2354 ▧ PRESCOTT, AZ 86302 ▧ TEL 800-515-7281 ▧ FAX 928-541-9570
E-MAIL BANDHU@SALUSAGLASSWORKS.COM ▧ WWW.SALUSAGLASSWORKS.COM

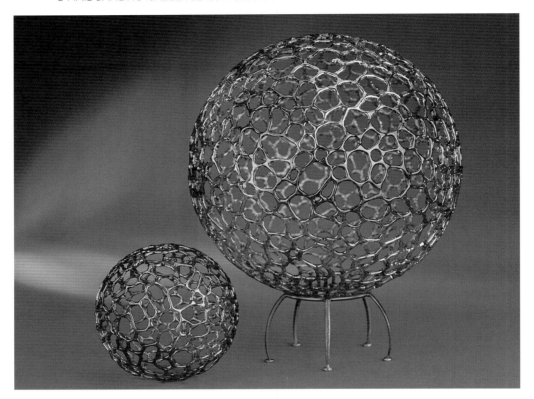

122

Top: *Rainbow Mottled Spheres,* 2004, lampworked glass, 6" and 11"Dia.
Bottom: *Amazing Kinetic Steam Engine,* 2004, lampworked glass, 36"H. Photographs: Christopher Marchetti.

MARSH SCOTT

2795 LAGUNA CANYON ROAD #C ▓ LAGUNA BEACH, CA 92651 ▓ TEL 949-494-8672
E-MAIL MARSH@MARSHSCOTT.COM ▓ WWW.MARSHSCOTT.COM

123

Top: *Desert Voices,* 2003, Kaiser Permanente, Palmdale, CA, stainless steel, 5 of 6 panels, each: 48"W × 48"H. Bottom left: *Wave Dance,* 2002,
public art for Laguna Beach, CA, stainless steel, 48"W × 66"H × 16" Dia. including base. Bottom right: *The Band,* 2003, stainless steel, each: 60"H × 20"W.

Representational Sculpture

126

Ilus Davis Maquette, Ilus Davis Park, Kansas City, final sculpture will be bronze, 9'H.

BRUCE WOLFE

BRUCE WOLFE LTD. ▨ 206 EL CERRITO AVENUE ▨ PIEDMONT, CA 94611
TEL 510-655-7871 ▨ FAX 510-601-7200 ▨ WWW.BRUCEWOLFE.COM

127

Left: *John Hannah Maquette*, Michigan State University, final sculpture will be bronze, 7.17'H. Top right: *Barbara Jordan*, Austin, TX airport, bronze, 7.17'H.
Center right: *Dr. Shumway*, Stanford School of Medicine, bronze, 20"H. Bottom right: *Mary Magdalene*, Santa Barbara Mission, bronze, 45"H.

HOPEN STUDIO INC.

BILL HOPEN ▪ AI QIU HOPEN ▪ 227 MAIN STREET ▪ SUTTON, WV 26601 ▪ TEL 800-872-8578 (U.S.)
TEL 304-765-5611 (INTERNATIONAL) ▪ E-MAIL HOPEN@MOUNTAIN.NET ▪ WWW.BILLHOPEN.COM ▪ WWW.AIQIUHOPEN.COM

128

Top left: *Blind Boone* by Ai Qiu Hopen, Warrensburg, MO, bronze, 125% life size.
Top right: *Sisters in Learning* (detail). Bottom: *Sisters in Learning* by Bill Hopen, Benedictine College, Atchison, KS, bronze, life size.

MARTHA PETTIGREW

201 WEST 21ST STREET ■ KEARNEY, NE 68845 ■ TEL/FAX 308-233-5504 ■ TEL 602-312-7979
E-MAIL DPETTIMAR@AOL.COM ■ WWW.MARTHAPETTIGREW.COM

Water Carrier. Photograph: Jafe Parson.

CRISTINA MIKULASEK

111 SE WHINERY ROAD ■ SHELTON, WA 98584 ■ TEL 360-427-9235 ■ FAX 360-427-7228
E-MAIL CHRIS@MIKULASEK.COM ■ WWW.MIKULASEK.COM

130

Top left: *Apassionata*, portrait of Beethoven, limited-edition bronze, life size. Right: *Home*, limited-edition bronze, 3'H, also available as an 8'H fountain or garden sculpture.
Bottom left: *Gone*, limited-edition bronze, half life size, also available as a life-size memorial.

TORK DESIGN GROUP

MARK LAGERGREN ■ ANTHONY BALL ■ 2505 FAIRWOOD AVENUE ■ COLUMBUS, OH 43207
TEL 614-492-1810 ■ FAX 614-492-1575 ■ E-MAIL TORKINFO@IWAYNET.NET ■ WWW.TORKWORKS.COM

131

Orchid, 2004, Franklin Park Conservatory, Columbus, OH, cast resin and copper, 16'H.

CYNTHIA SPARRENBERGER

SPARRENBERGER STUDIO ■ 5975 EAST OTERO DRIVE ■ ENGLEWOOD, CO 80112
TEL 303-741-3031 (STUDIO) ■ TEL 303-618-8974 (CELL) ■ E-MAIL CYNTHIA6@MAC.COM ■ WWW.SPARRENBERGERSTUDIO.COM

132

Top: *Late for School*, 2002, bronze, 11.5' × 5' × 4.5'.
Bottom left: *A Wing and a Prayer* (back), 2000, bronze, 63"H. Bottom right: *A Wing and a Prayer* (front). Photographs: Marcia Ward/The Imagemaker.

JANE RANKIN

19335 GREENWOOD DRIVE ▨ MONUMENT, CO 80132 ▨ TEL 719-488-9223 ▨ FAX 719-488-1650
E-MAIL JRANKIN@MAGPIEHILL.COM

133

Top: *Join the Parade* (partial view), 2003, bronze, life size.
Bottom left: *Wheels*, 2003, bronze, 39" × 38" × 19". Bottom right: *Joy*, 2002, bronze, 44" × 24" × 24".

MOANA PONDER

4110 HARTFORD STREET ▩ ABILENE, TX 79605 ▩ TEL 325-698-0866
E-MAIL MOANAPONDER1@AOL.COM ▩ WWW.PONDERSCULPTURE.COM

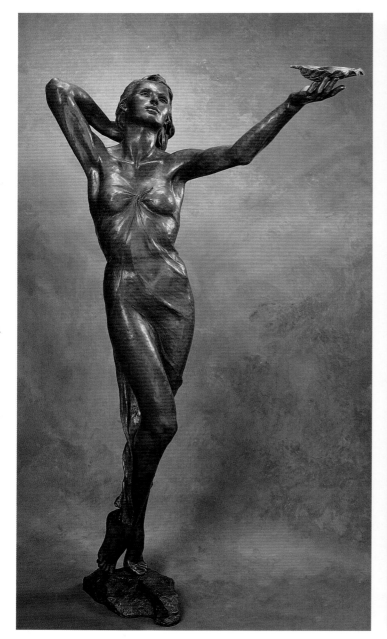

Left: *Seabreeze,* 2002, bronze with fountain option, 52"H.
Right: *Autumn Leaves,* 1999, bronze, 34"H. Photographs: Marc Bennett.

TROY KELLEY

TROY SCULPTOR INC. ■ BOX 301 ■ SALADO, TX 76571
TEL 254-947-8386 ■ FAX 254-947-9181 ■ E-MAIL TROYSCULPTOR@AOL.COM

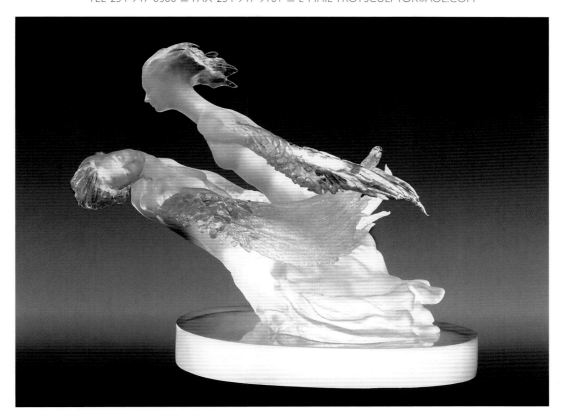

135

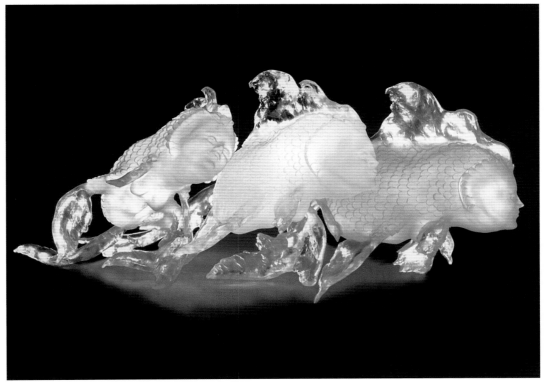

Top: *Dream of Flight*, 2002, acrylic, 24" × 14" × 21". Bottom: *Aquatic Dream*, 2002, acrylic, 17" × 14" × 30". Photographs: Johnny Shipman.

PAMELA SHAWLEY-WEAVER

EXPRESSIONS IN SCULPTURE ▨ 3597 EAST VALLEY ROAD ▨ LOGANTON, PA 17747 ▨ TEL 570-725-2807 ▨ FAX 570-725-2211
E-MAIL PAMELA@EXPRESSIONS-IN-SCULPTURE.COM ▨ WWW.EXPRESSIONS-IN-SCULPTURE.COM

136

Top left: *Incoming*, bronze, 16"H × 9"W × 10"D. Top right: *Soul Man*, bronze, 16"H × 10"W × 12"D.
Bottom left: *Cheers*, bronze, 17"H × 8"W × 10"D. Bottom right: *American Beauty*, bronze, 12"H × 7.5"W × 8"D. Photographs: Steve Tressler.

ANDREA WILKINSON

3502 SHADY VILLAGE ▪ KINGWOOD, TX 77345
TEL 281-358-4094 ▪ FAX 281-359-0033 ▪ E-MAIL ACLAYWORKS@YAHOO.COM

137

Top: *Fox Hunt*, 2003, bronze, 17.5"H x 31"L x 11"W. Bottom: *Poppy*, 2001, bronze, 32"H x 30"L x 18"W.

BIGBIRD-STUDIOS

PAT PAYNE ▓ 2121 ALAMEDA AVENUE ▓ ALAMEDA, CA 94501 ▓ TEL 510-521-9308
E-MAIL PPBIGBIRD@AOL.COM ▓ WWW.BIGBIRD-STUDIOS.COM

Top: *Eagle*, weathered welded steel, 53" × 74" × 26". Bottom: *Ascendant*, weathered welded steel, 77" × 72" × 48".

ROGER DiTARANDO

DiTARANDO & CO. ■ 1161 HARTFORD TURNPIKE ■ VERNON, CT 06066 ■ TEL 860-871-7635/860-870-1953
E-MAIL DITARANDO@AOL.COM ■ WWW.DITARANDO.COM

Top: *Herons*, welded and fabricated copper with cast bronze, height from left to right: 30", 52" and 36".
Bottom: *Goats*, welded and fabricated copper with cast bronze, 32"H x 35"L. Photographs: Dan Kelley.

MARK YALE HARRIS

C/O ARTWORK ▪ 1701 A LENA STREET ▪ SANTA FE, NM 87505 ▪ TEL/FAX 505-982-7447
E-MAIL ARTWORKSFE@AOL.COM ▪ ▪ WWW.MARKYALEHARRIS.COM

140

Top: *Recoil*, 2003, La Posada de Santa Fe, Rock Resorts, Santa Fe, NM, bronze, 46" × 33" × 42", edition of 8. Photograph: Stephen Yadzinski.
Bottom: *Pecos Red*, 2001, La Posada de Santa Fe, Rock Resorts, Santa Fe, NM, Texas red sandstone, 26" × 36" × 12".

JAMES SIMON

JAMES SIMON SCULPTURE STUDIOS ■ 305 GIST STREET ■ PITTSBURGH, PA 15219 ■ TEL/FAX 412-434-5629
E-MAIL MAIL@SIMONSCULPTURE.COM ■ WWW.SIMONSCULPTURE.COM

141

Liberty Avenue Musicians, 2003, Pittsburgh, PA, concrete, 15'H.
Liberty Avenue Musicians, dog and shoe (detail).

TUCK LANGLAND

12632 ANDERSON ROAD ▨ GRANGER, IN 46530
TEL/FAX 574-272-2708 ▨ E-MAIL TUCKANDJAN@AOL.COM

142

Top left: *Winter Solitude*, bronze with silver patina, 50"H.
Top right: *Generations*, bronze, 8.25'H. Photograph: Jafe Parsons. Bottom: *Crossroads*, 7'H bronze figures on Indiana limestone.

BARRY WOODS JOHNSTON

SCULPTUREWORKS INC. ▓ 2423 PICKWICK ROAD ▓ BALTIMORE, MD 21207
TEL 410-448-1945 ▓ FAX 410-448-2663 ▓ E-MAIL BARRY@SCULPTORJOHNSTON.COM ▓ WWW.SCULPTORJOHNSTON.COM

143

Top: *The Good Samaritan*, bronze. Bottom left and right: *The Good Samaritan* (details).

JON HAIR, OFFICIAL SCULPTOR OF THE U.S. OLYMPIC TEAM ▦ 20000 NORMAN COLONY ROAD ▦ CORNELIUS, NC 28031
TEL 704-892-7203 ▦ FAX 704-892-7208 ▦ E-MAIL JHSTUDIO@AOL.COM ▦ WWW.JONHAIR.COM

144

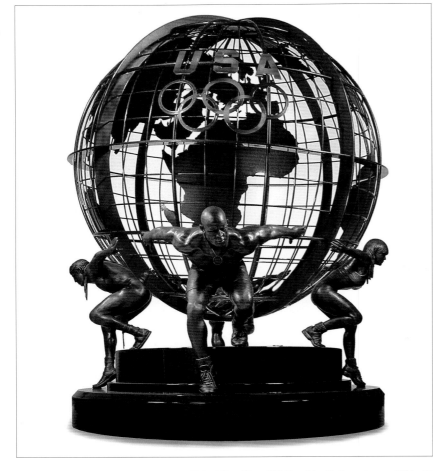

Top left: *Three Runners*, 12'H x 16'L, edition of 12. Top right: *Challenger*, bronze, 15'H, edition of 12. Bottom left: *Olympic Strength*, bronze
maquette for 30'H monument, 7'H. Center right: *Miccosukee Indian Boy*, bronze and polychrome, 9'H. Bottom right: *Dick Van Dyke*, bronze portrait bust, over life size.

Authenticating statement 36USC220506

JON HAIR STUDIO OF FINE ART, LLC

JON HAIR, OFFICIAL SCULPTOR OF THE U.S. OLYMPIC TEAM ▨ 20000 NORMAN COLONY ROAD ▨ CORNELIUS, NC 28031
TEL 704-892-7203 ▨ FAX 704-892-7208 ▨ E-MAIL JHSTUDIO@AOL.COM ▨ WWW.JONHAIR.COM

Top left: *Phoenix Rising*, bronze, 12'H x 9'W, edition of 12. Top right: *Capt. Christopher Newport*, bronze historic portrait (clay original shown), 24'H.
Bottom left: *Grizzly Bear*, bronze (clay original shown), 10'H x 13'W, edition of 12. Bottom right: *Defender*, bronze, 10'H x 12'W, edition of 12.

PAUL REIBER

PO BOX 732 ■ MENDOCINO, CA 95460 ■ TEL/FAX 707-964-7151
E-MAIL PREIBER@MCN.ORG ■ WWW.MENDOCINOFURNITURE.COM

Top: *Shell Fireplace Surround,* 1999, Chicago, maple, 74" × 43". Photograph: Mark Saffron.
Bottom left: *Fish Boat,* 2002, basswood, Jelutong, mahogany, gold leaf and pigment, 35" × 16" × 16". Bottom right: *3 figures,* basswood, up to 36"H. Photograph: Jay Odee.

JIM BUDISH

DENVER STUDIO ■ PO BOX 102377 ■ DENVER, CO 80250 ■ TEL 303-324-2081 ■ FAX 303-715-0430
E-MAIL SCULPT2001@AOL.COM ■ WWW.JIMBUDISH.COM

147

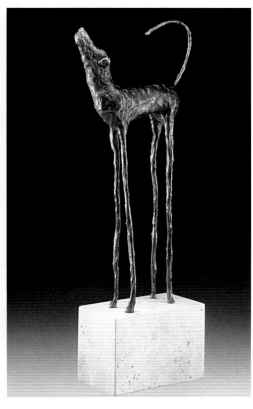

Top left: *Chauncey*, 20"H x 9"W (also 62"H x 28"W). Photograph: Marica Ward. Top right: *Little Joy*, 6"H x 3"W plus base (also 48"H x 24"W).
Bottom left: *The Couple*, 15.5"H x 14.5"W plus base (also 77"H x 74"W). Bottom right: *Zoë*, 16"H x 6"W plus base (also 72"H x 33"W). Photographs: Mel Shockner.

Liturgical Art

JEFF G. SMITH

ARCHITECTURAL STAINED GLASS, INC. ▓ PO BOX 1126 ▓ FORT DAVIS, TX 79734-1126
TEL 432-426-3311 ▓ FAX 432-426-3366 ▓ E-MAIL INFO@ARCHSTGLASSINC.COM ▓ WWW.ARCHSTGLASSINC.COM

150

Top left: *Holy Spirit Clerestory*, 5.8'H × 31.6"W; *Reconciliation Chapel Windows*, 15'H × 25.3'W; *St. Bridget Narthex Window*, 4.5'H × 4.3'W. Photograph: Chris Eden/Eden Arts.
Top right: *Reconciliation Chapel* (detail). Bottom: *St. Bridget Window* and *St. Bridget's Cloak* at main entry doors.

JEFF G. SMITH

ARCHITECTURAL STAINED GLASS, INC. ▨ PO BOX 1126 ▨ FORT DAVIS, TX 79734-1126
TEL 432-426-3311 ▨ FAX 432-426-3366 ▨ E-MAIL INFO@ARCHSTGLASSINC.COM ▨ WWW.ARCHSTGLASSINC.COM

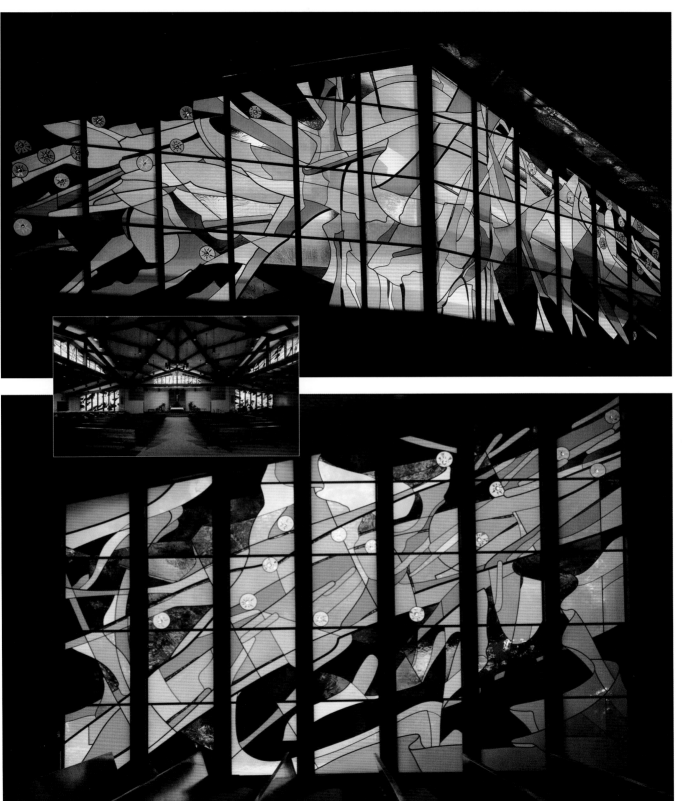

151

Top: *Creation Clerestory Window,* 10.4'H x 31.6'W. Photograph: Chris Eden/Eden Arts.
Inset: Nave and clerestory windows at Sanctuary. Photograph: Chris Eden/Eden Art. Bottom: *God's Gifts* at East Nave, 14.8'H x 21.1'W.

MARK ERIC GULSRUD

ARCHITECTURAL GLASS/SCULPTURE ■ 3309 TAHOMA PLACE WEST ■ TACOMA, WA 98466
TEL 253-566-1720 ■ FAX 253-565-5981 ■ E-MAIL MARKGULSRUD@ATTBI.COM ■ WWW.MARKERICGULSRUD.COM

152

Top left: Window wall, 2002, Hope Lutheran Church, Palm Desert, CA, custom hand-blown leaded glass. Top right: Window wall (detail).
Bottom: Window wall (exterior view). Photographs: Greg Epstein.

GUY KEMPER

KEMPER STUDIO ■ 190 NORTH BROADWAY ■ LEXINGTON, KY 40507
TEL/FAX 859-254-3507 ■ E-MAIL GUY@KEMPERSTUDIO.COM ■ WWW.KEMPERSTUDIO.COM

153

Sources (detail), Congregation of St. Agnes, Fond du Lac, WI. Fabricated by Derix Glasstudios, Taunusstein, Germany.

JOY SAVILLE

244 DODDS LANE ■ PRINCETON, NJ 08540 ■ TEL/FAX 609-924-6824
E-MAIL JSAVILLE@PATMEDIA.NET ■ WWW.JOYSAVILLE.COM

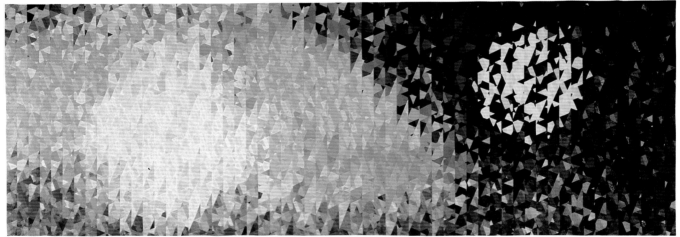

Top: *Day One, Genesis 1:1-5*, 2003. Center: *Day Four, Genesis 1:14-19*, 2003. Commissioned by The Jewish Center, Princeton, NJ, cotton, linen and silk, each panel: 6' x 16' x 1". Bottom: Installation of *Day One* and *Day Four*. Photographs: William Taylor.

ERLING HOPE

HOPE LITURGICAL WORKS ▨ 1455 SAG/BRIDGE TURNPIKE ▨ SAG HARBOR, NY 11963
TEL/FAX 631-725-4294 ▨ E-MAIL HOPELITWRK@AOL.COM

155

Top left: *Processional Cross #35,* 2000, maple, walnut and pigment, 16" × 16".
Right: *Processional Cross #34,* 1999, carved Baltic birch ply, vitreous mosaic tile fragments, gold leaf and pigment, 18" × 30".
Bottom left: *Texture #1: How Words Work,* 2000, mahogany, brass escutcheon pins describing a poem written in Braille, 11.5" × 9.5" × 2.5".

Furniture & Lighting

ANDY SÁNCHEZ

CUSTOM FURNITURE BY ANDY SÁNCHEZ ▨ 4 ARCHIBEQUE DRIVE ▨ ALGODONES, NM 87001
TEL 505-385-1189 ▨ FAX 505-771-1223 ▨ WWW.ANDYSANCHEZ.COM

158

Top: Cantilever coffee table, juniper, 48" x 26". Bottom: Juniper table with octagon marble base, 7'Dia, chairs by Drexel Heritage Furnishings. Photograph: Sandy Harvey.

MALAY PATEL

INSPIRED BY NATURE, INC ■ 353 EAST BAILEY ROAD ■ NAPERVILLE, IL 60565
TEL 630-709-9511 ■ E-MAIL MALAY@BYMALAY.COM ■ WWW.BYMALAY.COM

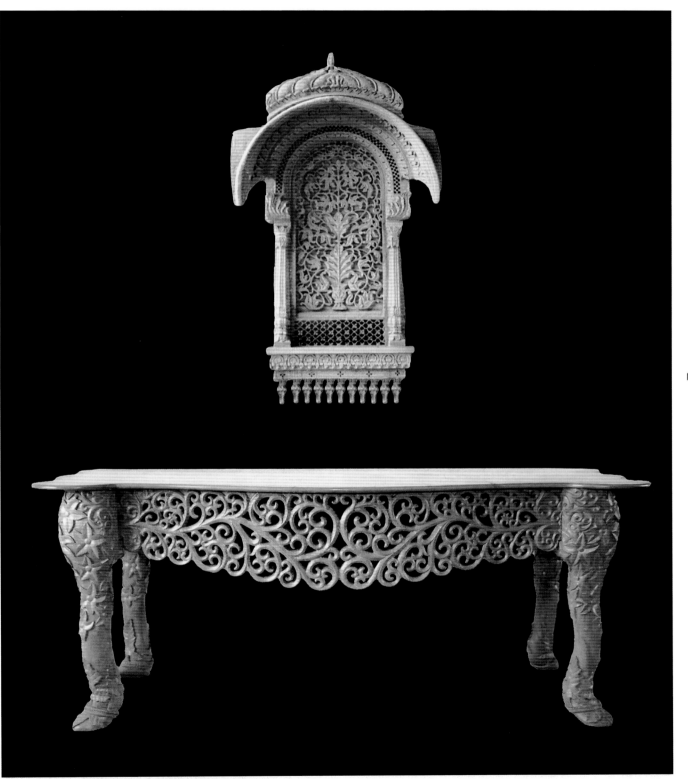

Hand-carved sandstone window, 2002, 42"H x 25"W x 10"D.
Hand-carved sandstone console table, 2003, 30.5"H x 71.5"W x 28"D.

PAM MORRIS DESIGNS EXCITING LIGHTING

PAM MORRIS ▓ GATE FIVE ROAD, STUDIO 100 ▓ SAUSALITO, CA 94965
TEL 415-332-0168 ▓ FAX 415-332-0169 ▓ E-MAIL LIGHTING@SONIC.NET

160

Left: Glass fireplace facade, kiln formed glass, fiber optic, 14'H. Top right: *Zen Zero Chandelier*, mixed media, 42"H. Bottom right: *Pool Table Wave Light*, steel, 72"L.

DALE JENSSEN

PO BOX 129 ■ TERLINGUA, TX 79852 ■ TEL/FAX 432-371-2312
E-MAIL JENSSENGALLERY@HOTMAIL.COM ■ WWW.DALEJENSSEN.COM

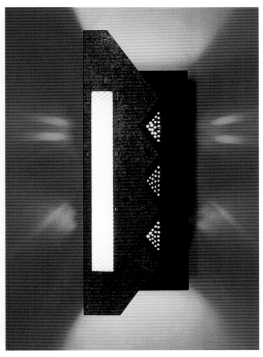

Top left: *Cloud Sconce*, 2002, galvanized steel, 18" × 18" × 8". Top right: *Zig Zag Sconce*, 2003, steel, acrylic and copper, 18" × 6" × 6".
Bottom: *Red Fun Chandelier*, 2003, wood, aluminum, acrylic, paint, brass and miscellaneous, 48" × 36" × 36".

FURNACE HOT GLASS WORKS LLC

CHRIS NORDIN ■ MICHELLE PLUCINSKY ■ 2225 DREXEL ■ DEARBORN, MI 48128
TEL 313-894-6000 ■ FAX 313-359-1837 ■ E-MAIL FURNACEHOTGLASS@AOL.COM ■ WWW.FURNACEHOTGLASS.COM

Top left and right: *Representing the Client's Personality*, 2003, Universal Images, Southfield, MI, blown glass and stainless steel, each: 4' × 10'. Photographs: Steve Lengnick, Plum Street Studio.
Bottom: *Jellyfish Chandeliers*, 1999, Charlie's Crab, Troy, MI, blown glass and stainless steel, 32" × 32". Photograph: GTODD Photography.

TRIO DESIGN GLASSWARE

RENATO FOTI ■ 253 QUEEN STREET SOUTH ■ KITCHENER, ON N2G 1W4 ■ CANADA ■ TEL 519-749-2814 ■ FAX 519-749-6319
E-MAIL RENATO@TRIODESIGNGLASSWARE.COM ■ WWW.TRIODESIGNGLASSWARE.COM

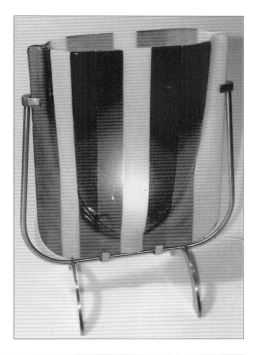

Top left: *Perspective* (detail), martini hall table, 15"W × any length × 31"H. Top center: Stainless steel cabinet with glass inserts, 38" × 24".
Top right: *Solid Perception*, glass table lamp, 15" × 12" × 3". Bottom: *Inverted Perspective Sink*, 19" × 19".

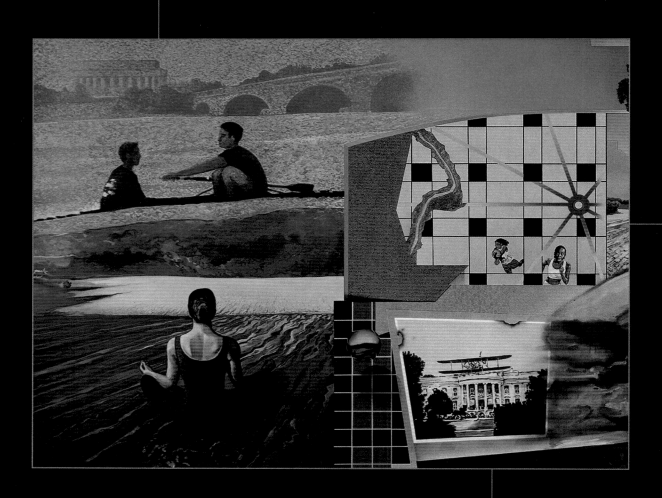

Murals & Trompe L'Oeil

STEWART WHITE

STEWART WHITE STUDIOS ▧ 1121 TYLER AVENUE ▧ ANNAPOLIS, MD 21403 ▧ TEL 410-263-7465
E-MAIL STEWHITE30@EARTHLINK.NET ▧ WWW.STEWARTWHITESTUDIOS.COM

166

Top left: *The Shops*, 1996, Altoona Railroaders Museum, acrylic on canvas, 12' × 30'.
Top right: *The Matson Container & Shipping Yards*, 2003, The National Museum of American History, acrylic on canvas, 14' × 26'.
Bottom: *Sandy Boulevard, Portland, Oregon*, The National Museum of American History, acrylic on canvas, 15' × 60'.

SPOLAR STUDIO

TONY SPOLAR ▩ 126 EAST MINERAL STREET ▩ MILWAUKEE, WI 53204 ▩ TEL 414-672-9847 ▩ FAX 414-831-2493
E-MAIL TONY@SPOLARSTUDIO.COM ▩ WWW.SPOLARSTUDIO.COM

167

Top: *The Survey Mural*, 2001, Miller Park, Milwaukee, WI, digitally designed and produced, printed on archival fine art canvas, 14' × 40'. Photograph: Jeff Salzer Photography.
Center: *The Boys*, 2002, private residence ceiling panel, seamless oil on canvas, 9' × 24'. Photograph: Dowling Studios.
Bottom: *Sculpted* murals, 2003, Master Lock World Headquarters, digital imagery with mixed media, 6' × 15' each, 8 murals total. Photograph: Jeff Salzer Photography.

TRENA McNABB

McNABB STUDIO, INC. ■ PO BOX 327 ■ BETHANIA, NC 27010
TEL 336-924-6053 ■ FAX 336-924-4854 ■ E-MAIL TRENA@TMCNABB.COM ■ WWW.TMCNABB.COM

Top: *Thank You for Your Service*, transparent, overlapping images painted in acrylic on canvas panels, Lopez Nursing Home, Veterans Administration Art in State Buildings Program, Land O' Lakes, FL, seven equilateral triangles, total size: 36" x 184" x 2". Bottom: *Thank You for Your Service* (detail).

DÉGAGÉ STUDIOS

TRUDY LYNN SIMMONS ▪ 1464 INGLESIDE AVENUE ▪ MCLEAN, VA 22101 ▪ 703-356-8002 ▪ FAX 703-356-7709
E-MAIL CSIMMONS@DEGAGE.COM ▪ WWW.DEGAGE.COM

169

Top left: Trompe l'oeil columns painted with a soft, distant scenic. Top right: *Painters Day Out.*
Bottom: Trompe l'oeil window and wine cellar extending the actual floor tile into the painting.

JOHN PUGH

PO BOX 1332 ■ LOS GATOS, CA 95031
TEL 408-353-3370 ■ FAX 408-353-1223 ■ WWW.ARTOFJOHNPUGH.COM

170

Top: *Valentine's Day*, Twentynine Palms, CA, full mural, 15' × 45'. Bottom left: *Trespasser*, private residence, Los Altos, CA, trompe l'oeil mural on door, 7.3' × 3'. Photograph: Brian Brumley. Bottom right: *River of Mercy* (detail), City of Merced, CA, full mural, 20' × 100'.

G. BYRON PECK/CITY ARTS

G. BYRON PECK STUDIOS ▨ 1857 LAMONT STREET NW ▨ WASHINGTON, DC 20010 ▨ TEL/FAX 202-331-1966
E-MAIL BYRONPECK@EARTHLINK.NET ▨ WWW.PECKSTUDIOS.COM ▨ WWW.CITYARTSDC.ORG

171

Top left: *Miller Building Mural*, Knoxville, TN, 90' × 21'. Top right: Mural replicating Tiffany window, American Embassy, Santiago, Chile, 8' × 16'.
Center: *American Legacy Mural*, 2004, acrylic, 8' × 18'. Bottom: *American Legacy Mural*, 2004, acrylic, 8' × 18'. Photographs: Greg Staley.

Building Artful Relationships: BJ Katz & Randy Schmitgen

ARTIST
BJ Katz

TITLE
Ideas Create Reality, 2003

COMMISSIONED FOR
American College Testing
Headquarters Training Center,
Iowa City, IA

TIMELINE: 9 months

DIMENSIONS: 11'H × 88'W

TRADE PROFESSIONAL
Randy Schmitgen,
Interiors/Senior Designer,
Flad & Associates

When artist BJ Katz met designer Randy Schmitgen at a trade show more than five years ago, a relationship began that eventually led to an exciting commission for a headquarters project in Iowa City. They talked from time to time about working together before eventually finalizing *Ideas Create Reality,* a project for the American College Testing (ACT) Headquarters training center. ▪ Katz and Schmitgen determined that they wanted something special for the space and had many discussions and brainstorming sessions before deciding to go with Katz's suggestion of a "river" theme, which tied into the quality and character of the wooded site where the buildings are located. "The natural terrain of Iowa was my inspiration; I often draw inspiration from nature," she notes. ▪ "The final product is definitely a master work of art," Schmitgen reports. "The glow, reflection and transparency of each piece are unique and inspiring. The coordination and constant communication between BJ and us early in the design process was critical. When the final art and design were communicated to ACT, they confirmed that it was exactly what was wanted." ▪ Katz agrees that working with the designers and architects from the very beginning was key to the success of this project. "Be specific and provide drawings, samples and maquettes so everyone is on the same page before production even begins," Katz advises. "We all communicated openly about what everyone wanted from the project, so the process was a real pleasure because there was so much enthusiasm about the artwork." ▪ The final result was 22 panes of glass cast to create a single flowing composition that forms the new "center" for three buildings on the campus. It is a dramatic art piece that truly enhances the space.

MARINA POPOVA

MARINA POPOVA AND ASSOCIATES INC. ▨ 87 ANGELL AVENUE ▨ MONTREAL, QC H9W 4V6 ▨ CANADA
TEL 514-630-9759 ▨ FAX 514-630-4009 ▨ E-MAIL INFO@MARINAPOPOVA.COM ▨ WWW.MARINAPOPOVA.COM

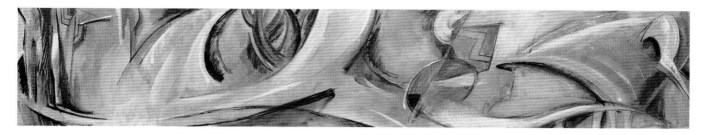

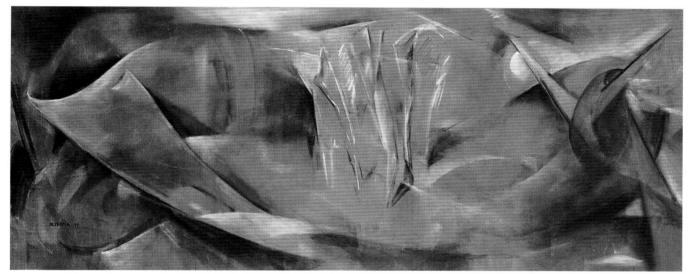

Top: *Movement*, 1998, Turning Stone Hotel & Casino, Verona, NY, 10' × 50'. Center: *Transformation*, 2001, Museum of Contemporary Art,
Moscow, Russia, 6.6' × 17'. Bottom left: *Cave Drawing Inspiration* (detail), 2000, private residence, Los Angeles, CA, 8.5' × 40'.
Bottom right: Trompe l'oeil mosaic (detail), 2003, Caesars Palace, Colosseum Theatre, Las Vegas, NV, 8.5' × 18.3'. Photographs: Patrice des Roches.

Paintings & Prints

JOSEPH SPANGLER

CITYBLOQUES ■ 2141 SOUTH FAIRFIELD AVENUE ■ CHICAGO, IL 60608
TEL 773-991-4537 ■ JOE@CITYBLOQUES.COM ■ WWW.CITYBLOQUES.COM

176

Top: *Chinatown Overpass*, 2001, oil on canvas, 60" × 60". Bottom: *Patience*, 2003, oil on canvas, 54" × 84".

YOSHI HAYASHI

YOSHI HAYASHI STUDIO ▧ 255 KANSAS STREET #330 ▧ SAN FRANCISCO, CA 94103 ▧ TEL/FAX 415-552-0755
E-MAIL YOSHIHAYASHI@ATT.NET ▧ WWW.YOSHIHAYASHI.COM

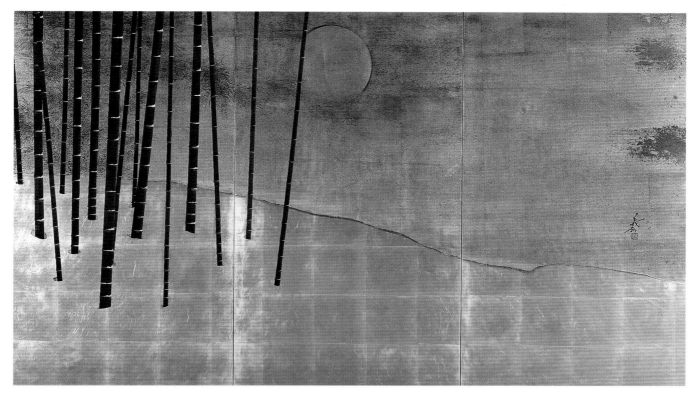

177

Top: *Snow Moon,* 2003, gold and silver leaf with oil paint, 42" x 72".
Bottom: *Mountain Moon,* 2001, gold, silver and copper leaf with oil paint, 48" x 80". Photographs: Ira D. Schrank.

NANCY "STEVIE" PEACOCK

NANCY PEACOCK ARTWORKS ■ PO BOX 47346 ■ SEATTLE, WA 98146 ■ TEL 206-242-8884
E-MAIL NANCYPEACOCK@COMCAST.NET ■ WWW.NANCYPEACOCK.COM

178

Top: *Monterey Jazz Quartet*, 2002, acrylic on canvas, 40" x 60".
Bottom: *Stanley Turrentine Quartet*, 1999, acrylic on canvas, 24" x 48". Photographs: Ken Wagner.

SUSAN SCULLEY

4731 NORTH PAULINA #3N ■ CHICAGO, IL 60640
TEL 773-728-6109 ■ FAX 773-728-9305 ■ E-MAIL SUSAN.SCULLEY@SCDCHICAGO.COM

Top: *The Sky Beyond*, 2002, oil stick on paper, 28" x 39". Bottom left: *Apricot Trees*, 2001, oil stick on canvas, 32" x 34".
Bottom right: *In the Hothouse*, 1998, oil stick on canvas, 40" x 40". Photographs: Steve Perry.

SILJA TALIKKA LAHTINEN

SILJA'S FINE ART STUDIO ▪ 5220 SUNSET TRAIL ▪ MARIETTA, GA 30068
TEL 770-993-3409 ▪ FAX 770-992-0350 ▪ E-MAIL PENTEC02@BELLSOUTH.NET

180

Top: *The Spirits of the Prairie*, 2003, artist collection, acrylic on canvas, 24" × 24". Bottom: *The Sun Paints the Sky with Fire*, 2003, artist collection, acrylic on canvas, 24" × 24".

GRANT JOHNSON

STIMULUS LLC ■ PO BOX 170519 ■ SAN FRANCISCO, CA 94117 ■ TEL 415-558-8339 ■ FAX 415-864-3897
E-MAIL GRANT@GRANTJOHNSONART.COM ■ WWW.GRANTJOHNSONART.COM

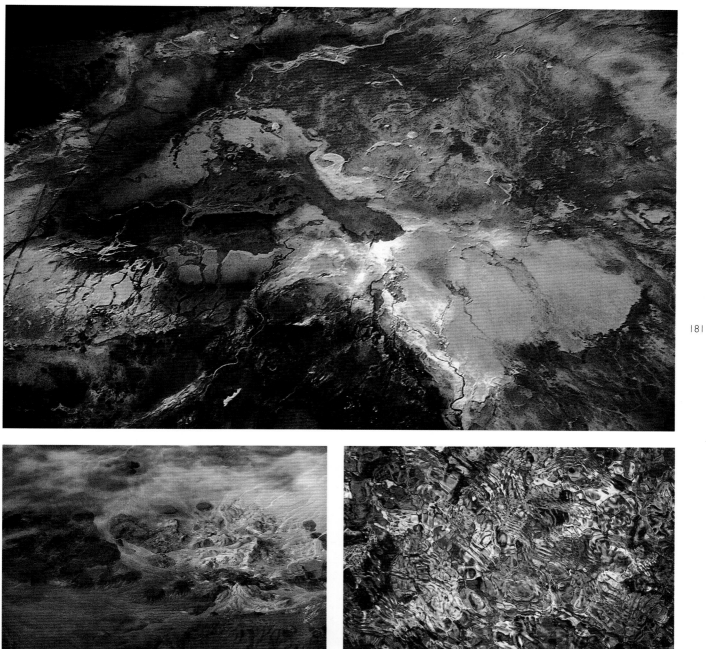

Top: *How I Spent My Summer Vacation, No Man's Land* series, 2001, archival pigment print on canvas, 48" × 72".
Bottom left: *Sandyland, No Man's Land* series, 2001, archival pigment print on canvas, 48" × 72".
Bottom right: *The Abstract Nature of Frozen Time, Water Color* series, 2000, archival pigment print on canvas, 48" × 72".

LOIS WALKER

149 HARBOR SOUTH ▨ AMITYVILLE, NY 11701 ▨ TEL 631-691-2376 ▨ FAX 631-691-1920
E-MAIL LOISVWALKER@AOL.COM ▨ WWW.ARTFULSTYLE.COM/WALKER

182

Top: *Habit*, 1989, acrylic on canvas, 36" x 36". Bottom: *Escape*, 1991, oil on canvas, 30" x 48". Photographs: Lisa Hermanson.

AMOS MILLER

AMOS MILLER STUDIO ▧ MIAMI, FL
E-MAIL STUDIOAM@BELLSOUTH.NET

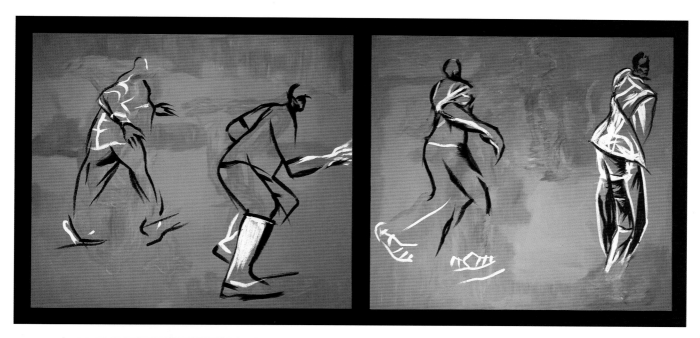

183

Top: Untitled, 2003, diptych, oil and acrylic on canvas, 64" × 144".
Bottom: Untitled, 2003, triptych, oil and acrylic on canvas, 72" × 144". Photographs: Daniel Portnoy.

BRENT LILLY

BRENTART.COM ▨ 10750 RIVER RUN DRIVE ▨ MANASSAS, VA 20112 ▨ TEL 703-298-2994
E-MAIL JEDI@BRENTART.COM ▨ WWW.BRENTART.COM

184

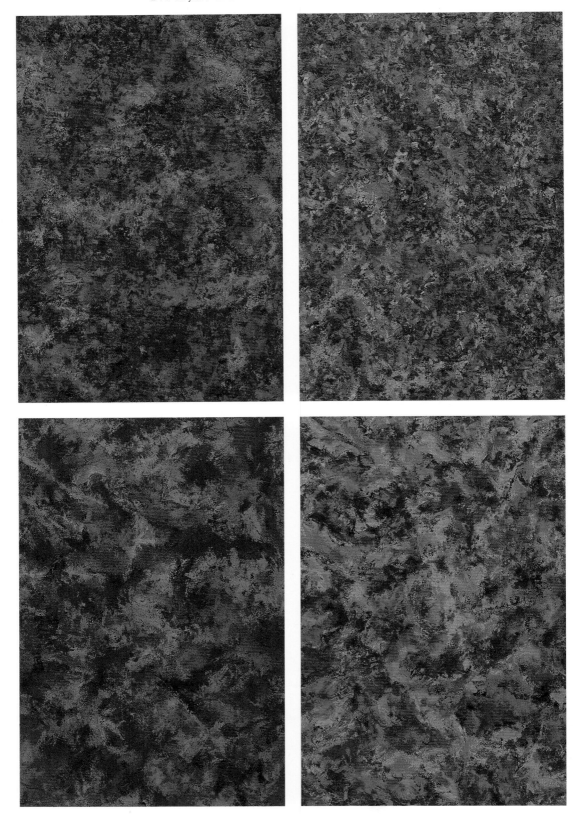

Top left: *Kalypso's Dream*, 2002, acrylic, 60" × 48". Top right: *At the End of the Day*, 2002, acrylic, 60" × 48".
Bottom left: *Code Red*, 2002, acrylic, 60" × 48". Bottom right: *Trade Winds*, 2003, acrylic, 60" × 48".

PAMELA COSPER

4439 ROLLING PINE DRIVE ▨ WEST BLOOMFIELD, MI 48323 ▨ TEL 248-366-9569
E-MAIL PAMELACOSPER@HOTMAIL.COM ▨ WWW.GO.TO/PCOSPER

185

Sunset Victory, 2003, acrylic, 37" × 49". Photograph: Tomiko Gumbleton.

JOHN SPEARS

2D-3D INC. ▨ 441 BARBERTOWN-POINT BREEZE ROAD ▨ FLEMINGTON, NJ 08822
TEL 908-996-6086 ▨ FAX 908-996-7401 ▨ E-MAIL SPEARS@BLAST.NET ▨ WWW.2D-3DINC.COM

186

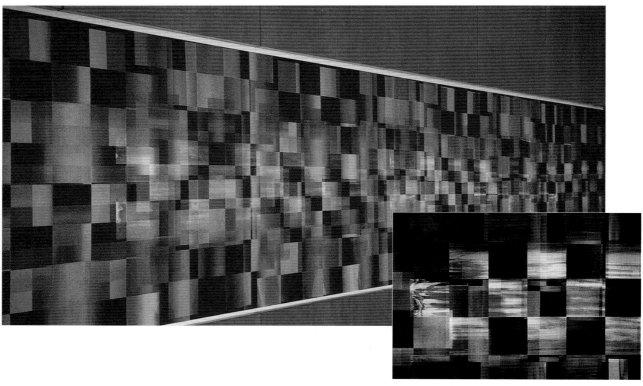

Top: *Celebration*, a series, 2004, Concourse Office Plaza, Podolsky Realty Partners, screen painting, 48" × 207". Inset: *Celebration* (detail).
Bottom: *Stain Glass*, a series, 2004, Concourse Office Plaza, Podolsky Realty Partners, screen painting, 48" × 207". Inset: *Stain Glass* (detail).

JOHN SPEARS

2D-3D INC. ▪ 441 BARBERTOWN-POINT BREEZE ROAD ▪ FLEMINGTON, NJ 08822
TEL 908-996-6086 ▪ FAX 908-996-7401 ▪ E-MAIL SPEARS@BLAST.NET ▪ WWW.2D-3DINC.COM

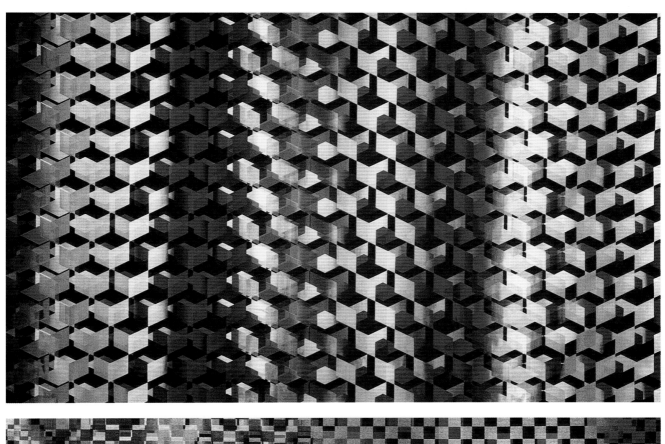

187

Top: *Building Blocks* (detail), a series, 2004, screen painting. Bottom: *Study of Pattern* (detail), a series, 2004, screen painting.

EVA CARTER

EVA CARTER GALLERY ▩ 132 EAST BAY STREET ▩ CHARLESTON, SC 29401 ▩ TEL 843-722-0506 ▩ FAX 843-722-7232
E-MAIL EVACARTER@EARTHLINK.NET ▩ WWW.EVACARTERGALLERY.COM

188

Top: *Extremes*, 2003, oil on canvas, 90" x 144".
Bottom left: *Aspen Magic*, 2002, oil on canvas, 60" x 48". Bottom right: *Above All Else*, 2001, oil on canvas, 64" x 50".

DAVID MILTON

1939 SOUTH HILLS PLACE ■ BELLINGHAM, WA 98229 ■ TEL 360-734-2225
E-MAIL DAVID@DAVIDMILTON.COM ■ WWW.DAVIDMILTON.COM

189

Top: *Journeys*, 2003, mixed media on wood panel, 72" x 36". Bottom: *Hidden Memories*, 2002, mixed media on wood panel, 48" x 36".

Fine Art Photography

TALLI ROSNER-KOZUCH

PHO-TAL, INC. ▓ 15 NORTH SUMMIT STREET ▓ TENAFLY, NJ 07670 ▓ TEL 201-569-3199 ▓ FAX 201-569-3392
E-MAIL TAL@PHOTAL.COM ▓ WWW. PHOTAL.COM

Top: *Orchid*, sepia. Bottom: *Lily*, sepia.

LEN MORRIS

LEONARD MORRIS, INC. ■ TEL 917-992-3313 ■ E-MAIL LENMORRIS@EARTHLINK.NET ■ WWW.LENMORRIS.NET

193

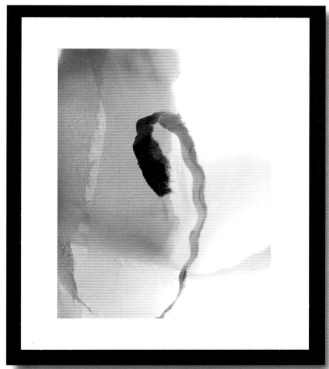

Top left: *Dance,* from the *Leaf* series, photograph of a leaf with paper. Top right: *PETALS ... petal,* from the *Lily* series, photograph of lily petals on paper.
Bottom left: *Beginnings,* from the *Paper Plate* series, photograph of a paper plate fragment on paper background.
Bottom right: *Possibilities,* from the *Classified* series, photograph of financial quotes on paper. All photographs are 16" x 20", limited editions of 125.

EWING PHOTOGRAPHY

GIFFORD EWING ▓ 800 EAST 19TH AVENUE ▓ DENVER, CO 80218
TEL 303-832-0800 ▓ FAX 303-832-0801 ▓ E-MAIL GALLERY@EWINGPHOTO.COM ▓ WWW.EWINGPHOTO.COM

194

Top: *Mount Herard,* 1990, Great Sand Dunes National Monument, CO, various sizes and murals available.
Bottom left: *Lone Buffalo,* 1997, Yellowstone, WY, various sizes and murals available.
Bottom right: *February Mist,* 1997, Franklin, ME, various sizes and murals available.

CAROL CARTWRIGHT

CARTWRIGHT PHOTOGRAPHY ▨ PO BOX 772 ▨ SALIDA, CO 81201 ▨ 719-221-1627
E-MAIL CCARTPHOTO@AOL.COM ▨ WWW.CARTWRIGHTPHOTOGRAPHY.COM

Top left: *Room with a View*, 2001, Ponderosa Ranch, Seneca, OR. Top right: *School Daze*, 2002, Ponderosa Ranch, Seneca, OR.
Bottom: *Spectrum*, 2002, Ponderosa Ranch, Seneca, OR. All images available as photographic or giclee prints on photographic paper or canvas. Various sizes available.

Building Artful Relationships: Robert Ellison & Ed Fritz

Alison Bies

ARTIST
Robert Ellison

TITLE
Sun Zone, 1998

COMMISSIONED FOR
Sonoma County
Administration Building,
Sonoma County, CA

TIMELINE: 18 months

DIMENSIONS: 14'H x 14'W x 12'D

TRADE PROFESSIONAL
Ed Fritz, Project Manager,
Sonoma County Architects Office

Large public sculpture design has been one of Robert Ellison's focuses for 30 years; his artistic goals include designing pieces that can be enjoyed by the community. He likes creating large, whimsical pieces in rich colors using materials such as steel, aluminum and concrete. Because of his passion for whimsy, he was the perfect artist to work with architects and engineers involved in the facelift of the entrance to the Sonoma County Administration Building. ■ The curved, billowing forms at the top of the abstract piece are a reference to the dynamic weather of the area. "A theme needed to be developed to include various aspects of life in Sonoma County, and that could be portrayed using my style of work," Ellison explains. "The sun, the shadows it creates and atmospheric symbols seemed to encompass this goal." ■ Ed Fritz, project manager for *Sun Zone,* was immediately taken with the sculpture Ellison created. "We first saw the entrance piece in the studio. It was amazing!" Fritz recalls. "It causes a lot of conversation, and I always see kids underneath it looking up, which is great because I think it makes those kids think." ■ Given the size, weight and dimensions of the piece, communication and flexibility were key to the project and the resulting relationships. ■ "Artists should focus on the essence of what the designers are looking for. Design professionals may bring something to the table that an artist may not have thought of," Ellison says. "It is a very fun and rewarding experience if you can speak the required technical language and, conversely, lure [the architectural team] into a more creative and abstract approach." ■ "There were some initial engineering problems with this piece. But, if you're flexible it can be resolved, as it was for us," Fritz notes. "This was a fun project, and something different from what I've done before."

DAR HORN

UNION ART WORKS ▓ 402 WEST 5TH STREET ▓ SAN PEDRO, CA 90731
TEL 310-833-1282 ▓ FAX 310-833-1592 ▓ E-MAIL DAR@DARHORN.COM ▓ WWW.DARHORN.COM

197

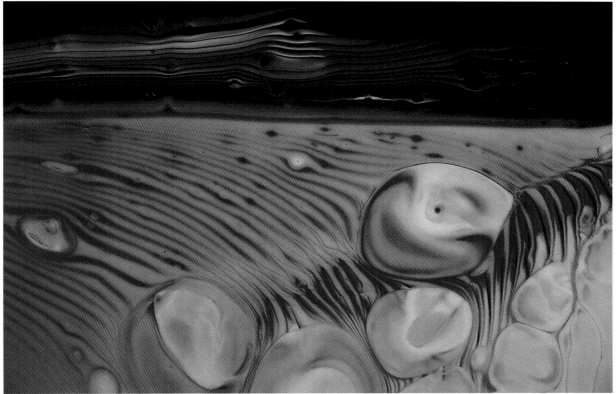

Top: *Stardust*, 2002, Ilfochrome™ print on aluminum panel, 20" x 30". Bottom: *Fire Fall*, 2002, Ilfochrome™ print on aluminum panel, 20" x 30".

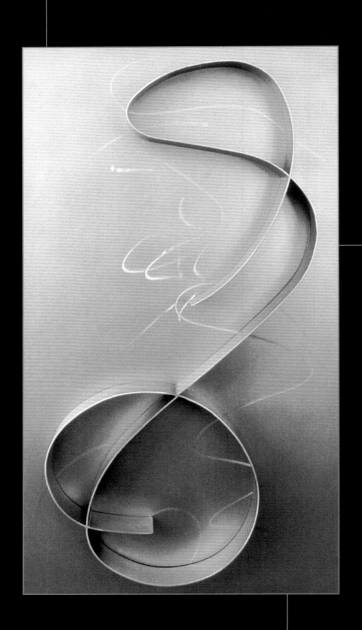

Art for the Wall | Metal

MARTIN STURMAN

MARTIN STURMAN SCULPTURES ▨ 3201 BAYSHORE DRIVE ▨ WESTLAKE VILLAGE, CA 91361
TEL 818-707-8087 ▨ FAX 818-707-3079 ▨ E-MAIL MLSTURMAN@SBCGLOBAL.NET ▨ WWW.STEELSCULPTURES.COM

200

Top: *Outdoor Floral*, 2003, stainless steel, 44" × 66" × 2". Bottom left: *Martini Table*, 2003, acrylic and steel, 27" × 12" × 12".
Bottom right: *Floral Screen*, 1995, stainless steel, 70" × 48" × 2". Photographs: Barry Michlin.

LINDA LEVITON

LINDA LEVITON SCULPTURE ■ 1011 COLONY WAY ■ COLUMBUS, OH ■ TEL 614-433-7486
E-MAIL GUILD@LINDALEVITON.COM ■ WWW.LINDALEVITON.COM

201

Top: *Copper Flora,* 2004, Shades of Green Hotel, Walt Disney World, Orlando, FL, copper, oil, acrylic, patina, dye and wood, 6' × 6'. Bottom: *Copper Flora* (3 details). Photographs: Jerry Anthony.

JOHN SEARLES

SEARLES SCULPTURE ▨ 13462 RED ARROW HIGHWAY ▨ HARBERT, MI 49125
TEL 708-646-4161 ▨ E-MAIL JOHNSEARLES@SEARLESART.COM ▨ WWW.SEARLESART.COM

 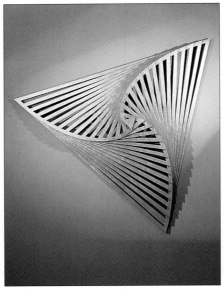 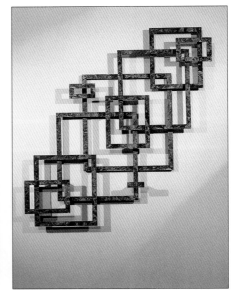

202

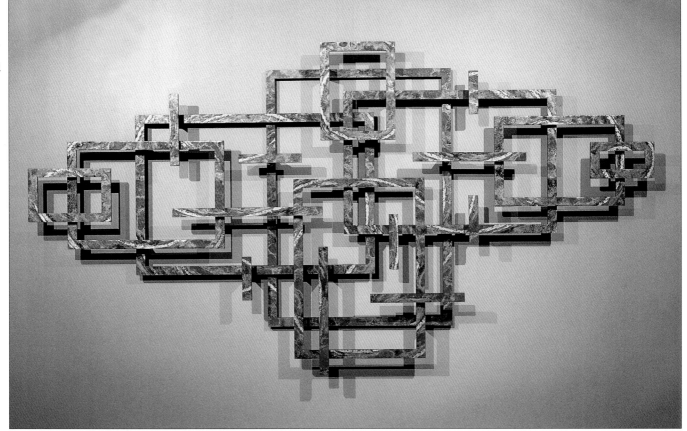

Top left: *Wavy Weaving*, 2003, copper with flame colors, 36" × 48" × 1". Top center: *Rotating Triangles*, 2003, aluminum, brushed finish, 55" × 55" × 55" × 8".
Top right: *Blue Rectangles*, 2002, copper with patina, 50" × 54" × 4". Bottom: *Thunderbird*, 2002, copper and brass with patina, 45" × 85" × 5".

RITA BLITT

RITA BLITT INC. ■ LEAWOOD, KS 66206 ■ TEL 800-627-7689
E-MAIL RITA@RITABLITT.COM ■ WWW.RITABLITT.COM

 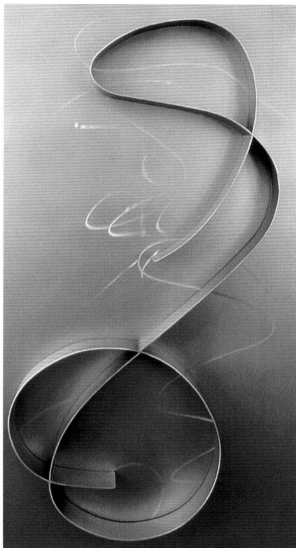

Top left: *Romeo*, 2003, private collection, New York City, stainless steel wall sculpture, 41" x 21" x 5".
Top right: *Juliet*, 2003, private collection, New York City, stainless steel wall sculpture, 41" x 21" x 5". Photographs: James Maidhof.
Bottom: *Romeo and Juliet*, 2003, White Recital Hall, Conservatory of Music, University of Missouri at Kansas City, stainless steel, 13' each.

DAVID M BOWMAN STUDIO

DAVID M BOWMAN ▨ BOX 738 ▨ BERKELEY, CA 94701 ▨ TEL 510-845-1072
E-MAIL DMBSTUDIO@EARTHLINK.NET ▨ WWW.DAVIDMBOWMANSTUDIO.COM

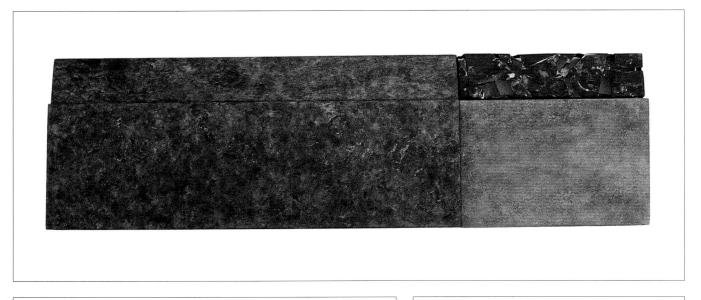

204

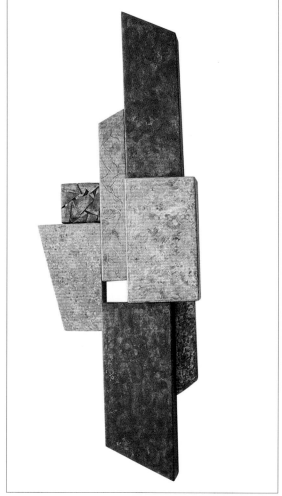

Top: *Wall Piece 03.83,* 2003, patinaed brass, 18" x 60".
Bottom left: *Wall Piece 04.03,* 2004, patinaed brass, 19" x 34". Bottom right: *Wall Piece 03.77,* patinaed brass, 12" x 36".

SUZANNE DONAZETTI

FREEFALL DESIGNS ■ 912 BEDFORD STREET ■ CUMBERLAND, MD 21502 ■ TEL 301-759-3618
E-MAIL SUZ@HEREINTOWN.NET ■ WWW.FREEFALLDESIGNS.COM

205

Top: *Redline 2*, private collection, painted woven copper, 32" × 72" × 5".
Bottom: *Four Seasons*, Bradley International Airport, Windsor Locks, CT. Photographs: David Romero/Vibrant Image.com.

Building Artful Relationships: Tuck Langland & Robert O'Boyle

ARTIST
Tuck Langland

TITLE
Circle of Life, 2004

COMMISSIONED FOR
Bronson Methodist Hospital,
Kalamazoo, MI

TIMELINE: 15 months

DIMENSIONS: 5'H sculptures
on 5'H columns

TRADE PROFESSIONAL
Robert O'Boyle, FASLA
Landscape Architect,
O'Boyle, Cowell,
Blalock & Associates Inc.

Visitors to the new Bronson Methodist Hospital were foremost in the minds of planning committee members when they decided to include a parklike setting in their design for the property. The idea was to present visitors (or simply passers-by) with a place for healing, meditation or inspiration. ▪ "With that in mind an entry plaza was developed for the integration of art within the landscape," reports landscape architect Bob O'Boyle. "We and our client agreed that the work must be specifically designed and created for the space." ▪ Enter Tuck Langland, a near resident of Michigan (he lives just over the border in Indiana) and well-known sculptor in the area. "My concept for the setting came from the fact that hospitals are places where people are born and die—so I suggested the theme of life." It was an idea Langland had been working with for some time, and

Bronson Hospital provided the perfect stage for the four bronze dancers he eventually crafted. ▪ The two male and two female dancers each represent a different ethnicity and point in the cycle of life. The first, an African woman, symbolizes the beginning of life. The second dancer takes the form of a European man and represents maturity. Third is the Indian sculpture of transformation, representing death. Finally, the Native American figure represents dormancy before the cycle begins again. ▪ "Tuck Langland's *Circle of Life* suite of four sculptures was perfect for the area," notes O'Boyle. "The project worked well because Tuck understood spatial concepts and the intent of the site—and he was willing to collaborate on the final design of the space. He was really the epitome of this criterion, and the results illustrate his success."

SUSAN McGEHEE

METALLIC STRANDS ▨ 540 23RD STREET ▨ MANHATTAN BEACH, CA 90266 ▨ TEL 310-545-4112 ▨ FAX 310-546-7152
E-MAIL SUSAN@METALSTRANDS.COM ▨ WWW.METALSTRANDS.COM

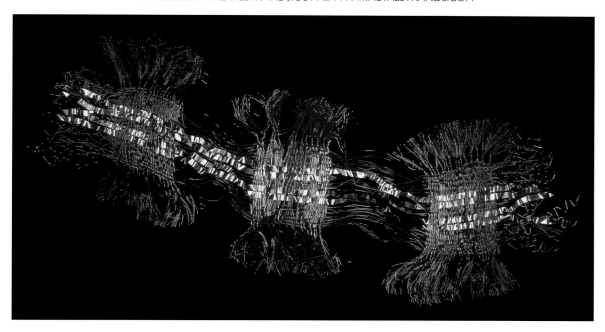

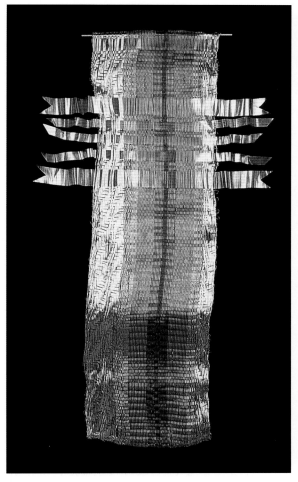 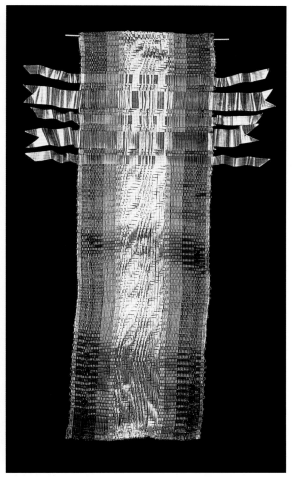

Top: *Liquid Fire Triptych*, woven anodized aluminum wire, 24" x 48". Bottom left and right: Two of eight weavings, 2003,
American Family Insurance building, Phoenix, AZ, woven anodized aluminum wire, each: 28" x 47". Photographs: Andrew Nuehart.

Art for the Wall |
Mixed & Other Media

BARBARA WEBSTER

STARFOREST QUILTS ▪ 1610 LICKSKILLET ROAD ▪ BURNSVILLE, NC 28714
TEL 828-682-7331 ▪ FAX 828-682-7987 ▪ E-MAIL BARBARA@STARFORESTQUILTS.COM ▪ WWW.STARFORESTQUILTS.COM

210

Top: *Pink Fog*, 2002, quilt made from a single photograph using Memory quilt block, 73"W × 72"H.
Bottom: *Approaching Summer*, 2003, Holy Cross Hospital, Silver Spring, MD, quilt composed of more than 240 photographs, 69"W × 54"H. Photographs: Tom Mills.

SUSAN VENABLE

VENABLE STUDIO ▓ 2323 FOOTHILL LANE ▓ SANTA BARBARA, CA 93105 ▓ TEL 805-884-4963 ▓ FAX 805-884-4983
E-MAIL SUSAN@VENABLESTUDIO.COM ▓ WWW.VENABLESTUDIO.COM

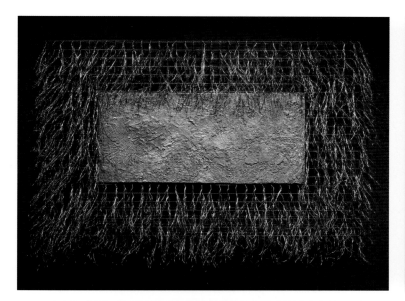 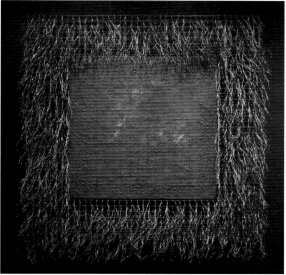

211

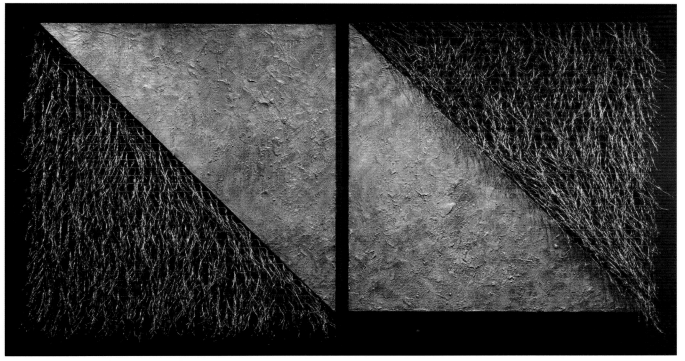

Top left: *Isis,* mixed media, 23" × 36". Top right: *Mysterioso,* mixed media, 40" × 40".
Bottom: *feverDance,* mixed media, 36" × 73". Photograph: William Nettles.

LYNN POSHEPNY

HORIZONS ▦ 5241 DOWNING ROAD ▦ BALTIMORE, MD 21212 ▦ TEL 410-323-9428
E-MAIL LYNN@HORIZONSART.COM ▦ WWW.HORIZONSART.COM

212

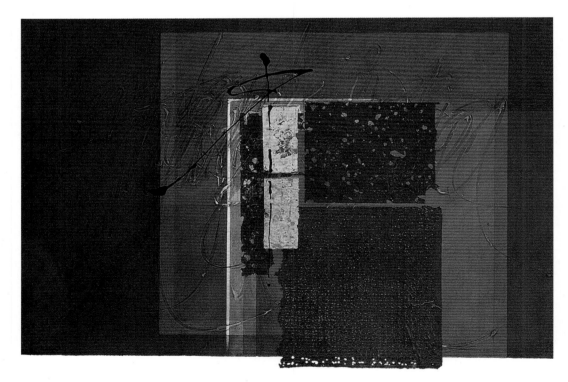

Top: *Free Movement*, 2003, acrylic and rice paper collage, 26"H x 41"W.
Bottom: *To Enact*, 2002, acrylic and rice paper collage, 26"H x 41"W. Photographs: Dan Meyers Photography.

TERRY DAVITT POWELL

1424 MILLS AVENUE ▨ REDLANDS, CA 92373 ▨ TEL 909-793-8141
E-MAIL TERRY@TDPOWELL.COM ▨ WWW.TDPOWELL.COM

213

Top: *Cinnamon*, mixed media on panel, 20" x 24" x 1.75". Bottom: *Oval Action 1, 2, 3*, mixed media on panel, 14" x 34" x 1.75".

DRAEGER UNUSUAL ART

STEVE DRAEGER ▦ S68 W12447 WOODS ROAD ▦ MUSKEGO, WI 53150 ▦ TEL 414-525-1130
E-MAIL DRAEGER@EXECPC.COM ▦ WWW.DRAEGERUNUSUALART.COM

214

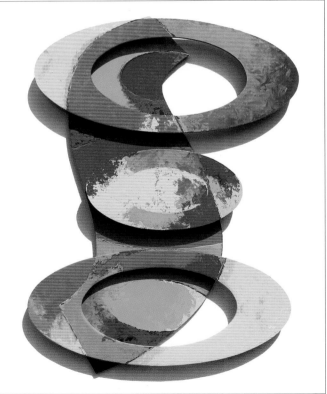

Top: *How'd Ya'll Know?*, 2002, wood, canvas and acrylics, 36" × 76". Bottom left: *What's Wrong with This Picture?*, 2002, wood, canvas, acrylics and transparent tinted urethane, 65" × 50". Bottom right: *Space Martini*, 2002, wood, canvas and acrylics, 51" × 68".

FRED SLAUTTERBACK

652 REDWOOD AVENUE ■ SAND CITY, CA 93955 ■ TEL 831-394-5170 ■ FAX 831-394-5346
E-MAIL FRED@SCFINEARTS.COM ■ WWW.SCFINEARTS.COM

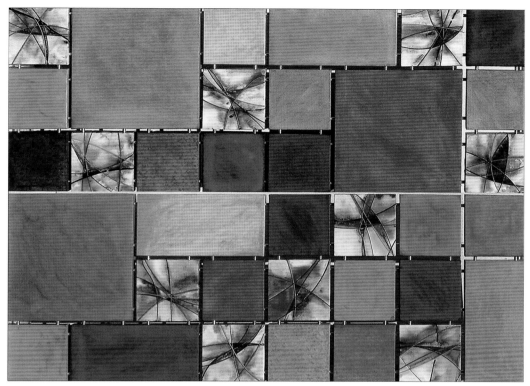

215

Top: *What's New,* 2003, thermoplastic and watercolor on paper; 35-panel grid, 55" × 75" × 2".
Bottom: *Ribbons,* 2003, thermoplastic and watercolor on paper, five panels, 93" × 117" × 3". Inset: *Ribbons* (detail).

RENE CULLER

RENE CULLER GLASS LLC ▪ 540 EAST 105TH STREET #122 ▪ CLEVELAND, OH 44108
TEL 216-851-5149 ▪ FAX 216-321-9428 ▪ E-MAIL RENE@RENECULLER.COM ▪ WWW.RENECULLER.COM

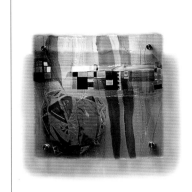

216

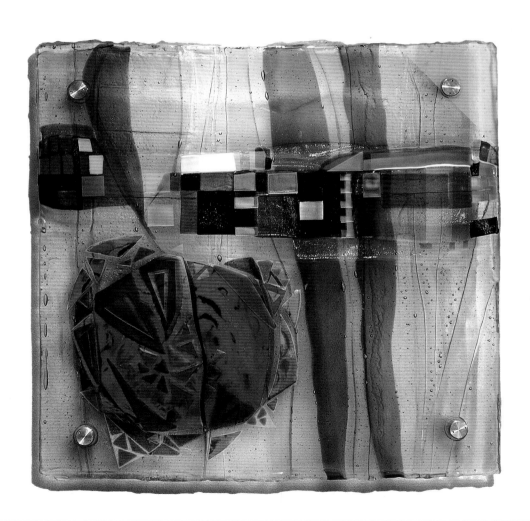

From Concentration to Dispersion, 2003, Cuyahoga County Library, Strongsville, OH, fused and slumped glass, each: 21" x 21".
Bottom: *From Concentration to Dispersion* (detail). Photographs: Robert Muller.

RAY ZOVAR

SILK PURSE ENTERPRISES, INC. ▨ 2499 KEENAN ROAD ▨ MCFARLAND, WI 53558
TEL 608-345-2991 ▨ FAX 608-838-6617 ▨ E-MAIL RAY@ZOVAR.COM ▨ WWW.ZOVAR.COM

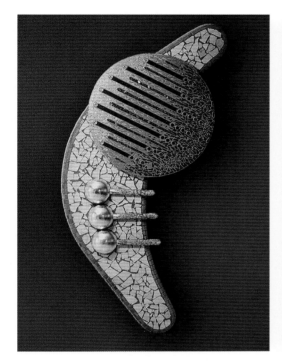

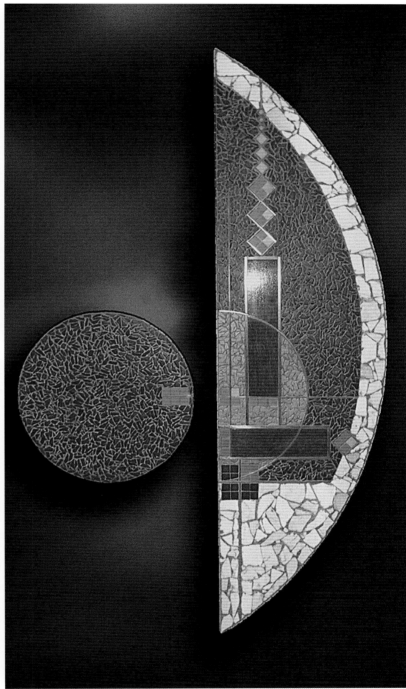

217

Top left: *Speed,* 2003, porcelain, granite, gold leaf over steel, stained glass, glass tile, copper and tumbled marble, 27" x 65". Right: *Frankish,* 2002, porcelain, lacewood, brass and tumbled marble, 18" x 63" with an 18"Dia. side piece. Bottom left: *Synergy,* 2003, porcelain, stained glass, brass, aluminum and gold leaf over steel, 29" x 45".

Building Artful Relationships: David Wilson & Michael Stevenson

Richard and Elizabeth Walker

ARTIST
David Wilson

TITLE
For Evelyn Smith, 2001-2002

COMMISSIONED FOR
Stamford Courthouse,
Stamford, CT

TIMELINE: 8 years

DIMENSIONS: 15'W × 24'H
each panel: 3' × 3'

TRADE PROFESSIONAL
Michael Stevenson
(Former) Design Principal
Ehrenkrantz, Eckstut & Kuhn

Evelyn Smith would have been proud of the architectural lobby windows David Wilson created and named in her honor. Smith, the former director of Connecticut's public art program, died of cancer during the design and construction of the Stamford Courthouse, a project she initiated. ■ "In 1994, I won the public art competition offered by the State of Connecticut through the Department of Public Works and The Connecticut Commission on the Arts," Wilson recalls. "But my initial artwork design was changed drastically after officials decided they wanted the building to be redesigned entirely. This gave me the opportunity to be part of the design team on the second building plan from day one." It was a project that would take nearly a decade to complete. ■ Michael Stevenson, architect for the Stamford Courthouse, notes that there were special qualifications for the main entrance lobby windows. "One of the distinguishing features of new courthouses is the enhanced security

that must be incorporated into the design, requiring a large space for people to wait as they enter the building. David's artwork adds tremendous richness and visual interest to the area." ■ The windows are built in a traditional courthouse style. "The design has a real sense of decorum, which I think is appropriate for a courthouse," Wilson says. Dichroic, beveled and mouth-blown pieces of glass are accompanied by bits of mirror and held in place with stainless steel pins and aluminum frames, giving the appearance that the panels are floating. ■ Stevenson says the project was one of his most successful collaborations with an artist. "It is important that artists understand how working on construction projects is fundamentally different from executing pieces to go in a gallery—scale, technical requirements, schedule, budget limitations and the ability to collaborate with others can become impediments. In David's case, he was very professional on all counts."

LINING ARTS INC.

WAYNE MANN ▨ CAREY THORPE ▨ 390 DUPONT STREET SUITE 200 ▨ TORONTO, ON M5R 1V9 ▨ CANADA
TEL 416-927-0353 ▨ FAX 416-922-0820 ▨ E-MAIL CTHORPE@LININGARTS.COM ▨ WWW.LININGARTS.COM

219

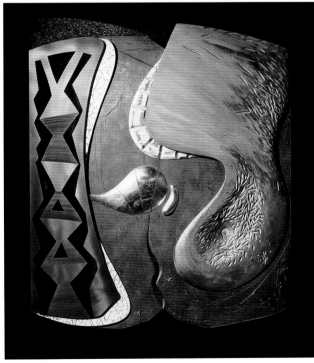

Top: Untitled, La Coquille Restaurant, Bermuda, aquatic scene on stainless steel. Bottom left: Untitled, Dresdner Bank board room,
Toronto, ON, mixed media. Photograph: Rob Davidson. Bottom right: Untitled, Rappongi Restaurant, Toronto, ON, mixed media. Photograph: Rob Davidson.

DENISE M. SNYDER

3017 ALDERWOOD AVENUE ▧ BELLINGHAM, WA 98225 ▧ TEL/FAX 360-647-1152
E-MAIL DSNYDER@ARTSCAN.COM ▧ WWW.ARTSCAN.COM/DSNYDER/

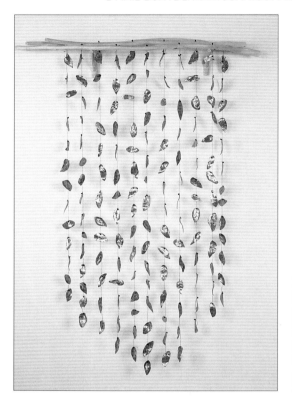 

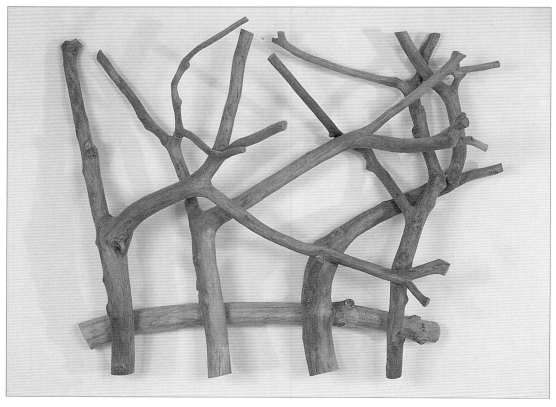

220

Top left: *Falling Leaves III*, 2002, copper, birch and beads, 24" × 35" × 5". Top right: *Woodman's Banner*, 2002, willow and hazelnut wood.
Photograph: Brett Baunton. Bottom: *Silhouette in Apple Wood*, 2002, apple and hazelnut woods, 32" × 25" × 13". Photograph: Brett Baunton.

GEORGE HANDY

2 WEBB COVE ROAD ▨ ASHEVILLE, NC 28804 ▨ TEL 828-254-4691 ▨ FAX 828-254-2227
E-MAIL GEORGE@GEORGEHANDY.COM ▨ WWW.GEORGEHANDY.COM

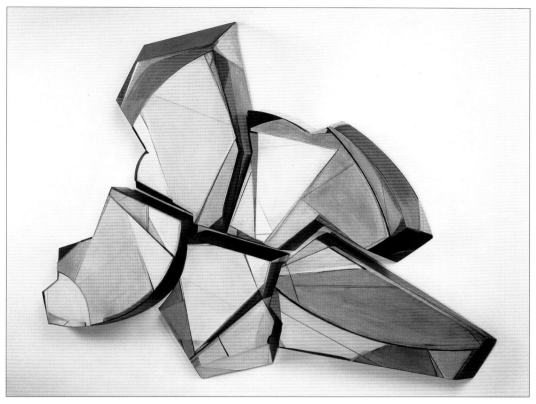

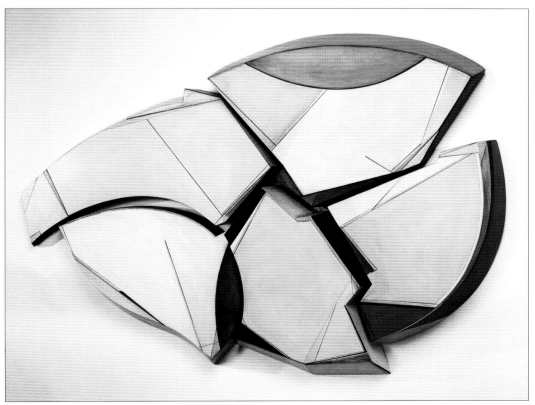

Top: *Arabesque,* 2004, high-relief wall sculpture, mixed media on wood, 56.5"H x 76"W x 3"–8"D.
Bottom: *Five Elements,* 2004, high-relief wall sculpture, mixed media on fiberglass resin, 46"H x 75.5"W x 4"–9"D. Photographs: Steve Mann.

Art for the Wall | Fiber

KAREN URBANEK

314 BLAIR AVENUE ▓ PIEDMONT, CA 94611-4004
TEL 510-654-0685 ▓ FAX 510-654-2790 ▓ E-MAIL KRNURBANEK@AOL.COM

Pebbles 2, 2004, naturally dyed silk fiber, polymer, 40"H x 53"W. Photographs: Don Tuttle Photography.

KATIE PASQUINI MASOPUST

235 RANCHO ALEGRE ROAD ▨ SANTA FE, NM 87508 ▨ TEL 505-471-2899 ▨ FAX 505-471-6537
E-MAIL KATIEPM@AOL.COM ▨ WWW.KATIEPM.COM

Sedona Cactus, 2003, fabric, machine-quilted fabric, 54" x 65". Photograph: Hawthorne Studio.

BARBARA BARRAN

CLASSIC RUG COLLECTION, INC. ▦ 1014 LEXINGTON AVENUE, 2ND FLOOR ▦ NEW YORK, NY 10021
TEL 212-249-6695/888-334-0063 ▦ FAX 212-249-6714 ▦ E-MAIL INFO@CLASSICRUG.COM ▦ WWW.CLASSICRUG.COM

226

Medallion, from Gee's Bend Quilt Collection, 2003, hand-tufted New Zealand wool, 70" x 87". Photograph: Hossein Montazaran.

LAURA MILITZER BRYANT

PRISM ARTS, INC ▨ 3140 39TH AVENUE NORTH ▨ ST. PETERSBURG, FL 33714
TEL 727-327-3100 ▨ E-MAIL LAURA@PRISMYARN.COM

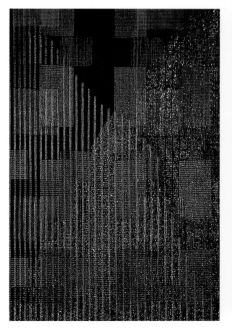

227

Top left: *System/Shift*, 2003, Northrup Grumman IT Headquarters, McLean, VA, weaving on copper, 8' × 5'.
Right: *Agra Infinity—1:1.6*, 2002, weaving, 70.5" × 47". Photograph: Rob Moorman. Bottom left: *System/Shift* (detail).

BIRDWORKS FIBER ARTS ▥ 2633 REYNARD WAY ▥ SAN DIEGO, CA 92103 ▥ TEL 619-294-7236 ▥ FAX 619-294-6873
E-MAIL CBIRD2400@AOL.COM ▥ WWW.BIRDWORKS-FIBERARTS.COM

La Luna, 2002, art quilt, 50" x 44.5". Photograph: Gary Conaughton.

BARBARA CADE

262 HIDEAWAY HILLS DRIVE ■ HOT SPRINGS, AR 71901 ■ TEL 501-262-4065 ■ E-MAIL CADE@IPA.NET

The Last Dance – Alaska Aspen, 2001, handmade felt and paper, wrapping, wool and linen, 50" x 32" x 2". Photograph: Cindy Momchilov.

Building Artful Relationships: Larry Zgoda & Father Thomas Paul

230   Richard Bruck

ARTIST
Larry Zgoda

TITLE
Marian Woods windows, 2000

COMMISSIONED FOR
Our Lady of the Angels Chapel,
Marian Village, Lockport, IL

TIMELINE: 1 year

DIMENSIONS:
Main window: 18'H x 10'W
Secondary windows: 9'H x 40"W

TRADE PROFESSIONAL
Father Thomas Paul,
Liturgical Consultant,
Franciscan Sisters of Chicago

As a Liturgical Consultant, Father Thomas Paul relies on GUILD sourcebooks to find original art best suited to a given environment. "Artwork that is original in its design and fabrication makes the space its own," he says. It was through the GUILD sourcebooks that Father Paul found glass artist Larry Zgoda. ▪ "The selection committee was familiar with my work and wanted a design much like the pieces I had done before—abstractions of the circle, triangle and square," Zgoda recalls. "The windows were more saturated in color than anything I had ever done. There was a lot of light and not a lot of foliage outside, so the colors had to be rich. We didn't want to have people wearing their sunglasses inside!" ▪ Father Paul finds special inspiration in Zgoda's artwork. "The windows really create the spiritual mood of the chapel. They enhance its beauty and allow visitors to come in contact with the mystery of God as light in darkness." ▪ Zgoda found his work with Father Paul and the design committee very helpful. "They were able to come up with symbolism for the chapel that I hadn't even considered. I'm very comfortable working in the kind of situation where the client is as involved with the design as the artist." ▪ As a result of their collaboration for the Our Lady of the Angels Chapel, Father Paul and Larry Zgoda have worked on two more projects together. ▪ "I would encourage other art consultants and designers to work with artists they've never worked with before," says Father Paul. "It's a wonderful way to find new sources for art. I'm very pleased with the creativity, design and responsiveness of Larry. He's created distinctive windows that will have a long-lasting effect on the residents and employees of Marian Woods."

MARILYN HENRION

505 LAGUARDIA PLACE #23D ▓ NEW YORK, NY 10012 ▓ TEL 212-982-8949 ▓ FAX 212-979-7462
E-MAIL MARILYNHENRION@RCN.COM ▓ WWW.MARILYNHENRION.COM

231

Top left: *Night Thoughts #3*, hand-quilted silk, cotton and metallics, 53"H × 51"W. Right: *Against the Sky II* (one panel of triptych), hand-quilted silk, 55"H × 16"W.
Bottom left: *Night Thoughts #2*, hand-quilted silk, cotton and metallics, 53"H × 51"W. Photographs: Karen Bell.

MYRA BURG

6180 WEST JEFFERSON, SUITE Y ▪ LOS ANGELES, CA 90016 ▪ TEL 310-399-5040 ▪ FAX 310-399-0623 ▪ WWW.MYRABURG.COM

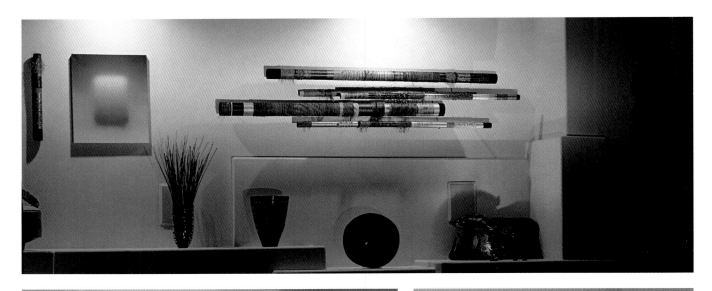

232

Top: *Quiet Oboes*, wrapped fiber, total size: 7.5' × 2.5'. Bottom left: *Indonesian Oboes*, wrapped fiber, total size: 7' × 8'.
Bottom right: *Jenny*, wrapped fiber and burnished aluminum, 3' × 12'. Photographs: Ron Luxemburg.

JOYCE P. LOPEZ

JOYCE LOPEZ STUDIO ▧ 1147 WEST OHIO STREET #304 ▧ CHICAGO, IL 60622
TEL 312-243-5033 ▧ FAX 312-243-7566 ▧ E-MAIL JOYCEPLOPEZ@SBCGLOBAL.NET ▧ WWW.JOYCELOPEZ.COM

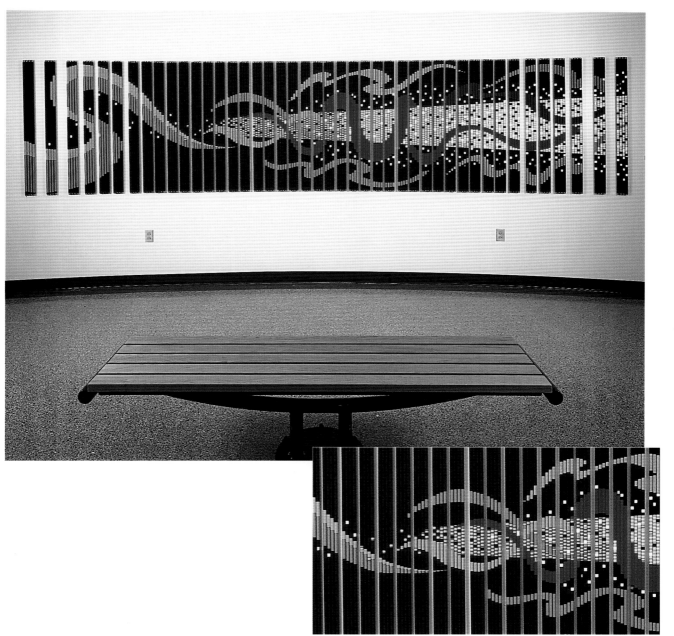

233

Seeing Music, 2003, Western Illinois University Simpkins Music Auditorium, fiber sculpture, 48" × 17' × 3". Inset: *Seeing Music* (detail). Photographs: Larry Dean.

PAVLOS MAYAKIS

4015 MATCH POINT AVENUE ▨ SANTA ROSA, CA 95407 ▨ TEL 707-578-4621 ▨ 866-629-2547 (TOLL FREE)
E-MAIL PAVLOS@PAVLOSMAYAKIS.COM ▨ WWW.PAVLOSMAYAKIS.COM

234

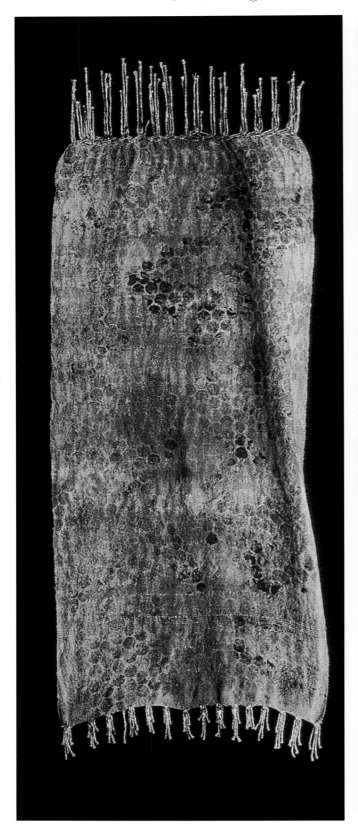 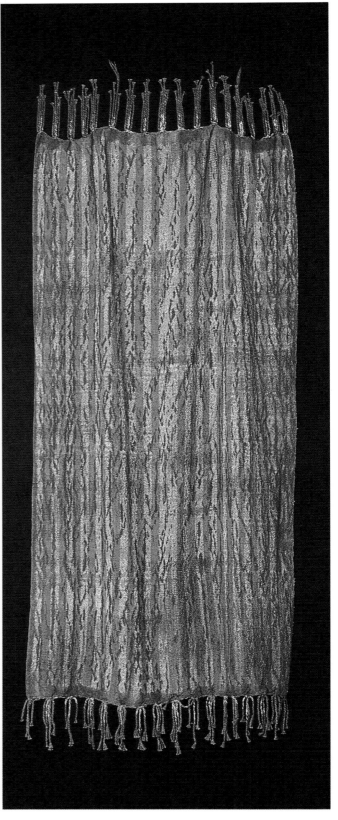

Left: *Shibori Bingo*, 2001, handwoven, dyed and stamped, 28" x 60". Right: *Ethno Shibori*, 2002, handwoven, dyed and over-dyed, 28" x 60". Photographs: Black Cat Studios.

SUSAN EILEEN BURNES

596 EARHART ROAD ■ ROGUE RIVER, OR 97537-5560
TEL 541-582-8967 ■ FAX 541-582-0273 ■ SEBURNES@EARTHLINK.NET

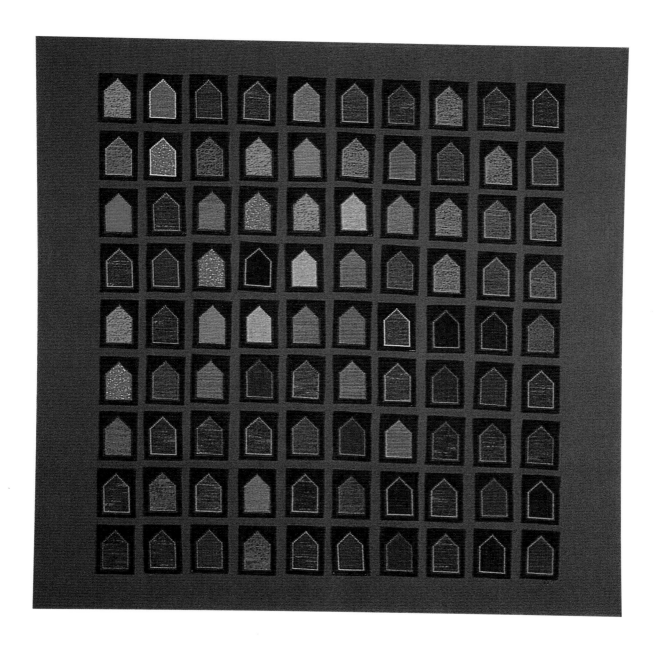

235

Magical, 2003, fiber, 24" × 24".

Resources

The Custom Design Center
A Project of GUILD.com

GUILD sourcebooks give architects, designers and art consultants the essential tools to find and commission original works of art. Within these pages you can find photographs showing a range of products, media and art forms, and contact information so that you can connect directly with the artists whose work you want to commission.

But GUILD offers another avenue to find hundreds of other artwork options: the Custom Design Center, an online complement to GUILD's paper-and-ink sourcebooks. Best of all, it's free to use!

Available through the GUILD.com website, the Custom Design Center features additional images of artwork by artists who have advertised in this sourcebook and others. In addition to artwork appropriate for corporate, public and liturgical spaces, the Custom Design Center also features hundreds of unique residential pieces.

USE GUILD'S CUSTOM DESIGN CENTER TO:

- Find that perfect piece of art by searching art category, medium or artist name
- Post Your Project specifications to hundreds of artists through our online form
- Send an e-postcard of a promising artwork to a client
- Create an online presentation for a client by saving images or links
- Get help from one of our trade sales consultants by e-mail or phone

Visit the GUILD Custom Design Center at **www.guild.com/cdc**, or call 877-344-8453 to discuss your idea with one of our consultants. They can recommend candidates for a specific job, assess the qualifications of individual artists or help draft a letter of agreement.

Above: Larry Zgoda, chapel entry doors, see page 25. This project resulted from a liturgical consultant's use of the GUILD Sourcebooks. See page 230 to read more about this one-of-a-kind collaboration.

ARTIST STATEMENTS

The pages that follow provide important information on the artists featured in *The Sourcebook of Architectural & Interior Art 19.* ▪ Listings in the Artist Statements section are arranged in alphabetical order according to the heading on each artist's page. These listings include the artist's contact information, as well as details about materials and techniques, commissions, collections and more. References to past GUILD sourcebooks are also included so that you can further explore the breadth of a particular artist's work. The heading at the top of each listing includes a page reference to the artist's display within the book. ▪ As you explore *The Sourcebook of Architectural & Interior Art 19,* use the Artist Statements section to enrich your experience. If something intrigues you while perusing the sourcebook—a shape, a form, an exotic use of the commonplace—please give the artist a call. Serendipity often leads to a wonderful creation.

240

Above: Clowes Sculpture, *Canticle to a Blue Planet*, see page 77. Photograph: Jeff Baird.

ARTIST STATEMENTS

AANRAKU STAINED GLASS
Page 24

2323 South El Camino Real
San Mateo, CA 94403
Tel 650-372-0527
Fax 650-372-0566
E-mail aanraku@abasg.com
www.bayareastainedglass.com

Hiroyuki Kobayashi, Ken Minasian and Jeffrey Castaline are the backbone of original design and fabrication at Aanraku Stained Glass. With nearly 100 years of experience between us, we create custom masterpieces in stained glass for our select clientele. Available for commission work for commercial, corporate, residential and liturgical clients.

SUSAN AHREND
Page 54

Cottonwood Design
321 Saint Joseph Avenue
Long Beach, CA 90814
Tel 562-438-5230
www.cottonwoodtile.com

I began Cottonwood Design in 1987, specializing in bas-relief patterned tiles for kitchens and baths. Since 2000, I have focused on creating tile murals for residential, commercial and public environments. I work in the traditional cuerda seca (dryline) technique with color palettes ranging from vibrant, full-color transparencies to soft, warm mattes. Within each palette I mix and play with the glazes to give my work a painterly or watercolor appearance. Frequent designs include florals, plein-air landscapes, animals and sea life. My murals can be found throughout California, enhancing kitchens and baths and enlivening once sterile hospital corridors. They have also been used as fund-raisers for non-profit organizations.

RECENT PROJECTS: Mural of dolphins, seals and other sea life, Ability First, Long Beach, CA

COMMISSIONS: Orthopedic Hospital, 2000, Los Angeles, CA; American Heart Association, 2000, Irvine, CA

AIRWORKS, INC.
Page 72

George Peters & Melanie Walker
815 Spruce Street
Boulder, CO 80302
Tel/Fax 303-442-9025
E-mail airworks@concentric.net
www.airworks-studio.com

We have worked as a team on a wide range of projects since we began collaborating in 1995. We have created many large-scale commissions that enliven and activate the environment in both interior and exterior spaces. We strive to make works that have a voice and character, and that uplift and reflect the positive aspects of human vision. We believe that public artwork should reflect a character of place, make a positive influence on the people who use and inhabit these areas and create an integrated platform for art in our public spaces.

RECENT COMMISSIONS: McGraw/Hill Companies, London, 2003; AstraZenica Pharmaceuticals, Wilmington, DE 2003; University of Arizona, Tucson, Library and Special Collections, 2002

GUILD SOURCEBOOKS: Architect's 13, 14, 15; Architectural & Interior Art 16, 17

241

MARY LOU ALBERETTI
Page 49

Alberetti Studios
16 Possum Drive
New Fairfield, CT 06812
Tel 203-746-1321
E-mail mlalb@aol.com
www.southernct.edu/~alberett/

My ceramic wall reliefs are inspired by the ancient architecture of Italy and southern Spain. By adding layers of color and texture to the clay surface, my aim is to evoke the timelessness of these ancient places. My reliefs can be freestanding or wall hung in individual or multiple groupings.

RECENT PROJECTS: Moorish Influences, 2004, Canterbury School, New Milford, CT

COLLECTIONS: Mint Museum of Art, Charlotte, NC; Fuller Museum of Art, Brockton, MA; GE World Headquarters, Fairfield, CT; ASU Nelson Museum, Tempe, AZ

EXHIBITIONS: Recent works, 2004, White Silo, Sherman, CT, 2002, HBO World Headquarters, New York, NY; Ceramic Leaders of Arizona, 2002, ASU Fine Arts Center, Tempe, AZ;

GUILD SOURCEBOOKS: Designer's 14, 15; Architectural & Interior Art 16, 17, 18

ARCHITECTURAL GLASS ART, INC.
Page 28

Kenneth F. vonRoenn, Jr.
815 West Market Street
Louisville, KY 40202
Tel 800-795-9429
Fax 502-585-2808
E-mail info@AGAinc.com
www.AGAinc.com

We focus on diverse applications of glass, thereby expanding the roles of glass in architecture. With a broad range of new techniques, we are able to meet the functional and aesthetic requirements of diverse architectural applications. These techniques have been developed and refined from new and emerging technologies, creating dynamic opportunities for glass to enhance architecture. We provide a complete range of services from design to fabrication to installation for a broad range of work. Our work is noted for its sympathetic integration with architecture and for its innovative application of new technologies.

RECENT PROJECTS: Home of the Innocents, Louisville, KY; Kentucky Museum of Arts & Design, Louisville, KY; Jewish Hospital Medical Center East

ART GLASS ENSEMBLES
Page 34

Christie A. Wood
208 West Oak Street
Denton, TX 76201
Tel 940-591-3002
Fax 940-591-7853
E-mail ensembles@compuserve.com

We at Art Glass Ensembles have been creating custom stained glass and mosaic glass artwork for a variety of clients since 1995. We specialize in creating stained glass artwork for private homes, working as the primary artist, as the fabricating studio for other artists or in collaboration with furniture makers, cabinetmakers, interior designers and clients. We welcome inquiries regarding projects, whether one of a kind or limited editions. Prices range from $10 sun catchers and recycled wine bottle art up to $5,500.

RECENT PROJECTS: CD-ROM of artwork entitled Opus One, November 2003, Dragonfly software; The Glass Menagerie, CD-ROM featuring animal artwork, March 2004, www.dfly.com

GUILD SOURCEBOOKS: Architectural & Interior Art 18

ARTIST STATEMENTS

B.S.K. DEVELOPMENT
Page 88

Stephen Geddes
Robert L. Moore
1453 Covered Bridge Road
Cincinnati, OH 45231
Tel 513-231-4309
Tel 513-921-7651
E-mail slgeddes@cinci.rr.com
www.bskdevelopment.com

We strive to create lasting sculpture characterized by strong form, careful detailing and harmonious siting. Grounded by years of experience in commercial and fine arts applications, we approach a project from multiple perspectives. We polychromed wood panels using a baseball theme to provide unifying architectural elements in unique spaces.

COMMISIONS: Owner's Suite, Great American Ballpark, Cincinnati, OH; St. Mary's Hospital, Huntington, WV; Children's Hospital, Cincinnati, OH; Wheeling Health and Wellness Center, Wheeling, WV; Turley Park, Carbondale, IL; Indiana University Library, Fort Wayne, IN

COLLECTIONS: Columbia Pictures, Disney, Dream Works, 20th Century Fox, Lucas Film Ltd., Universal Studios, Warner Brothers Studios

MICHAEL BAKER
Page 113

Michael Baker Studios
85 Gunter Drive
Colbert, GA 30628
Tel 706-354-4959
E-mail sculpture@michaelbaker.com
www.michaelbaker.com

My infatuation with the geometric shape in both its true and altered forms creates the basis for my fabricated stainless steel sculptures. Important in my design process is the balance of elements coupled with the appearance of positive and negative shapes. Giving the impression of being precariously balanced, these sculptures always form exciting and interesting three-dimensional arrangements. My work is suitable for anything from intimate garden settings to larger landscaped spaces as well as a wide variety of residential or commercial interiors.

COMMISSIONS: Loyola University Medical Center, 2003, Maywood, IL; Riverside Medical Center, 2003, Kankakee, IL; Allied Insurance Company, 2003, Des Moines, IA; Bridgeman Agency, 2003, Belleville, IL; ACRC Restaurant Corp., 2002, Deerfield, IL; private residence, 2002, Westport, CT; Wells Fargo Mortgage Corp., 2002, Charlotte, NC

BARBARA BARRAN
Page 226

Classic Rug Collection, Inc.
1014 Lexington Avenue, 2nd Floor
New York, NY 10021
Tel 212-249-6695/888-334-0063
Fax 212-249-6714
E-mail info@classicrug.com
www.classicrug.com

Featuring bold designs, strong colors, exciting textures and a sense of whimsy, my rugs are created in collaboration with my clients, so the finished piece reflects my design vision and complements the installation site. To achieve just the right look for each commission, the rugs are hand-tufted, hand-knotted, hand-hooked, hand-fabricated or flat-woven. I work in all styles, although quilt patterned, American Primitive and children's designs are among my favorites. In addition, I have the exclusive right to translate the Gee's Bend Quilts (currently touring museums throughout the U.S.) into rugs. *Elle Décor, American Farmhouse, The New York Times* and *Country Living* have featured my work. The Whitney Museum's Store Next Door, the American Folk Art Museum, the Smithsonian and other fine museum stores have carried my designs.

MICHAEL BAUERMEISTER
Page 101

6560 Augusta Bottom Road
Augusta, MO 63332
Tel/Fax 636-228-4663
E-mail michael@bauermeister.com
www.michaelbauermeister.com

I think of these tall vessels as figures. As such, I'm interested in their personalities and how they relate to one another. These vessels are made from cabinet-grade hardwoods and are finished with lacquer so they will not warp or crack. Most range in price from $1,000 to $3,000.

EXHIBITIONS: Smithsonian Craft Show, 2003, 2002, Washington, DC; Wood Turning Invitational, 2000-2003, American Art Co., Tacoma, WA; Turned Wood Invitational, 2002, 1999, 1998, Del Mano Gallery, Los Angeles, CA; Nuances d'ete, 2001, Carlin Gallery, Paris, France

AWARDS: 25th Annual Contemporary Crafts Purchase Award, 2003, Mesa Arts Center, Mesa, AZ; Best of Wood, 2002, American Craft Exposition, Evanston, IL; Niche Award, 2002; Award of Excellence, 2000, American Craft Council, Baltimore, MD

PUBLICATIONS: *Wood Art Today*, 2003; *Scratching the Surface*, 2002; *Object Lessons*, 2001; *American Craft*, June 1995

NICOLE BECK
Page 80

Nicole Beck Studios
805 South Oakley Boulevard
Chicago, IL 60612
Tel 312-563-0457
E-mail nbeckarts@aol.com
www.nicolebeck.com

A poetic distillation of the beauty found in nature and science, my inventive forms are well crafted and add a warmer, more organic flair to large-scale steel. I've collaborated closely with government, universities, corporations and private clients for both indoor and outdoor environments, including participatory works with students and community projects. Small works are also available. I maintain a fully-equipped studio and have been exhibited nationally in museums, galleries, corporate and public venues too numerous to list.

RECENT PROJECTS: *Artists in the Gardens*, 2004, Chicago Public Art Project; Chicago Percent for Arts Program; Chicago Sculpture, 2003; South Bend Airport, IN; Western Michigan University; Greensboro, NC

COMMISSIONS: DeVry University, Chicago, IL; ESPN Zone/Disney, Chicago, IL; Sarasota County, Sarasota, FL; Hand Center, St. Catherine Hospital, East Chicago, IL

SUSAN BEERE
Page 56

PO Box 70
Del Mar, CA 92014
Tel 760-942-9302
Fax 760-942-1702
E-mail susan@susanbeere.com
www.susanbeere.com

I create distinctive, bold designs and unique color juxtapositions in freeform sculpted tile and painted murals. In my works I seek to capture a unique sense of place—the essence of nature in birds, flowers and marine life. The pieces add imagination and vibrancy to any wall space. I have numerous collectors across the country and enjoy working closely with my clients to create their vision and mine. I have been told many times that my works engage and delight the viewer.

RECENT PROJECTS: *Toucans and Ginger Flowers*, 2003, private collection, Pasadena, CA; *Double Pisces*, private collection

PUBLICATIONS: *2,000 Outstanding Artists and Designers of the 20th Century*, 2003; *Architectural Ceramics*, 1999; *Handmade Tiles*, 1994, (cover of UK 1995 edition)

ARTIST STATEMENTS

BIGBIRD-STUDIOS
Page 138

Pat Payne
2121 Alameda Avenue
Alameda, CA 94501
Tel 510-521-9308
E-mail ppbigbird@aol.com
www.bigbird-studios.com

I love steel: its strength, its immediacy, even its tendency to fight back before yielding to form. Its structural limits seem boundless. Currently, I am also combining steel and cement using direct hands-on sculpting of animal and anthropomorphic figures. With steel and direct sculpting, the sculptor's imprint and the immediacy of method is not changed in foundry processing. I have had the pleasure of creating one-of-a-kind sculpture for the public and private sectors for over 25 years. The majority of my sculpture is suitable for indoor and outdoor placement. Prices range from $3,000-$35,000.

COLLECTIONS: Robin Williams; Gary Larson; Cypress Gardens; Broadway Plaza

EXHIBITIONS: Los Angeles Natural History Museum; El Paseo, Palm Desert, CA; One Bush, San Francisco

PUBLICATIONS: *La Sculpture En Acir*, 1992

GUILD SOURCEBOOKS: *Architectural & Interior Art 18*

CHARLOTTE BIRD
Page 228

Birdworks Fiber Arts
2633 Reynard Way
San Diego, CA 92103
Tel 619-294-7236
Fax 619-294-6873
E-mail cbird2400@aol.com
www.birdworks-fiberarts.com

Cadenced stories come alive in colorful textile works for public and private spaces. English and Spanish images and language enchant children of all ages and adults who love them. My lifelong studies of color, pattern and anthropology turn children's stories, rhymes and poetry into vivid, intimate, touchable art. I have been featured on *Telling Stories with Tomie de Paola*. Commissions are welcome. Prices range from $100-200/square foot.

COLLECTIONS: Neutrogena, Luce Forward, various private commissions

EXHIBITIONS: *Quilt Visions*, 2004, San Diego, CA; John Wayne Airport, 2004, Long Beach, CA; Rocky Mountain Quilt Museum, 2003, Golden, CO; Children's Museum San Diego/Museo de los Niños, 2002, San Diego, CA; La Jolla Fiber Arts Gallery, 2001, La Jolla, CA

RITA BLITT
Pages 198, 203

Rita Blitt Inc.
Leawood, KS 66206
Tel 800-627-7689
E-mail rita@ritablitt.com
www.ritablitt.com

My 13-foot stainless steel ribbon wall sculptures featured in this book have the honor of flanking the stage in the beautiful White Recital Hall of The Conservatory of Music, University of Missouri, Kansas City. I have inscribed my spontaneous lines on the surfaces of recently created stainless steel standing sculpture and on background mountings for some new ribbon wall sculptures, thus leaving the intimacy of my drawings on the finished product. The standing sculptures are installed in the Hilton Tokyo Bay Hotel, Shiba, Japan, and the Gold Coast Regional Art Center Sculpture Park, Surfer's Paradise, Australia. I have found great pleasure in fulfilling commissions throughout the world.

GUILD SOURCEBOOKS: *Architect's 7, 8, 10, 11; Designer's 11, 12, 13, 14; Architectural & Interior Art 16, 17; Artful Home 1*

243

KATHY BRADFORD
Page 38

North Star Art Glass, Inc.
142 Wichita
Lyons, CO 80540
Tel/Fax 303-823-6511
E-mail kathybradford@webtv.net
www.kathybradford.com

Sandblast carving and etching remain the major forces in my glass art. Over the years I have created many unique techniques to achieve certain imagery not found in the work of other glass artists. In the last few years, I have begun combining sand carving, etching and other glass detailing as appropriate to the composition. These compositions are unique, whimsical, energetic and powerful. I continually work with architects, designers and contractors to ensure proper and successful installations in many locations throughout the country. Everything possible is taken into account to create beautiful glasswork that will work in concert with the architecture of the location.

RECENT PROJECTS: Centura Health, Denver, CO; Aurora Firehouse #3, Aurora, CO; Oak Park Pavilion, St. Louis Park, MN; Russian Tea Room, New York, NY

LAURA MILITZER BRYANT
Page 227

Prism Arts, Inc
3140 39th Avenue North
St. Petersburg, FL 33714
Tel 727-327-3100
E-mail laura@prismyarn.com

Layers of geometry, texture and meaning color my woven works. Inspired by both landscape and architecture, I achieve visual impact through shifting systems of overlapped grids and loosely interpreted images. Brilliantly dyed planes intersect, merge and diverge to create a sense of space and place. I often include metallic threads in the weaving, which complement the copper plates that are treated with patina liquids. Colorations and surface treatments on the copper echo the lines and colors in the weavings. Copper-mounted works hang securely against the wall with an invisible system; free hanging weavings hang from Velcro attachments at the top. I use museum-quality dyes for all threads.

RECENT PROJECTS: Northrup Grumman IT Headquarters, McLean, VA

AWARDS: Recipient of the NEA and Florida State Artist grants

JIM BUDISH
Page 147

Denver Studio
PO Box 102377
Denver, CO 80250
Tel 303-324-2081/Fax 303-715-0430

Chicago Area Studio
PO Box 652
Highland Park, IL 60035
Tel 847-236-1625/Fax 247-236-1653
E-mail sculpt2001@aol.com
www.jimbudish.com

A Colorado native, I studied sculpture at The Arts Students League of Denver and the Loveland Academy of Fine Arts and participated in ISC workshops at the Art Institute of Chicago. I began my artistic career sculpting representational figurative works, studying with many of the highly regarded sculptors working in and around Loveland and Denver, Colorado. With time, however, I realized that it was neither my desire nor my ambition to sculpt "photographs" in bronze. I wanted to create my own new and unique direction in representing the human form and the forms of the multitude of special creatures surrounding us, exploring the unique attitude, emotion and personality of each, while attempting to capture the joie de vivre that I believe is lurking somewhere inside of all of us.

ARTIST STATEMENTS

MYRA BURG
Page 232

6180 West Jefferson, Suite Y
Los Angeles, CA 90016
Tel 310-399-5040
Fax 310-399-0623
www.myraburg.com

Somewhere between tapestry and jewelry, "quiet oboes" and sculptural installations adorn spaces in a free-floating, peaceful way. Hand-wrapped fiber and burnished metals are combined to create inspired sculptural pieces that meet the clients' needs and wants within the requirements of the space. The bigger the challenge, the more the fun. Collaborations are welcome.

RECENT PROJECTS: *Japonaise,* Universal, Japan; *Galactic Curve,* Universal, Japan; *Quiet Oboes,* Caribé Hilton, Puerto Rico; Travelocity, Dallas, TX

EXHIBITIONS: SOFA, Chicago; LA County Museum of Art, CA; Howard Hughes Center, Los Angeles, CA; Orange County Museum of Art, CA

AWARDS: First place, 2002, *Artfest of Henderson;* first place, *Beverly Hills Affaire in the Gardens,* 2001, 1999, 1998

GUILD SOURCEBOOKS: *Designer's 10, 13, 14, 15; Architect's 14, 15; Architectural & Interior Art 16, 17, 18; Artful Home 1, 2*

RUTH BURINK
Page 104

Burink Sculpture Studio
1550 Woodmoor Drive
Monument, CO 80132
Tel/Fax 719-481-0513
E-mail ruth@burinksculpture.com
www.burinksculpture.com

Stone is a truly beautiful and satisfying medium in which to work. I don't force my sculptures; instead, I allow them to emerge gracefully from the magnificent stone. The abstract nature of my work engages the viewer, instigating a dialogue between art and viewer. I collaborate closely with clients to design and create original sculpture—from tabletop to monumental—that meets their needs. I carve directly in stone and often cast bronze from a stone original.

EXHIBITIONS: Biennale Internazionale dell'Arte Contemporanea, Florence, Italy; Colorado Governor's Invitational

RECENT COMMISSIONS: Penrose Hospital, Colorado Springs, CO; St. Theresa Parish, Houston, TX

COLLECTIONS: St. Joseph Hospital, Denver, CO; Sammy Yu, Sidney, Australia; Loveland Arts Commission, Loveland, CO

PUBLICATIONS: *Sculptural Pursuit Magazine*

SUSAN EILEEN BURNES
Page 235

596 Earhart Road
Rogue River, OR 97537-5560
Tel 541-582-8967
Fax 541-582-0273
seburnes@earthlink.net

My work is about the movement of colors and patterns, the repetitions of feeling that come through in nature and in life experiences. Using traditional technique, I create original wall pieces of unique, contemporary fiber art. I stitch by hand rows upon rows of fine wool, silk, cotton and rayon threads onto even-weave fabric. These simple geometric forms relate to each other as they evolve into rhythmic, textural patterns of light, shadow and flowing colors. Each individual element is then hand-sewn onto painted and stretched canvas, forming a whole that is greater than the sum of its parts.

AWARDS: First place, 2001, Rocky Mount Art Center; First place, 2003, AAUW Art Exhibition, Grants Pass Museum of Art

244

RIIS BURWELL
Page 109

3815 Calistoga Road
Santa Rosa, CA 95404
Tel 707-538-2676
E-mail riisburwell@riisburwell.com
www.riisburwell.com

The dynamic balance between order and chaos in nature serves as the inspiration for the abstract metal sculpture I create. Each peice, from wall sculpture to tabletop to large-scale work, is hand-fabricated. I primarily use bronze, steel and stainless steel for both indoor and outdoor sculpture. My work can be found in private and corporate collections within the United States and abroad.

COMMISSIONS: Suffolk Construction Company, 2003, MA; Vineyard Creek Spa & Conference Center, 2002, CA; Burbank Airport Plaza, 2001, CA; Congregation Beth Ami, 2000, CA

EXHIBITIONS: *Contemporary Constructions,* Los Angeles County Museum; Olive Grove Sculpture Gallery at Auberge du Soliel, Sandy Carson Gallery, Denver, CO

GUILD SOURCEBOOKS: *Architect's 13, 14, 15; Architectural & Interior Art 16, 17, 18*

BARBARA CADE
Page 229

262 Hideaway Hills Drive
Hot Springs, AR 71901
Tel 501-262-4065
E-mail cade@ipa.net

Collectible rocks, luscious vegetation, textured trees and dramatic skies: two- and three-dimensional sculptural landscape elements inspired by your geographic location, maybe using your favorite photograph. Use elements together or individually. I continue to be inspired by themes in nature, translating my photographs into tapestries of woven and felted wool, often incorporating other fiber techniques.

COMMISSIONS: St. Luke's Hospital, 2003, The Woodlands, TX; the Kraft Center, 1997, Paramus, NJ

COLLECTIONS: Weyerhaeuser Company, Tacoma, WA; Tacoma Art Museum, Tacoma, WA

EXHIBITIONS: *Reality Check,* Ohio Craft Museum, 2001, Columbus, OH

GUILD SOURCEBOOKS: *Designer's 8, 9, 10, 11, 12, 15; Architectural & Interior Art 17, 18; Artful Home 1*

CANNETO STUDIOS INC.
Page 93

Stephen Canneto
1450 Roads End Place
Columbus, OH 43209
Tel 614-237-9078
Fax 614-237-9059
E-mail canneto@cannetostudios.com
www.cannetostudios.com

My mission is to bring the viewer more closely in touch with our social and physical environment by creating art that explores the dynamic tension between people, nature and technology. By collaborating with owners, designers and the public, we bring meaning, identity and enjoyment to the spaces my works occupy. Canneto Studios provides design, structural analysis, documents, project management and installation. My creations include sculpture for public, corporate and residential sites, functional furnishings and memorials.

COMMISSIONS: Fallsgrove, Rockville, MD; Ohio Departments of Education, Rehabilitation and Correction; Southeast, Inc., Columbus, OH

COLLECTIONS: Cities of Beachwood and Columbus, OH; Dresden, Germany; Seville, Spain; Herzliya, Israel; Franklin University; Goodyear; Huntington National Bank

GUILD SOURCEBOOKS: *Architect's 7*

ARTIST STATEMENTS

EVA CARTER
Page 188

Eva Carter Gallery
132 East Bay Street
Charleston, SC 29401
Tel 843-722-0506
Fax 843-722-7232
E-mail evacarter@earthlink.net
www.evacartergallery.com

My work is not indicative of any specific place or thing but an attempt to communicate an emotional and spiritual response to that experience. The process of painting creates its own unique surprises. Some are kept, others are destroyed, and through that process of destruction new possibilities emerge. It is the intuitive product of dreams, visions and mystery that moves us to a place beyond ourselves. Employing Abstract Expressionism, I am inspired by my experiences from the Southwest, Tennessee and the low country of South Carolina.

COLLECTIONS: Gibbes Museum of Art, Charleston, SC; Carol Reece Museum, Johnson City, TN; Federal Reserve Bank of Charlotte, Charlotte, NC; Chubb, Atlanta, GA

PUBLICATIONS: *The Post & Courier,* January 2003; *Charleston Magazine,* June 2002; *A Frame of Mind,* July 2000

WARREN CARTHER
Pages 14, 20, 40

Carther Studio Inc.
80 George Avenue
Winnipeg, MB R3B 0K1
Canada
Tel 204-956-1615
Fax 204-942-1434
E-mail warren@cartherstudio.com
www.cartherstudio.com

Through glass, I explore light in varied and unusual ways, manipulating the quality of light as it is filtered through the translucent layers of my work. My respect and understanding of the structural capabilities of glass, combined with my interest in working sculpturally within the architectural environment, lead me to produce unique work that crosses the boundaries between art and architecture. Innovative techniques in structure, abrasive blast carving, laminations and color application distinguish my often large-scale work. Numerous commissions and publications throughout the world have helped me create a reputation for the ability to produce strikingly unique work for public and private spaces.

COMMISSIONS: Canadian Embassy, Tokyo, Japan; Swire Group, Hong Kong; Charles de Gaulle Airport, Paris, France; Anchorage International Airport, AK

CAROL CARTWRIGHT
Page 195

Cartwright Photography
PO Box 772
Salida, CO 81201
719-221-1627
E-mail ccartphoto@aol.com
www.cartwrightphotography.com

I have had extensive training in photographic methods and techniques in programs and workshops throughout the United States. I use creativity and sensitivity to capture the rhythmic nature of subjects. My archival images are printed using photographic processes or digital giclée printmaking.

RECENT PROJECTS: Photographing 85 city artworks, 2003, Ames, IA

COLLECTIONS: Mary Greeley Medical Center, Ames, IA

EXHIBITIONS: *Art of the New West,* 2003, Dahl Art Center, Rapid City, SD; *Year of the Horse,* 2002, Octagon Center, Ames, IA; *La Petite IX,* 2002, Coburg, OR; *Ten Women, Ten Views,* Des Moines, IA; *Day or Night,* 2001, Make Ready Press, Montclair, NJ

AWARDS: First Place, 2003, Superintendent's Award, 2001, Iowa State Fair Photography Salon

PUBLICATIONS: *Rocky Mountain School of Photography* catalog, 2003-2004

CARVINGS BY C.B. MARTIN
Page 64

Carol B. Martin
1155 Industrial Avenue
Escondido, CA 92029
Tel/Fax 760-746-5896
E-mail cbcbm@san.rr.com

I cannot imagine a better medium than wood to show the rich beauty of nature. This can take an incredible variety of forms, from a classic 14th-century acanthus design to the grace and simplicity of the Japanese Ikebana style of flower arrangement. Sometimes it is the small touches that make all the difference. A sprig of pine, a long-stemmed rose, perhaps, and a blank panel becomes the highlight of an elegant room. I have been carving professionally for 15 years and have had the honor of being selected twice as judge at the Design in Wood Show sponsored by the San Diego Fine Woodworkers Association. I look forward to working with your cabinetmaker and finisher if you have concerns about matching existing work.

JILL CASTY
Page 71

Jill Casty Design
494 Alvardo Street
Monterey, CA 93940
Tel 831-649-0923
Fax 831-649-0713
E-mail jillcdesign@hotmail.com
www.jillcastydesign.com

I think of my art as a combination of flowing grace and good-natured exuberance. While always personal and inventive, it is still sensitive to a site's spirit and spaces, and to the important vision of client and architect. My aerial pieces range from the joyful glow of atrium mobiles to large-scale projects involving innovative sets of hanging art for multiple areas of a site. My festive standing sculptures (up to 30 feet high) are abstract yet pique the imagination with site-related allusions. I employ, and often blend, diverse materials such as metals, Plexiglas and glass.

RECENT PROJECTS: Country Club Plaza, Sacramento, CA; City of Montclair, CA; SuperMall of the Great Northwest, Auburn, WA; Northwest Plaza, St. Louis, MO

GUILD SOURCEBOOKS: *Architect's 10, 11, 12, 13, 14, 15; Architectural & Interior Art 16, 17, 18*

DOUGLAS CHICK
Page 96

2541 Cheswick Drive
Troy, MI 48084
Tel 248-642-1508
Fax 248-642-4005
E-mail dchick642@aol.com
www.DougChickSculpture.com

In my sculpture I strive to create an uplifting—almost spiritual—feeling. Figures lightly touch their bases and show a strong sense of movement. I model in wax, clay and plaster and then cast my work in bronze. While I work on both small and large pieces, I enjoy the larger pieces the most—the bigger the better. Recently, I created and installed a 6.8'H bronze sculpture entitled *Fabled Flight* at West Bloomfield Township Public Library in Michigan. It is a limited edition of 25. I am currently working on a 7'H piece for a church in Troy, MI. To see some of my other sculptures and reliefs, please visit my website at www.DougChickSculpture.com. I welcome the opportunity to discuss commissions.

COMMISSIONS: Troy School District, Schroeder Elementary, Troy, MI; Troy Public Library; West Bloomfield Township Public Library; North Hills Christian Church, Troy, MI.

ARTIST STATEMENTS

CLOWES SCULPTURE
Pages 77, 240

Jonathan and Evelyn Clowes
8 March Hill Road
Walpole, NH 03608
Tel/Fax 603-756-9505
E-mail jon@clowessculpture.com
www.clowessculpture.com

Jon and I have been creating sculpture together for over 30 years. Our work is lyrical, graceful and emblematic of the joy we find collaborating together. We design for clients in the hotel, healthcare, corporate and cruising markets, as well as for private homes. Our experiences collaborating with clients, architects and art consultants have been enriching and fruitful—so much so that we have come to specialize in site-specific designs. A Clowes piece has a distinct mark of elegance in form and how it speaks to its environment. The organic shapes and flowing curves formed in wood, metals and composites contrast with the colors of blown glass, stone and other materials we use.

COMMISSIONS: Pfizer; Royal Caribbean International; Tokyo Hilton Hotel; Indianapolis Museum of Art; Visalia Convention Center; Monadnock Paper Inc.; Manchester, NH, District Courthouse; Antioch New England Graduate School; Hope Hospice, Ft. Myers, FL

DAVID CODDAIRE
Pages 106-107

755 East 10th Street
Oakland, CA 94606
Tel 510-451-7353
Fax 510-451-7351
E-mail tallironvases@mindspring.com
www.tallironvases.com

My metal sculpture is a direct interpretation of the human figure. My intent is to maintain the approximate scale of five feet to six feet and convey movement and stature in a manner undertaken by the likes of dancers and circus performers.

RECENT PROJECTS: Weston Hotel Chapel, Maui Hawaii; Renaissance Hotel lobby, Montreal, QC; Marriott Hotel lobby, Nashville, TN

COLLECTIONS: Mr. A. Moretti, Rome; Mrs. S.W. Smith, New York City; Mr. D. Goldman, Los Angeles, CA; Mr. and Mrs. L. Dorfmeir, New York City

EXHIBITIONS: Paradise Ridge Winery, 2004, Santa Rosa, CA; Phoenix Gallery, 2003, Park City, UT; D. Silverstein Gallery, 1997, New York, NY

PUBLICATIONS: *Design Times*, 1999; *Sculpture* magazine, 1995

GUILD SOURCEBOOKS: *Artful Home 1, 2*

PAMELA COSPER
Pages 185, 236

4439 Rolling Pine Drive
West Bloomfield, MI 48323
Tel 248-366-9569
E-mail pamelacosper@hotmail.com
www.go.to/pcosper

My art expresses feelings through textures, patterns, symbols and color. My style is impressionistic or abstract, often with hints of realism. I enjoy the challenge of painting for a client—creating works for specific environments that capture a client's heart. Custom one-of-a-kind work is my favorite. Paintings range in price from $250 to $5,000.

COMMISSIONS: Recent commissions include what I like to call "life story portraits," in which the painting tells the story of a person or family's feelings and experiences. My latest commission is entitled *The Journey*.

RECENT PROJECTS: Transforming five rooms into environments, including a desert, a never-ending garden, heaven and an underwater scene. For each room I utilized wood, paint and fiberglass.

246

JONATHAN COX
Page 100

Cox Fine Art
768 Private Drive 3952
Willow Wood, OH 45696
Tel 740-867-0658
Fax 304-696-6505
E-mail coxj@marshall.edu
www.jonathancoxsculpture.com

My father gave me my first toolbox when I was four. He cleared the trees from the land that he bought from my grandmother and then used the trees to build the house in which I was raised. Before I was 14, we had built five boats together. The process that I pursue with my large-scale sculptures begins with wood and the skills that I learned as a child. From there I add the materials that will best communicate the idea: marble, granite, bronze, clay, polyester.

COMMISSIONS: Kinetic Park, 2003-2004, Huntington, WV

COLLECTIONS: Huntington Museum of Art, Huntington, WV

AWARDS: Florida Individual Artist Fellowship, 1999, Florida Department of State; West Virginia Individual Artist Fellowship, 2002, West Virginia Commission on the Arts

RENE CULLER
Page 216

Rene Culler Glass LLC
540 E 105th Street #122
Cleveland, OH 44108
Tel 216-851-5149
Fax 216-321-9428
E-mail rene@reneculler.com
www.reneculler.com

I work with glass because absorbed light animates and enlivens my compositions. Many layers of color or pattern, created by fusing and then slumping, yield dimension and dynamism. High-fire enamel painting, scraffito and line drawing embellish the surface and interior. I enjoy working with clients to create meaningful projects. Prices start at $2,000.

RECENT PROJECTS: Cleveland Clinic Hotel, OH; Blackwell Hotel, OSU, Columbus, OH

COMMISSIONS: Distinguished Service Award, Cleveland Orchestra, OH; Cuyahoga County Public Library, various branches, OH

COLLECTIONS: The Renwick Gallery, Smithsonian Institution, Washington, DC

AWARDS: Artist's Fellowships, Development Awards, the Ohio Arts Council

PUBLICATIONS: *Women Working in Glass*, 2003; *International Glass Art*, 2003

DAVID M BOWMAN STUDIO
Page 204

David M Bowman
Box 738
Berkeley, CA 94701
Tel 510-845-1072
E-mail dmbstudio@earthlink.net
www.davidmbowmanstudio.com

We build wall pieces from brass sheet so that they have up to four inches of relief and appear massive while actually being light enough to hang on any type of wall. We patina the brass using sculptural patina techniques so they are durable and weather well outdoors. My ideal composition is a balanced yet asymmetrical abstract form that can hang in any orientation. Prices for pieces generally range from $1,500 to $4,000. We have made more than 500 pieces for residential, corporate and public spaces, and I always welcome the opportunity to design for a specific space.

GUILD SOURCEBOOKS: *Designer's 8, 11, 13, 14; Architectural & Interior Art 16*

ARTIST STATEMENTS

DAVID WILSON DESIGN
Pages 26, 218

David Wilson
202 Darby Road
South New Berlin, NY 13843-2212
Tel 607-334-3015
Fax 607-334-7065
E-mail mail@davidwilsondesign.com
www.davidwilsondesign.com

My work seeks to reinvent the ancient craft of stained glass and place it in the context of contemporary architecture. Simplicity, restraint, changing light, projected image and night view all inform design development. I encourage a reciprocal dialogue in a collaborative design process and offer, in association with WRW Studio LLC, a complete service of design, fabrication and installation.

COMMISSIONS: St. John Baptist Catholic Church, 2003, Howell, MI; U.S. Courthouse, 2003, Erie, PA; NEC Monorail Station, Newark Liberty International Airport, 2002, Newark, NJ

EXHIBITIONS: *Design Excellence, Public Patronage of Art and Architecture*, 2004, 2003, AAF, Washington, DC; *A New Millennium, A New Light*, 2003, Louisville, KY

GUILD SOURCEBOOKS: *The Guild 1, 2, 3, 4, 5; Architect's 6, 7, 8, 9, 11, 13, 14, 15; Architectural & Interior Art 16, 17, 18*

DEANNE SABECK STUDIOS
Page 35

Deanne Sabeck
Jeffery Laudenslager
574 Arden Drive
Encinitas, CA 92024
Tel/Fax 760-943-0988
E-mail deanne@deannesabeck.com
www.deannesabeck.com
www.laudenslagersculpture.com

Deanne: I explore the pure nature of light with materials including reflective glass, photo imagery and text. I create mysterious and evocative installations that question perception and reality.

Jeffery: Kinetic sculpture is my primary expressive tool. All are wind driven and use no motors. I use metals such as stainless steel and titanium. Public and private commissions welcome.

COMMISSIONS: Florblanca Resort, 2002, Santa Teresa, Costa Rica; Scripps MacDonald Center, 2001, La Jolla, CA; Torrey Pines Business Park, 2000, Del Mar, CA; San Diego International Airport, 1998

EXHIBITIONS: *Elemental*, 2004, Karen Lynn Gallery, Boca Raton, FL; *In Pursuit of Eros*, 1997, Mona Museum, Los Angeles, CA; *Riparte*, 1996, Rome, Italy; solo exhibit, New Leaf Gallery, Berkley, CA

PUBLICATIONS: *Sedona Home & Garden*, 2003; *Sedona Monthly*, 2003; *Contemporary Glass*, 2001

DÉGAGÉ STUDIOS
Page 169

Trudy Lynn Simmons
1464 Ingleside Avenue
McLean, VA 22101
Tel 703-356-8002
Fax 703-356-7709
E-mail csimmons@degage.com
www.degage.com

For 14 years, we have beautified homes, places of worship, government buildings and businesses throughout the United States with decorative artistry . Under the direction of Trudy Simmons (an artist, colorist and interior designer), we have a staff of full-time artists who create an imaginative range of artworks, from tile mural works to fine painted murals and trompe l'oeil for indoors and outdoor environments. Murals are often painted on canvases and shipped for installation on walls and ceilings.

RECENT PROJECTS: Recent projects include a Honeywell-Poms lobby mural and two 30' exterior tile murals, one of which depicts Atlantis and the other, a playful beach scene. Underwater bar stools with tiled tops feature patterns that match our waterline tiles.

ARISTIDES DEMETRIOS
Pages 78, 83

2694 Sycamore Canyon Road
Santa Barbara, CA 93108
Tel 805-565-2217
Fax 805-565-7721
E-mail arisdemetrios@aol.com
www.demetriossculpture.com

After successfully completing a series of monumental public sculptures, I turned my attention to smaller works for private collectors. In the last few decades I have designed, fabricated and installed a large number of commissioned works for the gardens of private collectors, including a great many bronze fountains. In addition, I have had several gallery and museum shows featuring my figurative and abstract bronze sculptures and my painted or patinaed steel sculptures, most of which are now owned by private collectors across the United States.

RECENT COMMISSIONS: *Surge*, 2002, Dehart/Cohen collection, Santa Barbara, CA; *Joie de Vivre, 9 Acrobats*, Emmons collection, Santa Barbara, CA; *Verging Ribbons X*, 2000, Governor and Mrs. Mark Warner collection, VA

RECENT AWARDS: Santa Barbara Beautiful Award for the most beautiful work of public art, an 18' bronze fountain, *Mentors*, 2002, for the Santa Barbara City College

DILLON FORGE
Pages 5, 58, 60

Michael Dillon
14250 Birmingham Highway
Alpharetta, GA 30004
Tel 770-649-8012
Fax 678-366-0542
E-mail dillonforge@mindspring.com
www.dillonforge.com

My methods stem from a strong background in sculpture, where metal is transformed using heat, hammer and intuition. When I approach functional work, such as tables, railings and gates, I focus on a design that will both reflect the clients personal vision and elevate the object into a work of art. My primary medium is iron; however, I also work with stainless steel, brass and bronze. I have been featured in *Southern Accents* magazine and on HGTV'S *Modern Masters*. I have completed grand stair railings and gates for exclusive homes in Atlanta, Nassau, historical Biltmore Forest in Asheville, NC, and Pawleys Island, SC. My work is produced specifically for each client, whether commercial or residential. My goal is to forge a relationship with each client to bring forth a collaborative vision for highly crafted works of art.

JUDY DIOSZEGI
Page 70

Judy Dioszegi, designer
1295 Margate Lane
Green Oaks, IL 60048
Tel 847-367-8395
Fax 847-367-8395 *51
E-mail jdiox2@aol.com
www.jdioszegi.com

Since 1976, we have specialized in designing and fabricating banners, tapestries and mobiles for corporate, residential, liturgical and public spaces. Collaborating with architects, designers and individual clients, we produce site-specific creations that enhance environments through color, shape and attention to architectural surroundings. Materials range from richly textured fabrics in tapestries to durable, vibrant nylon for mobiles and atrium pieces. Projects are unique, and prices vary according to design and complexity. Inquiries are welcome.

AWARDS: Industrial Fabrics Association International: Outstanding Achievement Award, 2002; two Outstanding Achievement Awards, 2001; Design Award, 1998, 1994; Modern Liturgy: Bene Award, 1996-97

GUILD SOURCEBOOKS: *Architect's 8, 10, 12, 14; Architectural & Interior Art 17*

247

ARTIST STATEMENTS

ROGER DiTARANDO
Page 139

DiTarando & Co.
1161 Hartford Turnpike
Vernon, CT 06066
Tel 860-871-7635/860-870-1953
E-mail ditarando@aol.com
www.ditarando.com

About 25 years ago, I began studying the sculptural relationship between man and animal. This philosophy underlying primitive construction methods and exploring our primal relationships continues to be an area of personal fascination. I want to augment the attitude, approach and style of creative thinking of clients and co-workers. I've expanded the scope of how to apply my skills by working and learning with architects, landscape architects, art consultants, exhibit designers, historic and educational planners and others. While using a variety of techniques in unique combinations, I strive to be the traditionalist who breaks the rules and the innovator who pays homage to the past. My work adorns everything from gardens to museums, and in it you will find a boldness of design, a sense of humor, an abiding respect for nature and an appreciation for the mysteries no man can unravel.

SUZANNE DONAZETTI
Page 205

Freefall Designs
912 Bedford Street
Cumberland, MD 21502
Tel 301-759-3618
E-mail suz@hereintown.net
www.freefalldesigns.com

I paint on copper with metallic leaf, inks, acrylics and pigments. I weave the painted copper into tapestries, framed pieces and folding screens. I enjoy working with copper and am enchanted by the layers and complexity that result from weaving the paintings together. My vision is to create large-scale art to bring a sense of healing and meditation to the viewer.

RECENT PROJECTS: Bradley International Airport, Windsor Locks, CT; Time Inc. Conference Center, New York, NY; Longmont United Hospital, Longmont, CO; Weinberg Medical Center, Mercy Hospital, Baltimore, MD

COMMISSIONS: Dental Center, 2003, Denver, CO; Private residence, 2003, Anchorage, AK; Hotel Takamatsu, 2001, Tokyo, Japan; Alaska Court System, 2001, Anchorage, AK; New Mexico Emergency Management Center, 2000, Santa Fe, NM; Hilton Hotel, 1999, Sapporo, Japan

GUILD SOURCEBOOKS: *Designer's 9, 12, 13, 14, 15; Artful Home 1*

DRAEGER UNUSAL ART
Page 214

Steve Draeger
S68 W12447 Woods Road
Muskego, WI 53150
Tel 414-525-1130
E-mail draeger@execpc.com
www.draegerunusualart.com

My signature three-dimensional wall sculptures are composed mainly of wood, stretched canvas and acrylics, which are laid on thickly for extra texture and dimension. My love and appreciation for the spontaneity of abstract art combined with pop art elements have inspired me to create these individual and dimensional sculptures for over 15 years. The three-dimensional aspect brings extra life, movement and individuality to each piece. I impose no meaning or concepts to my art—I want my art to be whatever the viewer's imagination creates and to give the viewer a new perspective each time the piece is studied. My client base is the domestic United States. My work is well suited for custom residential design projects and has been incorporated in a variety of commercial and corporate settings.

BANDHU DUNHAM
Page 122

Salusa Glassworks, Inc.
PO Box 2354
Prescott, AZ 86302
Tel 800-515-7281
Fax 928-541-9570
E-mail bandhu@salusaglassworks.com
www.salusaglassworks.com

I always wanted to be a mad scientist or an alchemist. By 15, I had an extensive chemistry lab in my parent's basement. Since the beakers at the hobby store were never cool-looking enough, I taught myself the basics of lampwork glassblowing. Later, I dropped out of Chemical Engineering at Princeton to become an artist. Nature inspires me, the interplays between art and science always interest me, and glass merges these fields like no other material. After 29 years, fanciful steam engines and other kinetic sculptures represent a full turn of the circle, back to the colorful, magical mysteries that captivated my childhood self. He's still in there, and he wants you to come play, too.

COLLECTIONS: Corning Museum of Glass, Sphere Museum, Niijima Glass Center

VALERIE EGLAND
Page 63

Eclipse Art
870 School Road
San Juan Bautista, CA 95045
Tel 831-623-2664
Fax 831-623-1719
vegland@hollinet.com
www.valerieegland.com

Often narrative in nature, my pieces are born out of an interactive discussion with the builder, architect designer and/or client. Together we work to clarify function, design and anticipated aesthetic result. I target long-term aesthetic muscle through the complexity of concept, design and execution. Feeling at home with conceptual and mixed-media art, I create representational pieces to reflect an innovative approach to materials. The sculpture materials I use are elementally important but do not dominate. Most important is satisfying the commission parameters such that the finished piece falls naturally into its function on site while maintaining artistic integrity.

ROBERT W. ELLISON
Pages 16, 89, 196

Ellison Studio
6480 Eagle Ridge Road
Penngrove, CA 94951
Tel 707-795-9775
Fax 707-795-4370
E-mail robert@robertellison.com
www.robertellison.com

I have over 30 years of experience providing full-service design, fabrication and installation of site-specific, large-scale sculpture and sculptural architectural accompaniments. Collaborations with architects, landscape architects and public agencies have resulted in well-received works with a great variety of form, format and imagery. Many metals, fiberglass, electronics, clockworks and lighting are used to create sculptural solutions for any environment. Prices range from $20,000 to $750,000.

COMMISSIONS: Dublin Public Library, 2002, Dublin, CA; City Park Lincolnshire Shopping Center, 2002, Chicago, IL; Bay Area Rapid Transit, 2002, San Francisco, CA; Harvest Community Park, 2001, Greenwood Village, CO; Jack London Aquatic Center, 2000, Oakland, CA; Great America Building, 2000, Cedar Rapids, IA; Alameda County Recorder's Office, 1999, Oakland, CA; Rohnert Park Cultural Arts Center, 1999, Rohnert Park, CA

ARTIST STATEMENTS

DALE ENOCHS
Page 85

8635 South Ketcham Road
Bloomington, IN 47403
Tel/Fax 812-824-8181
E-mail denochs@bluemarble.net
http://home.bluemarble.net/~denochs

The primary material that I shape is indigenous to the area in which I work, the oolitic limestone quarries of south central Indiana. This stone speaks of time, substance, strength, endurance and the earth from which it comes. It has been a primary source in architecture and sculpture for millennia. Matching the inherent qualities of the stone with contrasting materials and exploiting ideas with scale, form and texture, my work pays homage to the past but speaks in a contemporary voice. It is appropriate for interior or exterior settings, as a water feature or as an independent statement. I relish the collaborative process with architects and clients and approach each project with an attention to detail, both conceptual and physical.

EWING PHOTOGRAPHY
Page 194

Gifford Ewing
800 East 19th Avenue
Denver, CO 80218
Tel 303-832-0800
Fax 303-832-0801
E-mail gallery@ewingphoto.com
www.ewingphoto.com

As the trends and movements in photography seem to sway toward alternative techniques and digital imagery, my work captures the purity and natural beauty of landscapes through more traditional photographic methods. I capture the majority of my images in black and white, developing all of the images and printing on archival silver paper. All of my prints are numbered and are part of a limited-edition series that may vary depending on the size of the image and subject matter.

EXHIBITIONS: Group show, October 2004-March 2005, National Museum of Wildlife Art, Jackson Hole, WY; *Opening the Season,* 2004, Virginia Lynch Gallery, Rhode Island School of Design, Providence, RI; *Heart of the West Campaign,* 2003, The Nature Conservancy Colorado Chapter, Boulder, CO; *B&W Works by Gifford Ewing and Kim Weston,* 2003, Shaw Gallery, Northeast Harbor, ME

ROB FISHER
Pages 75, 94, 120

228 North Allegheny Street
Bellefonte, PA 16823
Tel 814-355-1458
Fax 814-353-9060
E-mail glenunion@aol.com
www.robfisheramericandream.com

I have received commissions in Japan, Saudi Arabia, St. Thomas and throughout the United States. I work primarily in stainless steel, aluminum and light, and have created pieces for private residences, corporations and public spaces. My sculpture is suspended, freestanding and wall-mounted, and is both interior and exterior.

PUBLICATIONS: *MIT Technology Review,* 2004; *Buildings* Magazine 2004; *USA Today,* 2003; *New York Times; Attache,* US Airways: In-flight magazine, 2003; *Philadelphia Style,* 2003; *Philadelphia* magazine, 2003; *Philadelphia Inquirer,* 2003; *Interior Design* 2003

GUILD SOURCEBOOKS: *Architect's 9, 11, 12, 13, 14, 15; Architectural & Interior Art 16, 17, 18; Artful Home 1*

RECENT PROJECTS: Florida Atlantic University, Boca Raton, FL; Penn Stater Conference Center/Hotel, State College, PA

ROB FISHER
Pages 75, 94, 120

228 North Allegheny Street
Bellefonte, PA 16823
Tel 814-355-1458
Fax 814-353-9060
E-mail glenunion@aol.com
www.robfisheramericandream.com

COMMISSIONS: Arrivals Hall, Philadelphia International Airport, 2003, Philadelphia, PA; National Education Association Headquarters, 2003, Washington, DC; Harbor Branch Oceanographic Institute, 2003, Fort Pierce, FL; AstraZeneca Pharmaceuticals Visitor Center, 2002, Wilmington, DE; Gateway Center, 2002, Corporate Office Properties, Columbia, MD; Booz Allen Hamilton Headquarters, 2001, McClean, VA; Sherman Medical Center, 2001, Chicago, IL; Grounds for Sculpture, 2000, Hamilton, NJ; Jackson National Life Headquarters, 2000, Lansing, MI; Banco Popular Headquarters, 1999, St. Thomas, Virgin Islands

EXHIBITIONS: *Art Miami,* 2004; Century Club, 2003, New York; Environment Art Academy, GCA, 2002, Tokyo, Japan; *Grounds for Sculpture,* 2001, Hamilton, NY; Nexus Gallery, 2000, Philadelphia, PA; Pier Walk, 1998, Chicago, IL; NTT Intercommunication Center Museum, 1997, Tokyo, Japan

STEVE FONTANINI
Page 61

Steve Fontanini Architectural
and Ornamental Blacksmithing
PO Box 2298
11400 South Hoback Junction Road
Jackson, WY 83001
Tel 307-733-7668
Fax 307-734-8816
E-mail sfontani@wyoming.com
www.stevefontaniniblacksmith.com

I am a designer and builder of forged metalwork for home and business. My crew and I create architectural metalwork such as stair railings, gates, fireplace accessories and even furniture. Bronze, stainless steel, mild steel or aluminum can be forged, cast, machined or welded into any shape or design. I will design items to fit your environment, taste and style. My work is found throughout the U.S.

AWARDS: Silver award, 2002, National Ornamental & Miscellaneous Metals Association

PUBLICATIONS: *Teton Home Magazine,* Spring/Summer 2003, Fall/Winter 2001-2002, premiere issue 2000; *Cowboys & Indians Magazine,* January 2002, Summer 1996

RON FOSTER & MICHAEL LINSLEY
Page 112

Kaleidosculpture
2921 Pebble Drive
Corona del Mar, CA 92625
Tel 949-650-0662
Fax 949-650-6890
E-mail ron@kaleidosculpture.com
E-mail michael@kaleidosculpture.com
www.kaleidosculpture.com

Kaleidosculpture™ is a whole new concept in art and sculpture. It fuses kaleidoscope theory—multiple, duplicated, single-plane symmetrical images placed at opposing angles—with color theory, bringing to life a three-dimensional, interactive kaleidoscope effect that uniquely mimics and complements its surroundings. Like kaleidoscopes, each sculpture changes dramatically depending on the viewing angle. Creators Ron Foster, a former Vietnam combat illustrator and successful commercial artist, and Michael Linsley, a versatile ceramist with a flair for diverse techniques and styles, combine their talents and an infinite array of materials, colors and textures to spectacularly ignite any locale through this innovative, incomparable medium.

ARTIST STATEMENTS

FURNACE HOT GLASS WORKS LLC
Page 162

Chris Nordin
Michelle Plucinsky
2225 Drexel
Dearborn, MI 48128
Tel 313-894-6000
Fax 313-359-1837
E-mail furnacehotglass@aol.com
www.furnacehotglass.com

At FURNACE we aim to create a successful body of work tailored to the needs of our clients. From furniture to architectural accents, we incorporate traditional Venetian techniques with a modern flair. Our work includes, but is not limited to, blown and cast glass, metal, wood and mixed media. We have experience in all phases of design, construction and installation, with jobs completed on time and within budget. Working closely with architects, designers and individuals, we encourage inquiries for residential commissions, site-specific designs and interior design projects. We create individual, unique, contemporary works. See for yourself at WWW.FURNACEHOTGLASS.COM.

RECENT PROJECTS: Opus One Restaurant, 2004, Detroit, MI; offices at Universal Images, 2003-2004, Southfield, MI

GALVIN GLASS WORKS LTD.
Page 41

Andrew Galvin
339 East Avenue, Suite 400
Rochester, NY 14604
Tel 585-325-6910
Fax 585-546-1394
E-mail ggwltd@aol.com
www.galvinglassworks.com

Galvin Glass Works features fused and cast glass. Using layers of sheet glass to create one-of-a-kind large-scale pieces, we design and fabricate work for private commissions. This work includes lighting fixtures for a four-story building and several private residences, a bar top and room divider for a local bar/restaurant, and frit-fused glass murals that act as faux windows for a bathroom. We specialize in glass tabletops and design and fabricate custom glass awards for large-scale corporations.

COMMISSIONS: Bar top and dividers, 2002, Pearl Restaurant, Rochester, NY; mural, 2001, private residence, Brighton, NY; wall sconces, 2003, The Valley Building, Rochester, NY; tabletops, 2003, private residences, La Hoya, CA, Rochester, NY, and Canandaigua, NY

GAYA GLASS
Page 36

Dan King-Lehman
Eve King-Lehman
4742 North Street
Somis, CA 93066
Tel 805-386-4069
E-mail art@gayaglass.com
www.gayaglass.com

We create custom glass sinks and backsplashes using fused and kiln-formed methods. Each project is a personal quest to find the best style and technique for that space, based on the needs and desires of all involved.

RECENT PROJECTS: Dr. & Mrs. Cowden, 2003, Monte Sereno, CA

COMMISSIONS: David & Ellie Gross, 2003, Novato, CA; Diana Clark, 2003, Brentwood, CA

EXHIBITIONS: *Color Catalog*, 1995, Loveland Museum, Loveland, CO; solo exhibition, 1992, Grants Pass Museum, Grants Pass, OR

AWARDS: *Art in the Park*, 2003, Ojai, CA; first place award, 1985, Desert West, Lancaster, CA

PUBLICATIONS: *Contemporary Warm Glass*, 2000; *New Glass Review*, 1992, 1991, 1989, 1987

250

DANIEL GOLDSTEIN
Page 74

224 Guerrero Street
San Francisco, CA 94103
Tel 415-621-5761
Fax 415-643-8369
E-mail danieljgoldstein@yahoo.com

I have successfully collaborated with architects and designers for over 25 years. My suspended sculptures of glass and steel, as well as my mobiles in aluminum, have been commissioned for public, corporate and private environments.

RECENT PROJECTS: Astra Zeneca headquarters, Wilmington, DE; Alcoa Aluminum headquarters, Pittsburgh, PA; BART station, Colma, CA; Norcal Headquarters, San Francisco, CA

COLLECTIONS: Chicago Art Institute, IL; Brooklyn Museum, NY; Berkeley University Art Museum, CA; Carnegie Museum, Pittsburgh, PA

EXHIBITIONS: Durka Chang Gallery, 2002, San Francisco, CA; Brauer Museum of Art, 2000, Valparaiso, IN; National Gallery of Victoria, 1998, Melbourne, Australia

PUBLICATIONS: *Art-Science Fusion*, 2001; *Beyond Belief: Modern Art & the Religious Imagination*, 1998;

GUILD SOURCEBOOKS: *Architect's 7, 8, 10, 11, 12, 13, 14; Architectural & Interior Art 17*

RALF GSCHWEND
Pages 18, 69

Ralfonso.com
301 Clematis Street, #3000
West Palm Beach, FL 33401
Tel 561-655-2745
Fax 561-655-4158
E-mail ralfonso@ralfonso.com
www.ralfonso.com

Kinetic art has been my passion for the last 25 years. I primarily design wind, water or motor-driven sculptures for public places such as restaurant, hotel and corporate interior lobbies or atriums. I also design for outdoor plazas, fountains and parks. Custom commissions, as well as numerous ready designs, are available. My moving sculptures range from two-foot interior limited-edition models that start at $2,500 to large ceiling or wall-suspended mobiles that start at $9,000 to monumental originals that start at $50,000. Ralfonso sculpture leasing is available. Please contact me for a free Ralfonso CD with videos, images and descriptions of my work.

RECENT PROJECTS: *Moving on Up*, 15' sculpture for the New Star building in St. Petersburg, Russia

EXHIBITIONS: *Art in Motion*, Biennale, Holland; Chinese Academy of Science, Beijing, China

MARK ERIC GULSRUD
Page 152

Architectural Glass/Sculpture
3309 Tahoma Place West
Tacoma, WA 98466
Tel 253-566-1720
Fax 253-565-5981
E-mail markgulsrud@comcast.net
www.markericgulsrud.com

Primarily site-specific, my commissions range internationally and include public, private, corporate and liturgical settings. Media include custom hand-blown leaded glass; sand-carved, laminated and cast glass; handmade ceramic; stone; and carved wood. I encourage professional collaboration and am personally involved in all phases of design, fabrication and installation. My primary concern is a sympathetic integration of artwork with environment.

GUILD SOURCEBOOKS: *GUILD 3, 4; Architect's 7, 8, 9, 10, 11, 12, 13, 14, 15; Architectural & Interior Art 16, 17, 18*

ARTIST STATEMENTS

GEORGE HANDY
Page 221

2 Webb Cove Road
Asheville, NC 28804
Tel 828-254-4691
Fax 828-254-2227
E-mail george@georgehandy.com
www.georgehandy.com

Recently, I've completed my fifth public art commission. These are interactive holographic artworks that engage the viewers and promote conservations and community, thus fulfilling my goal as an artist who designs for public spaces. Shown in this book are my residential/corporate sculptures, which combine numerous planes and complex angles that create a visual dynamic. Layers of translucent colors build a patina, revealing a matrix of drafting lines, and showing the revisions and history of my working process.

RECENT PROJECTS: UNC-Asheville, Asheville, NC; Charlotte Transit Authority; North Carolina Zoo, Asheboro, NC; Charlotte Parks Department, NC

COMMISSIONS: Warner Brothers, *Batman Forever* set design; Charlotte Health Department

COLLECTIONS: Smithsonian Institution Permanent Collection; Renwick Museum; RJ Reynolds

AWARDS: North Carolina Regional Artist Grant, 2004

JOAN ROTHCHILD HARDIN
Page 55

Joan Rothchild Hardin Ceramics
393 West Broadway #4
New York, NY 10012
Tel 212-966-9433
Fax 212-431-9196
E-mail joan@hardintiles.com
www.hardintiles.com

My award-winning, hand-painted ceramic art tiles add interest and richness to residential, corporate and public settings. Over the years, I have learned ways of layering glazes on the tiles to create depth and variety not usually seen in the medium.

COMMISSIONS: Three veterinary hospitals, New York, NY; *al benessere*, New York, NY; private residences across the country

COLLECTIONS: American Art Clay Company, Indianapolis, IN

EXHIBITIONS: *Moravian Tile Works*, 2002, 2003; *Ceramic Tile*, 2002, 2003, New York, NY; *21st Century Tiles*, 2002, Minnesota Crafts Council; *Tiles in America*, 2002, Clay Fine Arts Gallery, Cheyenne, WY;

PUBLICATIONS: *A Glaze of Color*, 2004; *Ceramic Art Tile for the Home*, 2001

GUILD SOURCEBOOKS: *Designer's 14, 15; Architectural & Interior Art 16, 17, 18*

MARK YALE HARRIS
Page 140

c/o ARTwork
1701 A Lena Street
Santa Fe, NM 87505
Tel/Fax 505-982-7447
E-mail ARTworksfe@aol.com
www.markyaleharris.com

My figurative works combine soft lines with geometric shapes and a disproportion that suggests the duality of humanity. In a distinctly different vein are the animal sculptures, which capture moments in time and the whimsy of nature preserved. All of my original forms are created in stone, and selected works are available in limited-edition bronze.

COMMISSIONS: Edward Peace, Congressman, IN; Hester Capital Management, Austin, TX

EXHIBITIONS: Top Ten Texas Artists of 2003, Austin Visual Arts Association, Austin, TX; National Juried Exhibition, 2002, Holter Museum, Helena, MT; *Animals in the Atrium*, 2001, National Sculpture Society, New York, NY

PUBLICATIONS: Preview 2003: Bosque Conservatory Art Council catalog; Sculpture in the Park catalog, 2002; Flash of Spirit catalog, 2002

YOSHI HAYASHI
Pages 8, 177

Yoshi Hayashi Studio
255 Kansas Street #330
San Francisco, CA 94103
Tel/Fax 415-552-0755
E-mail yoshihayashi@att.net
www.yoshihayashi.com

I was born in Japan and learned the rigorous techniques of Japanese lacquer art from my father. I carry the spirit, history and inspiration of this process with me today as I reinterpret the ancient lacquer traditions for my screens and wall panels. My designs range from delicate, traditional 17th-century Japanese lacquer art themes to bold, contemporary geometric designs. By skillfully applying metallic leaf and bronzing powders, I add both illumination and contrast to the network of color, pattern and texture. Recent commissions include works for private residences in the United States and Japan.

COMMISSIONS: Restaurant, 2003, San Diego, CA

EXHIBITIONS: *Japanese Screens Revisited*, 2003, lobby, San Francisco, CA

GUILD SOURCEBOOKS: *THE GUILD 4, 5; Designer's 6, 7, 8, 9, 10, 11, 12, 13, 14, 15; Architectural & Interior Art 16, 17, 18; Artful Home 1*

ARCHIE HELD
Page 84

Archie Held Studio
5-18th Street
Richmond, CA 94801
Tel 510-235-8700
Fax 510-234-4828
E-mail archieheldstudio@comcast.net
www.archieheld.com

I work primarily in bronze and stainless steel, with water as a central element. I enjoy incorporating contrasting materials, surfaces and textures in my work.

COMMISSIONS: SCSI Corporation, Australia; Alliant Energy World Headquarters, Madison, WI; Louis Vuitton Moet Hennessey, San Francisco, CA; SAP Technology, Pennsylvania; T Mimarlik, Istanbul, Turkey; Chevron World Headquarters, San Ramon, CA; Sacramento Metropolitan Arts Commission, Sacramento, CA; Playboy Mansion, Los Angeles, CA; Robert Mondavi Winery, Napa, CA; WW Grainger, Inc. World Headquarters, Las Vegas, NV; Midway Trading, Canada; Sky Tokyo Club, Japan; Harrah's Resort Casino, Reno, NV; City of Los Angeles, Department of Water and Power, Los Angeles, CA; Krups, Germany

MARILYN HENRION
Page 231

505 LaGuardia Place #23D
New York, NY 10012
Tel 212-982-8949
Fax 212-979-7462
E-mail marilynhenrion@rcn.com
www.marilynhenrion.com

Whether exploring the visual aspects of music or the metaphor of poetry, my art quilts vibrate with the lush intensity of a Matisse painting, the complexity of an Indian miniature, the mystery of a Russian icon or the elegance of a Japanese kesa (the robes worn by monks), just a few of the many sources that inspire me. Celebrating textiles as my medium of choice, I employ a wide range of materials—including silks from India and Chinese brocades, metallics and exotic cotton prints—animating their surfaces with meticulous hand quilting. My work is included in museum, corporate and private collections, including the Museum of Arts & Design, New York, NY; U.S. Ambassadors' residences in Rabat, Lucent Technologies, Avaya Communications, Kaiser Permanente, Carnegie Abbey Country Club and the Dana Farber Cancer Institute. I am included in the Smithsonian Institution's Archives of American Art.

ARTIST STATEMENTS

KAREN HEYL
Pages 42, 44, 76

1310 Pendleton Street, ML#2
Cincinnati, OH 45202
Tel 513-421-9791/760-489-7106
E-mail heylstone2@aol.com
www.karenheyl.com

My award-winning mural relief sculpture combines old world stone carving techniques with contemporary design, lending itself to a variety of architectural applications, both monumental and small. Using varied textural surfaces, I create aesthetic sophistication with simplified sensual forms.

RECENT PROJECTS: *Ecological Sampler,* six limestone panels at 5' x 3.5' x 3" mounted on 30'H steel easel, Orange County Convention Center, Orlando, FL; *Nature's Guardians,* two limestone panels at 4'x 8'x 10" flanking entryway into housing development, privately funded public art project for the city of Brea, CA

COMMISSIONS: *Organic Life Forms,* courtyard sculpture, 2002, private residence, Ft. Thomas, KY; *Parrots,* 2002, garden sculpture, private residence, Mason, OH; Cellular micrographs, 2000, Vanderbilt University Medical Research Center, Nashville, TN

GUILD SOURCEBOOKS: *Architect's 9, 12, 13, 14, 15; Architectural & Interior Art 16, 17, 18; Artful Home 1, 2*

ERLING HOPE
Pages 148, 155

Hope Liturgical Works
1455 Sag/Bridge Turnpike
Sag Harbor, NY 11963
Tel/Fax 631-725-4294
E-mail hopelitwrk@aol.com

Versed in a wide range of materials and techniques, I use a multidisciplinary approach to explore the influence of objects, images and the built environment on the contemporary liturgical experience. I serve as Director of the Society for the Arts, Religion and Contemporary Culture, and have served as artist-in-residence at Andover Newton Theological School's Institute for Theology and the Arts.

RECENT PROJECTS: 14 Bronze Stations of the Cross, Immaculate Heart of Mary Catholic Church, Grand Junction, CO

COLLECTIONS: Good Shepherd Episcopal Church, Silver Springs, MD; Trinity Evangelical Lutheran Church, North Bethesda, MD; Insurance Board Disciples of Christ, UCC

AWARDS: Merit Award, 2003, *Inform Magazine;* Religious Arts/Visual Arts Award, Interfaith Forum on Religion, Art and Architecture

GUILD SOURCEBOOKS: *Architect's 13; Architectural & Interior Art 16*

HOPEN STUDIO INC.
Page 128

Bill Hopen
Ai Qiu Hopen
227 Main Street
Sutton, WV 26601
Tel 800-872-8578 U.S.
Tel 304-765-5611 (international)
E-mail hopen@mountain.net
www.billhopen.com
www.aiqiuhopen.com

We at Hopen Studio have devoted ourselves to sculpting the figure for narrative and emotional communication. We create works that focus on the warmth and meaning of human relationships and the strength and character of individuals in our portraits. We listen very carefully to our clients, creating images that speak clearly to them; each work must also be graceful and expressive to satisfy us as artists. We are able to create custom-designed bronzes in months, not years. Simply pick up the phone and call us—we will discuss your project at length, without obligation. View our works online and call any one of our clients. We are proud of our record of award-winning work. It is always installed on time and within budget and always exceeds expectations.

252

DAR HORN
Page 197

Union Art Works
402 West 5th Street
San Pedro, CA 90731
Tel 310-833-1282
Fax 310-833-1592
E-mail dar@darhorn.com
www.darhorn.com

My images are uniquely beautiful. The intensely saturated colors and richly detailed forms combine to engage viewers and draw them into the image—and seemingly into vistas and worlds not even imagined. These Ilfochrome™ prints are mounted on aluminum panels and have a purported archival life of 200 years. Various sizes are available.

PAUL HOUSBERG
Page 27

Glass Project, Inc.
875 North Main Road
Jamestown, RI 02835
Tel 401-560-0880
E-mail info@glassproject.com
www.glassproject.com

Paul Housberg creates art glass features for hospitality, corporate, religious and public spaces. Central to his work is the power of light, color and texture to shape and define a space. Please visit his website for additional information. The artist welcomes inquiries regarding any planned or contemplated project.

RECENT PROJECTS: Logan International Gateway, Boston, MA; Le Meridien Hotel, Minneapolis, MN; Temple Habonim, Barrington, RI; Peninsula Hotel, Chicago, IL; William J. Nealon Federal Building and U.S. Courthouse, Scranton, PA

GUILD SOURCEBOOKS: *Architect's 6, 7, 8, 9, 10, 11, 13, 15; Architectural & Interior Art 16, 17, 18*

HOWDLE STUDIO INC.
Page 48

Bruce Howdle
225 Commerce Street
Mineral Point, WI 53565
Tel 608-987-3590
E-mail bhowdle@chorus.net
www.brucehowdle.com

I have been a ceramic sculptor since 1976. I have produced work ranging from thrown forms up to six feet in height to 30-foot relief murals utilizing nine tons of clay. I fire with a sodium process that melts the clay surface, preserving the integrity of the media and creating a very durable piece. My work is suitable for freestanding or installed wall locations. My pieces are in large public institutions, banks, corporations, private offices and homes. Prices range from $1,500 to $150,000. I collaborate closely with clients and provide detailed drawings of my proposed projects.

GUILD SOURCEBOOKS: *Architect's 7, 9, 10, 11, 12, 13, 14, 15; Architectural & Interior Art 16, 17, 18*

ARTIST STATEMENTS

IE CREATIVE ARTWORKS
Page 73

1399 Railspur Alley, Granville Island
Vancouver, BC V6H 4G9
Canada
Tel 604-254-4374
Fax 604-683-4343
E-mail studio@iecreative.ca
www.iecreative.ca

What do you get when you cross a rocket scientist lured from nuclear physics by the muse of sculpture with a crazy animator who paints up a storm at every opportunity? You get ie creative artworks: two artists who—when it comes to art—love it all. Our company excels in large public sculptures, elegant murals, transformative installations, unique film animations and kooky inventions—like the Robotic Ball Tosser for our dog Joe or the elaborately automated "Martini Machine"! At ie creative, we have a philosophy of producing artworks that engage a wide audience. Our sense of fun is nicely balanced by our aesthetic sophistication. Without actually putting words in anyone's mouth, it's fair to say that our clients do say nice things about us.

INDIANA ART GLASS
Page 33

Gregory R. Thompson
6400 Brookville Road
Indianapolis, IN 46219
Tel 317-353-6369
Fax 317-359-9630
E-mail greg@indianaartglass.com
www.indianaartglass.com

Our artisans and craftsmen produce unique, high-end custom architectural glass products to meet or exceed our clients' visual communication needs by adapting the medium of glass to any circumstance. Specializing in cast glass and detailed glass etching, we enjoy the challenge of diverse products—including developing new ideas with glass. We can also include other materials such as metal, stone and water to produce quality pieces of functional glass art.

RECENT PROJECTS: St. Vincent Hospital, Carmel, IN; Eli Lilly Corporate Headquarters, Indianapolis, IN; Riverview Hospital, Noblesville, IN; Hyatt Regency Resort and Spa, Lake Tahoe, NV

COMMISSIONS: Firefighters Credit Union, Indianapolis, IN; Premiere Credit, Indianapolis, IN

EXHIBITIONS: HD Boutique, 2003, South Beach; Penrod Arts Festival, 2002, Indianapolis; Hospitality Design Exposition, 2002 Las Vegas, NV

JAMES T. RUSSELL SCULPTURE
Pages 114-115

James T. Russell
1930 Lomita Boulevard
Lomita, CA 90717
Tel 310-326-0785
Fax 310-326-1470
E-mail james@russellsculpture.com
www.russellsculpture.com

In a seamless transition, my sculpture becomes part of its environment. The highly polished stainless steel spires and curves penetrate gently into their space. Building upon my four decades of monumental sculpture, I respond to the world and my artwork continues to grow.

COMMISSIONS: Coast Aluminum and Architectural, 2003, Santa Fe Springs, CA; Astra Zeneca Pharmaceuticals corporate headquarters, 2002, Wilmington, DE; Chico Municipal Airport, 2001, Chico, CA

COLLECTIONS: Motorola Corporation, Beijing, China; Allstate Insurance Corporation, Glendale, CA; Riverside Art Museum, Riverside, CA; A.T. Kearney Inc., Chicago, IL

PUBLICATIONS: Landscape Architect, 2000; Focus Santa Fe, 2000; Art Calendar, 1999

GUILD SOURCEBOOKS: Architect's 7, 8, 12, 13, 14, 15; Architectural & Interior Art 16, 17, 18

DALE JENSSEN
Page 161

PO Box 129
Terlingua, TX 79852
Tel/Fax 432-371-2312
E-mail jenssengallery@hotmail.com
www.dalejenssen.com

Having fun combining form and function is my M.O. Using fabricated and/or found elements in a variety of materials, I create work that is infused with sensuality and humor. I am happy designing in any architectural style, be it contemporary, retro, arts and crafts, southwestern or my own quirky amalgam of them all. While I predominantly work alone, meticulously crafting each piece from start to finish, I occasionally employ trusted subcontractors and offer custom powder-coated finishes on my creations. In addition to the sconces and chandeliers, I also make table, floor and hanging lamps, lampshades, illuminated sculptures and installation pieces.

RECENT PROJECTS: Sconces, Star of Mt. Pleasant Shopping Center, Mount Pleasant, TX; chandeliers, sconces and hanging lamps, Lajitas Resorts, Lajitas, TX; sconces, Marathon Hotel, Marathon, TX

GUILD SOURCEBOOKS: Artful Home 1

GRANT JOHNSON
Page 181

Stimulus LLC
PO Box 170519
San Francisco, CA 94117
Tel 415-558-8339
Fax 415-864-3897
E-mail grant@grantjohnsonart.com
www.grantjohnsonart.com

A fascination with form dominates my work, specifically the evolution of form resulting from the interaction of natural and human forces with the landscape. My art is environmental and celebrates nature as the abiding intelligence at work in the universe. I currently use reconnaissance image processing technology to interpret my terrestrial and high-altitude aerial photographs as large prints on canvas and watercolor paper. I personally produce each print in my studio. Trained as a painter and photographer before becoming involved with new media, I received the first graduate degree in experimental video awarded by the Rhode Island School of Design in 1975. My work has been shown worldwide and is found in numerous private collections. Visit www.grantjohnsonart.com to view series, portfolios and more information.

BARRY WOODS JOHNSTON
Page 143

SculptureWorks Inc.
2423 Pickwick Road
Baltimore, MD 21207
Tel 410-448-1945
Fax 410-448-2663
E-mail barry@sculptorjohnston.com
www.sculptorjohnston.com

My sculptures have won awards and commissions for over 25 years. Energy, movement and drama radiate from my works. Educated in architecture, I mastered the figure at the Pennsylvania Academy, the National Academy of Design and in Florence, Italy.

RECENT PROJECTS: Faith, Hope and Love; The Wooer

COMMISSIONS: Portrait of Gil, private collection, 2003, Atlanta, GA; The Relief of Mother Theresa, 2003, Baltimore, MD; The Good Samaritan, 2003, Baltimore, MD

COLLECTIONS: Virginia's Outdoor Gallery; The Vatican; Georgetown University; James Michener Museum of Art

EXHIBITIONS: Hampton, VA, 2004

AWARDS: Sun Trust Award, 2004; Allied Artists of America, Inc., 2003

GUILD SOURCEBOOKS: Architect's 13, 14, 15; Architectural & Interior Art 16, 18

ARTIST STATEMENTS

JON HAIR STUDIO OF FINE ART, LLC
Pages 144-145

Jon Hair, Official Sculptor of the U.S. Olympic Team
20000 Norman Colony Road
Cornelius, NC 28031
Tel 704-892-7203
Fax 704-892-7208
E-mail jhstudio@aol.com
www.jonhair.com

I am creating several major new works in 2004: a 30-foot monument, *Olympic Strength*, for the U.S. Olympic Committee—the largest bronze monument in Colorado; a 20-foot monument for the Olympic Truce Foundation in Athens, Greece; a 24-foot statue of Captain Christopher Newport, perhaps the largest historic portrait bronze in America; a 28-foot *Boilermaker* for Purdue University; the world's largest standing bronze lion for Queen's University; and a portrait bust of Hollywood legend Dick Van Dyke.

COMMISSIONS: U.S. Olympic Committee; International Olympic Committee; Dick Van Dyke; Purdue University; the Miccosukee Indian Tribe; Husqvarna Corporation; United Cerebral Palsy; Elon University; Christopher Newport University; Furman University; Presbyterian College; Queens University; St. Andrews College

TED JONSSON
Page 82

Humongous Arts
805 NE Northlake Way
Seattle, WA 98105
Tel 206-547-4552
Fax 206-324-7326
E-mail sculptureworks@aaahawk.com

When using less to achieve more, a refined simplicity of form, devoid of unintentional ambiguity, requires elegant crafting and fastidious finishing. I achieve these results through a conceptual design process combining the skills of sculptor, engineer and architect to design, fabricate and install site-specific sculpture and fountains. I have over 35 years of experience, with major commissions in national, state, corporate and private collections. Contemporary, distinctively innovative, durable sculptures range in scale from gallery to fountain to monumental.

COMMISSIONS: Kennely Commons Fountain, 2004, Green River Community College; Jon and Mary Shirley, 2001, Medina, WA; S.A.P. Labs Fountain, 1998, Palo Alto, CA; Federal Reserve Bank of San Francisco, Seattle Branch, 1991; Manoogan Collections, Marley Station, 1987, Glen Burnie, MD; Fair Oaks Center, 1980, Arlington, VA; Alaska Council on the Arts, 1976, University of Alaska, Anchorage

HANK KAMINSKY
Pages cover, 1, 87

808 South Government Avenue
Fayetteville, AR 72701
Tel 479-442-5805
Fax 479-442-3927
E-mail sculptor@kaminsky.com
www.sculptor.kaminsky.com

I think of my sculptures as landscapes and use words as structures on the topography. Some of my pieces are waterfalls inspired by the rock bluffs around my home in the Ozark Mountains. Words appear beneath the flowing water as if they were written into the earth itself. The robust surface textures of my work are the stuff of the hand-built clay process, leading to a sand-cast bronze sculpture. Often I work directly in sand molds to shape words and forms before casting in bronze. When I conceive public art, I go into the community as an ethnographer, wanting to understand the ideas that are important to people. The sculpture, then, mirrors the thoughts, values and dreams of the people who have commissioned the piece.

BJ KATZ
Pages 37, 172

Meltdown Glass Art & Design
3225 North Washington Street
Chandler, AZ 85225
Tel 480-633-3366
Fax 480-633-3344
E-mail bjkatz@meltdownglass.com
www.meltdownglass.com

Kiln-cast glass is the new frontier in art glass. Using this method, glass is molded and, at times, colored and shaped in large industrial kilns at temperatures up to 1,600 degrees. Artwork can be fired multiple times until the desired effect is achieved. My creative process is spontaneous. I begin with an overall concept and design for each work of art, but the nuances of each piece happen at the time of creation. My artwork is "in process" until it feels fully evolved.

RECENT PROJECTS: American College Testing, Iowa City, IA; QVC Store, Mall of America, Minneapolis, MN; Phelps Dodge Corporate Headquarters, Phoenix, AZ; Desert Ridge Marketplace, Phoenix, AZ; Texas Children's Hospital, Houston; public art project, Phoenix Children's Hospital, AZ

GUILD SOURCEBOOKS: *Architect's 14, 15; Designer's 14, 15; Architectural & Interior Art 16, 17, 18; Artful Home 1*

TROY KELLEY
Page 135

Troy Sculptor Inc.
Box 301, Salado, TX 76571
Tel 254-947-8386
Fax 254-947-9181
E-mail troysculptor@aol.com

My work covers a variety of subjects, including busts in cast bronze and a dream series of cast acrylic pieces.

RECENT PROJECTS: I have been commissioned to sculpt two monumental-size cast bronze figures to be installed June 2004, in the new Killeen, TX, airport terminal.

COMMISSIONS: *Mustangs*, 2002, Wichita, KS; *Late Again*, 2001, Salado, TX; *Little Emily*, 2000, Austin, TX; *Dr. Harry Wilmer*, 1998, Salado, TX; *F. Mayborn*, 1990, Temple, TX; *Sirena*, 1986, Salado, TX

COLLECTIONS: Cities of Salado, Temple and Killeen, TX; private collection, Wichita, KS

EXHIBITIONS: *Texas 100*, 2001, Austin, TX; *Works in Progress*, 2000, Venice, Italy; Loveland Sculptor Invitational, 1994, Loveland, CO

AWARDS: Distinctive Public Art, 2003; Public Art League of Texas

LITA KELMENSON
Page 102

199 North Marginal Road
Jericho, NY 11756
Tel 516-822-3219
E-mail litakel@yahoo.com

My work is an emotional journey that seeks insights into life's variables. These wood structures, enhanced with other materials such as rubber and tailpipes, create a union between meaning and form that evokes a visual dialogue with the viewer. The carved and constructed units are made of eight quarter sugar pine, which is, at times, laminated into large blocks or cut to form delicate ribbon-like enclosures. Surface textures and expressive lines also articulate the essence of each idea. Permanent public collections include the Jane Voorhees Zimmerli Art Museum at Rutgers University, New Brunswick, NJ. Among numerous private collections is the Mari Galleries of Westchester, Ltd., Mamaroneck, NY. My work has been shown extensively in gallery and museum settings along the East Coast.

ARTIST STATEMENTS

GUY KEMPER
Page 153

Kemper Studio
190 North Broadway
Lexington, KY 40507
Tel/Fax 859-254-3507
E-mail guy@kemperstudio.com
www.kemperstudio.com

My work is distinctive for its emotional and painterly expressiveness. Freeing stained glass from the constraints of traditional technique, I design windows unlike any others in the world. My strength lies in listening: to the client, the architect and the space itself. The right questions must be asked with a quiet mind to hear the right answers. Using only the finest materials, I strive for a design of harmonious essentials that will outlast fashion. I guarantee my work for my lifetime.

RECENT PROJECTS: 100' x 14' glass wall for the Greater Orlando International Airport, St. Joseph's Chapel, Ground Zero, New York, NY

GUILD SOURCEBOOKS: *Architect's 9, 10, 11, 14, 15; Architectural & Interior Art 16, 17, 18*

KERSEY'S GLASS WORKS
Page 29

Stephen Kersey
Mary Kersey
23960 Clawiter Road
Hayward, CA 94545
Tel 510-782-7813
Fax 510-782-2062
E-mail mkersey@kerseyglass.com
www.kerseyglass.com

For the past 30 years, we have developed and mastered a broad range of unique textures and techniques. Beginning with sand-carved and glue-chipped windows, doors, side lights, shower enclosures and murals for private residences, we soon began supplying our art glass to designers and architects whose projects also included polishing, painting and guilding. In 1985 we added fused, slumped, enameled and kiln-textured glass to our repertoire. We also produce fused and slumped glass countertops and bowls.

RECENT PROJECTS: Bridgeview Condos, San Francisco, CA; private residence, Monterey, CA; private residence, Omaha, NE; Chinese Presbyterian Church, San Francisco, CA

COMMISSIONS: Lake Hotel, Yellowstone National Park, WY; San Francisco Children's Library; Children's Hospital, Oakland, CA; Oakland Coliseum, CA

SILJA TALIKKA LAHTINEN
Page 180

Silja's Fine Art Studio
5220 Sunset Trail
Marietta, GA 30068
Tel 770-993-3409
Fax 770-992-0350
E-mail pentec02@bellsouth.net

My work draws from the myths, landscape, folk songs and textiles of my native Finland. I am especially inspired by Lapland Shamanism in my paintings, collages, wall panels, prints and drums. I am always trying to create a better painting today than I did yesterday. Price range: $400-$30,000.

EXHIBITIONS: Nuutti Galleria, 2003, Virrat, Finland; Kennesaw College, 2003-2004, Atlanta, GA; Elevations Gallery, 2003, Atlanta, GA; Ward-Nasse Gallery, 2003-2004, New York, NY

AWARDS: Award of Artistic Merit, 2003, Italy; Award of Merit, *Not Just Another Pretty Face*, WCA Show, 2003, Sanford, FL

PUBLICATIONS: *Print World Directory*, 2003; *Encyclopedia of Living Artists*, 2002; *Who's Who of American Artists; Who's Who of Women Artists*

GUILD SOURCEBOOKS: *Gallery 1, 2, 3; Designer's 9, 10, 11; Architectural & Interior Art 17, 18*

TUCK LANGLAND
Pages 142, 206

12632 Anderson Road
Granger, IN 46530
Tel/Fax 574-272-2708
E-mail tuckandjan@aol.com

After 40 years of creating figurative sculptures and portraits, my list of museum collections and public sculptures is considerable. I enjoy the give and take of working with creative design teams of architects, landscape architects and others. My recent work ranges from small indoor figures to heroic multiple-figure groupings. Recent projects include a fountain for the center of a university, a group called *Circle of Care* for the Hillman Cancer Center, four figures on columns for Bronson Hospital and many smaller figures for private and public gardens. Recent portraits include the Mayo brothers for the Mayo Clinic and the former president of Indiana University for a new mall on campus. I am currently creating a sculptural relief of a young family and a garden piece.

LINDA LEVITON
Page 201

Linda Leviton Sculpture
1011 Colony Way
Columbus, OH
Tel 614-433-7486
E-mail guild@lindaleviton.com
www.lindaleviton.com

Creating modular wall sculpture that evokes the color and texture of nature is central to my art. These designs can be hung to form one large piece or mounted as smaller separate units, creating ease and flexibility for large installations as well as changing interior spaces. Using etching, dyes, patinas and paint, I can texture and color metal to form subtle or vibrantly colored designs.

COMMISSIONS: Palisades of Bethesda, MD; Interstate Hotels & Resorts Corporate Office, Fairfax, VA; Symantec Corporation, New York, NY; University of Southern California; Northeastern Utilities, CT; St. Vincents Hospital, Indianapolis, IN

COLLECTIONS: Northwest Airlines, Detroit, MI; Tait, Weller & Baker, Philadelphia, PA; State of Ohio

EXHIBITIONS: SOFA, 2003, Chicago, IL

AWARDS: Grant, 2003, Ohio Arts Council

PUBLICATIONS: "Modern Masters," HGTV; *Color on Metal*, 2001

NORMA LEWIS
Page 108

Norma Lewis Studios
30500 Aurora del Mar
Carmel, CA 93923
Tel 831-625-1046
Fax 831-625-5733
E-mail normaart@dlewis.com

I work primarily in bronze. My sculptures are not sentimental. They embody integrity of material, grace of weight and simplicity of form. I do not force the dialogue, but wait for the shapes to introduce themselves and then embrace and build on what they suggest. The forms are complete in themselves without explanations or justifications for being. My works can be found in private and corporate collections worldwide.

RECENT PROJECTS: Brookstone Development, Phoenix, AZ; Monterey Museum of Art, Monterey, CA; Library & Technology Center, Monterey Peninsula College, Monterey, CA

GUILD SOURCEBOOKS: *Architect's 14, 15; Designer's 13, 14, 15; Architectural & Interior Art 16, 18*

ARTIST STATEMENTS

JACQUES LIEBERMAN
Page 52

484 Broome Street
New York, NY 10013
Tel 646-613-7302
Fax 646-613-7305
E-mail jacqueslieberman@mac.com
http://homepage.mac.com/jacqueslieberman

In a quest for ever-expanding avenues, my exuberant, lively, colorful imagery has been created as photographs, serigraphs, lithographs, paintings, digital prints, a fabulous collection of textiles as art to wear, and now original, extremely vivid ceramic tiles that can be framed or installed. My diversified creations can be found around the globe, including Argentina, Belgium, Brazil, Canada, China, Ecuador, England, France, Germany, Holland, Honduras, Hong Kong, Israel, Italy, Mexico, Spain, Sweden, Turkey, Taiwan and, naturally, the United States. My work has been featured on television and in the press. The human spirit has an infinite capacity to absorb universal elements and restructure them into fresh combinations. Therein lies the excitement of constant renewal.

PUBLICATIONS: *Art Business News; Art World News; Indulge Magazine; Arts Magazine; New York Arts Journal*

256   GUILD SOURCEBOOKS: *Designer's 11, 15; Architectural & Interior Art 16*

LINING ARTS INC.
Page 219

Wayne Mann
Carey Thorpe
390 Dupont Street Suite 200
Toronto, ON M5R 1V9
Canada
Tel 416-927-0353
Fax 416-922-0820
E-mail cthorpe@liningarts.com
www.liningarts.com

Lining Arts Inc. has a 20-year history as a creative consultancy that delivers artistic solutions for design projects of every size. Our expertise ranges from wall finishes and trompe l'oeil to murals and sculpture. We work with architects, interior designers, art consultants, corporations, developers or individuals to design visually compelling solutions for any space. Panel systems and a unique canvas technique can be used to ship our inspiring products right to your door. View our web site for client list, corporate profile and portfolio at www.liningarts.com.

STEVEN LIGUORI
Page 91

Liguori Designs
818 Park Paseo
Las Vegas, NV 89104
Tel 702-525-0506
E-mail sliguori01@aol.com

I sculpt in a variety of media, predominantly in bronze. My work is intensely focused on detail, from jewelry-sized pieces to monumental public art. I strive to portray the human condition in both my historical representations and my abstract monuments.

COMMISSIONS: Mary Dutton Park, 2003, Las Vegas, NV; Bureau of Reclamation, 2002, NV; Hoover Dam, 1999, Hoover Dam, NV; Veteran's Memorial Park, 1995, Hollywood, FL; Nevada Veteran's Cemetary, 1991, Boulder City, NV

COLLECTIONS: The White House Permanent Collection, Washington, DC; The Boulder City Museum, NV; The Bureau of Reclamation, Hoover Dam, NV

EXHIBITIONS: George Sturman Gallery, Las Vegas, NV; Hoover Dam Gallery, Boulder City, NV

AWARDS: Best of Show, Las Vegas Art Museum; Spirit Award, State of Nevada; Artist Emeritus, Henderson Art Association

JOYCE P. LOPEZ
Page 233

Joyce Lopez Studio
1147 West Ohio Street #304
Chicago, IL 60622
Tel 312-243-5033
Fax 312-243-7566
E-mail joyceplopez@sbcglobal.net
www.joycelopez.com

My interior fiber work is created from chromed steel tubes, which are hand wrapped with colorful French thread. The artwork hangs easily from provided wall mounts. With tapestry-like precision and design, this work is inspired by sources as varied as Pompeii, nature, brocades, numbers, other cultures, etc. I have worked professionally for 20 years as both a fiber artist and a photographer. My work is priced from $300 to $85,000.

COMMISSIONS: State of Illinois; State of Washington; City of Chicago; Nokia Collection, Dallas, TX; Sony Corporation; Health South, Alabama; private collections

EXHIBITIONS: International Exhibition of Photography, 2003, Turkey; Soho Photo, 2002, New York; *Tradition and Innovation-Fiber*, 2001, Latvia; International Tapestry Exhibition, 2000, Beijing, China

AWARDS: Art in Architecture, 2003, 2000, Illinois; Art in Public Places, 2002, 1995, Washington; Governor James Thompson State of Illinois Merit Award, 2002

BRENT LILLY
Page 184

Brentart.com
10750 River Run Drive
Manassas, VA 20112
Tel 703-298-2994
E-mail jedi@brentart.com
www.brentart.com

I cultivated my talent from early childhood, well into the Washington Color School period of the 1960s and 70s. I use Modular paints in rich, true, scientifically formulated colors that flow from tubes onto my palette knives. By layering cool colors over warm, I create an optical color shift where complementary colors are in close proximity. My paintings are non-objective, non-political and ultra-expressionistic. They command attention in commercial areas and mesmerize viewers with a high-impact statement of color. Perhaps one can see in these paintings the silent burst of a supernova giving birth to galaxies and new life elsewhere. I am available to create commissioned works of art that thrust our thoughts and senses through the threshold of the 21st century in a fresh new way.

EXHIBITIONS: Washington Ethical Society Art exhibition, 1974, Washington, D.C.; Catapetl Gallery, 1975, Frederick, MD; William Pogue Gallery Ltd. 1978. *Art-O-Matic*, 2002, Washington, DC; Manassas Art Guild Walk Show, 2003, Manassas, VA; Washington Project

ELIZABETH MacDONALD
Page 45

Box 186
Bridgewater, CT 06752
Tel 860-354-0594
Fax 860-350-4052
E-mail epmacd@earthlink.net
www.elizabethmacdonald.com

I produce tile paintings that suggest the patinas of age. These compositions are suitable for indoor or outdoor settings, and take the form of freestanding columns, wall panels or architectural installations. Public art commissions include: Wilbur Cross High School, New Haven, CT; and the Department of Environmental Protection, Hartford, CT.

COMMISSIONS: Conrad International Hotel, Hong Kong; St. Luke's Hospital, Denver, CO; Chapel at Mayo Clinic, Scottsdale, AZ

AWARDS: State of Connecticut Governor's Arts Award

GUILD SOURCEBOOKS: *THE GUILD 1, 2, 3, 4, 5; Architect's: 6, 7, 8, 9, 10, 11, 12, 13, 14, 15; Designer's: 6, 8, 9, 10, 11, 12, 13, 14, 15; Architectural & Interior Art 16, 17, 18; Artful Home 1, 2*

ARTIST STATEMENTS

ELLEN MANDELBAUM GLASS ART
Pages 13, 22

Ellen Mandelbaum
39-49 46th Street
Long Island City, NY 11104-1407
Tel/Fax 718-361-8154
E-mail emga@ix.Netcom.com
www.emglassart.com

I have worked in glass for more than 20 years, listening to the unique requirements of each individual commission and respecting deadlines and budgets. The beauty of stained glass colors and light remain at the heart of my work. There is something infinite about this art with the colors that change because of the weather and the sky. It is a great pleasure to design and share my glass with the architect and the people who use the building.

RECENT PROJECTS: Holy Spirit Catholic Community, Naperville, IL; Marian Woods, Hartsdale, NY; South Carolina Aquarium, Charleston, SC; Adath Jeshurun Synagogue, Minneapolis, MN

COMMISSIONS: Congregation Har Shalom, Potomac, MD; Toni Sikes residential window, New York, NY; Christ United Methodist Church, Honolulu, HI; Greater Baltimore Medical Center Hospital, Baltimore, MD

GUILD SOURCEBOOKS: GUILD 1, 2, 3, 5; Architect's 6, 8, 9, 10, 11, 12, 13, 14, 15; Architectural & Interior Art 16, 17, 18

KATIE PASQUINI MASOPUST
Page 225

235 Rancho Alegre Road
Santa Fe, NM 87508
Tel 505-471-2899
Fax 505-471-6537
E-mail katiepm@aol.com
www.katiepm.com

Photographs are the starting point of my work. I make a drawing from the photograph and then add different layers, creating a more abstract design. I add transparencies to give a double exposure or use additional colors to create a surreal experience. I also might fracture the plane in order to suggest movement. My newest work consists of free hanging panels that invite the viewer to closely explore the space formed by the separate panels. I construct my pieces of fabrics, machine appliqué and machine quilt with a thin wool bat. Prices are $500 a square foot.

COLLECTIONS: The Discovery Channel; The James Collection; Nebraska University; The Cargilss, Wyazata, MO

PUBLICATIONS: Fractured Landscapes, Ghost Layers and Color Washes, C&T Publishing, Concord, CA

MAX-CAST
Page 90

Steve Maxon
Doris Park
PO Box 662, 611 B Avenue
Kalona, IA 52247
Tel 319-656-5365
Fax 319-656-3187
E-mail max-cast@kctc.net
www.max-cast.com

Our company, Max-Cast, is a unique combination of sculpture studio and full-service art foundry, staffed by a highly professional team of talented artists. Our artistic ability and technical expertise allow us to carry out nearly any sculptural project. Whether you are an artist looking for a first-class foundry to cast your art in bronze, iron or aluminum, or an architect seeking unique design elements, we will work closely with you to bring your concept to fruition. As artists, we can create your heart's desire. As technicians, we can perfect your sculpture in bronze. From historical restoration to portraiture, we will share your vision and make it a reality.

257

PAVLOS MAYAKIS
Page 234

4015 Match Point Avenue
Santa Rosa, CA 95407
Tel 707-578-4621/866-629-2547 (toll free)
E-mail pavlos@pavlosmayakis.com
www.pavlosmayakis.com

I hand-weave and surface design unframed and framed ARTpieces as wall art. Producing rich colors and striking that important balance between the elements in a controlled, yet somewhat spontaneous manner, comes naturally to me. Working with multiple dye classifications and pigments, I especially enjoy working with fiber reactive dyes in tandem with vat dyes. My work appears throughout the United States and Europe, and has been featured in the 2002-2003 New Art International and The Artful Home 1: Art for the Wall. Awards include a Mendocino College fulltime faculty scholarship and the Mendocino College Foundation Scholarship of Promise. I welcome collaborations with architects, designers and individuals.

E. JOSEPH McCARTHY
Page 46

E. Joseph McCarthy Studio
76 Hope Street
Greenfield, MA 01301
Tel/Fax 413-772-8816
E-mail cts@crocker.com
www.crocker.com/~cts/

For over 25 years, I have been designing and painting fine ceramic tile environments for corporate, public and private clients. Specializing in large-scale murals, I custom design each piece to fit into the configurations of a specific location. These tile works can be individually mounted as framed paintings. Recently, my works have expanded to include oils and acrylics on large canvases. These newly compiled works of art parallel my tile abstracts.

COMMISSIONS: Sherman Hospital, IL; Edsel B. Ford Center, MI; Savannah Hotel, Barbados; Valley Children's Hospital, CA; Tampa International Airport, FL; Merck and Company, NJ; Kahalan Madarin Orient Hotel, HI; Celebrity Cruise Line, FL

GUILD SOURCEBOOKS: The Guild 5; Architect's 9, 12, 13, 15; Designer's 7, 11, 13, 14, 15; Architectural & Interior Art 16

SUSAN McGEHEE
Page 207

Metallic Strands
540 23rd Street
Manhattan Beach, CA 90266
Tel 310-545-4112
Fax 310-546-7152
E-mail susan@metalstrands.com
www.metalstrands.com

I wove with fiber for many years. Fourteen years ago I started using all metals instead of fiber. I still employ the traditional tools, techniques and patterns from when I worked in fiber. Weaving metals allows me to form a piece into a dimensional shape that will retain its form and undulating vitality. I primarily use anodized aluminum wire because although it looks like copper, it has the advantage of being lightweight and retains its color and shine. The pieces are easy to install and maintain.

GUILD SOURCEBOOKS: Designer's 12, 13, 14, 15; Architecture & Interior Art 16, 17, 18; Artful Home 1

ARTIST STATEMENTS

TRENA McNABB
Page 168

McNabb Studio, Inc.
PO Box 327
Bethania, NC 27010
Tel 336-924-6053
Fax 336-924-4854
E-mail trena@tmcnabb.com
www.tmcnabb.com

I paint large site-specific, allegorical paintings. My work is a multilayered montage of brightly lighted, realistically rendered, thematically related scenes and images. I use multiple, overlapping and transparent images to portray specific stories. Dimensionality is important to me and is achieved in many ways: sectional pieces wrap around corners; suspend from the ceiling on swivels; extra canvas, plexiglass, twine, or sawdust are often sewn or adhered to the canvas. Different textures, such as matte and gloss, are also often found on a single painting. My large-scale works for public and corporate spaces are represented in permanent collections in government buildings, major corporations, hospitals, banks and museums. International commissions include works for corporate facilities in China, Japan and Germany.

AMOS MILLER
Page 183

Amos Miller Studio
Miami, FL
E-mail studioam@bellsouth.net

I paint in oil and acrylic on canvas. My primary focus is to record and convey images of our time, or current events. I follow the news from around the world through various mass media, often using newspaper photos and stories as starting points for my pictures. My work has appeared in numerous exhibitions and is collected throughout the U.S., France, Jamaica and South Africa.

EXHIBITIONS: Art Basel, 2003, Miami Beach, FL

AWARDS: Gallery Victoria, Naples, FL; Best of Show, Artescape National Painting Competition, 2003

MERRYWOMAN STUDIOS
Page 50

Christine Merriman
7076 US Route 4
PO Box 153
Bridgewater, VT 05034
Tel 802-672-2230
E-mail merrywoman@vermontel.net
www.vermontel.net/~merrywoman

As a creative yet dyslexic corporate L.A. Art Director coming into Raku, I discovered Raku to mean "happy accident." And that describes my life! The Raku process offers me religion—Zen. It also offers me a personal relationship with fire, the true magician. Together we create Raku art tile presentations. I offer everything from limited orders of standard field tiles to provocative pieces of fine art. All are designed with an agreed-upon budget in mind. Whether the budget is limited or large, the point of installation private or public, all have loved these jewel-like, luscious Raku art tiles.

RECENT PROJECTS: *Blind Woman's Bathroom*, 2003, private residence, Wachung, NJ; *Mendocino Seas*, 2001, Mendocino, CA; *Samurai Couple*, 2002, Middleburg, MD

COMMISSIONS: Private commissions, kitchens and baths, Washington, DC and surrounding areas; *The Valleys of Central Vermont*, 2004, Woodstock, VT; *Calvin Coolidge Mural*, 2003-04, Plymouth, VT

DAVID MILTON
Page 189

1939 South Hills Place
Bellingham, WA 98229
Tel 360-734-2225
E-mail david@davidmilton.com
www.davidmilton.com

My abstract expressions resonate with the vibrant colors and rhythms of my native South Africa. My art is driven by the exploration of the emotional elements of life, evoking their power. Through texture, blending and layering, I create multi-dimensional views into the complex world of feelings. The use of line creates movement and depth, propelling perception beyond the two-dimensional canvas. Blending, layering and texturing create multiple dimensions. My varied styles, along with my collaborative experience, facilitate working with individuals on customized projects. My paintings are in private collections from California to the Caribbean. I accept commissions in a broad range of sizes. A portfolio of paintings and sculpture is available upon request. Current paintings range from 12" x 12" to 67" x 102".

GUILD SOURCEBOOKS: *Architectural & Interior Art 18, Artful Home 1*

CRISTINA MIKULASEK
Page 130

111 SE Whinery Road
Shelton, WA 98584
Tel 360-427-9235
Fax 360-427-7228
E-mail chris@misulasek.com
www.mikulasek.com

My work in sculpture is the result of a love of the human figure and spirit, coupled with a love of fine craftsmanship. I am a romantic realist in style and a perfectionist by nature. For 20 years I've made sculptures that will speak as eloquently to humans 1,000 years from now as they do in our time.

RECENT PROJECTS: Life-size founder's portrait, PEMCO Headquarters, Seattle, WA; 8' bronze enlargement of *Home* for Olympic Sculpture Park, Seattle, WA

COMMISSIONS: Port Townsend Library, WA; Tor Spindler Memorial, Monterey, CA; four original carousel horses, Alberta Ltd., CA; portraits of Lincoln and Beethoven, Day Fine Art Publishing

COLLECTIONS: Vanderbilt, New York City; Lyme Academy, CT; Burton Collection, FL; Brenner Collection, Italy; Tom Houston Collection, TX

AWARDS: Alex Ettl Prize, National Sculpture Society; Phoenix Foundation Fellowship

MOBERG STUDIO ART GALLERY
Page 92

2921 Ingersoll Avenue
Des Moines, IA 50312
Tel 515-279-9191
Fax 515-279-9292
E-mail galleryinfo@mobergstudio.com
www.mobergstudio.com

For more than 25 years, Moberg Studio has offered unique custom artwork for the home or business. We collaborate with architects, designers and clients to design original artworks to enhance any interior or exterior environment. The Moberg Studio Art Gallery offers both the formal exhibition of artwork by a variety of artists in a range of mediums, as well as the opportunity for clients to commission custom pieces. The work of Moberg Studio Art Gallery artists is featured in private, public, corporate and liturgical collections. We will design innovative and personal artwork that's perfect for your art project needs. Please contact us if you are looking for site-specific work or would like to order an existing original work from the gallery or website.

PUBLICATIONS: "Home Planning Ideas," 2003, *Better Homes and Gardens*; "Modern Masters," 2003, HGTV; *Identity* magazine, 1996

ARTIST STATEMENTS

LEN MORRIS
Page 193

Leonard Morris Inc.
Tel 917-992-3313
E-mail lenmorris@earthlink.net
www.lenmorris.net

As an artist, part of my job is to create opportunities for people to see and think differently. I create and photograph assemblages of objects that are often viewed as disposable. In the four series featured in this book, my photographs reveal an extraordinary beauty in what may have otherwise been overlooked. They are generic in subject, but specific in concept: familiar objects viewed with consideration and passion.

RECENT PROJECTS: Corporate and private collectors around the world, including the Boca Raton Museum; The Miyako Osaka Hotel, Japan; WNYC Radio, New York

MOTAWI TILEWORKS
Page 47

Nawal Motawi
170 Enterprise Drive
Ann Arbor, MI 48103
Tel 734-213-0017
Fax 734-213-2569
E-mail motawi@motawi.com
www.motawi.com

Motawi Tileworks art tile studio was founded by Nawal Motawi in 1992. Over the last decade, we have created hundreds of installations for homes, businesses and public institutions. Aesthetically, our emphasis is on historically inspired design, particularly the early twentieth-century English and American decorative arts. We prefer projects that utilize our large collection of relief designs, our expertise with matte glazes or our cuenca polychrome technique. We specialize in custom-designed, beautifully glazed residential fireplace installations and murals.

RECENT PROJECTS: Mural, Grand Californian Hotel, 2000, Anaheim, CA

PUBLICATIONS: *Arts and Crafts Style and Spirit: Craftspeople of the Revival,* 1999; *Old House Interiors,* November 2003; *Interior Design,* October 2003

JAMES C. MYFORD
Page 110

320 Cranberry Road
Grove City, PA 16127
Tel 724-967-1612
Tel/Fax 724-458-9672
E-mail jcmyf@zoominternet.net

My sculptures are found in corporate, museum, university, public and private collections throughout the United States. They are also in collections in Japan, Sweden, Venezuela, Australia and Brazil. My cast and fabricated aluminum sculptures, though often outwardly abstract, are closely linked to nature and reality. The energy and vitality expressed in my compositions reflect a subtle inner strength and spirit that expand and interact gracefully with space. My sculptures range in size from smaller indoor works to major outdoor site-specific commissions. Indoor works start at $1,000; outdoor works range from $10,000 to $75,000. A large selection of unique works for indoors and out can be viewed, by appointment, at my residence.

GUILD SOURCEBOOKS: *Architect's 9, 10, 11, 12, 13, 14, Architectural & Interior Art 16, 17*

259

MARY BATES NEUBAUER
Page 105

#3 North Bullmoose Circle
Chandler, AZ 85224
Tel 480-821-1611
Fax 480-821-8218
E-mail mary.neubauer@asu.edu
www.sculpture-digital.net

I am enchanted by the natural world, creating large-scale sculptures from models of biological and botanical images. Cast in bronze, my sculptures possess a unique presence; their texture and luminosity give them a sense of animation. Bright, painterly patinas and lively textural surfaces reveal their spirituality, tactile beauty and enduring quality.

COMMISSIONS: Phoenix Airport Sculpture Garden, Phoenix, AZ; Tangerine Road, Oro Valley, AZ; River Road, Tucson, AZ

COLLECTIONS: Barclay Simpson Sculpture Garden, CA; City of Loveland, CO; DiRosa Sculpture Garden, CA

EXHIBITIONS: Bentley Garden, Scottsdale, AZ; International RP Exhibition, Georgetown, TX; Documentation, WomanMade Gallery, Chicago, IL; Arizona Biennial, Tucson Art Museum, AZ

AWARDS: Fulbright Fellowship, Ford Fellowship

PUBLICATIONS: *ArtNews, Art in America, Sculpture*

BRUCE A. NIEMI
Page 111

Niemi Sculpture Gallery & Garden
13300 116th Street
Kenosha, WI 53142
Tel 262-857-3456
Fax 262-857-4567
E-mail sculpture@bruceniemi.com
www.bruceniemi.com

I create one-of-a-kind stainless steel and bronze abstract sculptures. "Aesthetically powerful," "graceful" and "energized with balance" are the terms that best describe both my small interior pieces and my large-scale public pieces. I work well with architects, designers and developers and am able to meet budgets and timetables. The 20-acre Niemi Sculpture Gallery & Garden continues to provide a great atmosphere in which to view interior and exterior sculpture by over 30 national artists.

COMMISSIONS: North American Group, 2003, Chicago, IL

COLLECTIONS: Friends of Art Collection, Milwaukee Art Museum, WI

EXHIBITIONS: River Walk, 2003-2004, Milwaukee, WI; North Shore Sculpture Park, 2003-2005, Skokie, IL

GUILD SOURCEBOOKS: *Architect's 10, 11, 14, 15; Architectural & Interior Art 16, 17, 18*

ORKA ARCHITECTURAL ART GLASS
Pages 30-31

Sharon Roadcap-Quinlivan
Lorri Roadcap-Clower
Jeremy Roadcap
1181 Jensen Drive
Virginia Beach, VA 23451
Tel 757-428-6752
Fax 757-428-6750
E-mail lroadcap@orka.com
www.orka.com

ORKA Architectural Art Glass was established ten years ago to explore and define the genuine detail that can be achieved in the composition and presentation of carved architectural art glass. We are equipped with 25 years of art glass carving, ten years of painting, sculpting and graphic design, a state-of-the-art facility and qualified relationships with a legion of specialized and innovative suppliers and consultants all of which enable us to execute the smallest to the largest architectural projects.

RECENT PROJECTS: Orlando National Airport, main terminal, Orlando, FL

COMMISSIONS: Goldman Sachs Headquarters, 2004, Jersey City, NJ; University of Iowa, Sports Hall of Fame, 2003, Iowa City, IA

AWARDS: 1999 Dupont Benedictus Award nominee

GUILD SOURCEBOOKS: *Artful Home 2*

ARTIST STATEMENTS

PAM MORRIS DESIGNS
EXCITING LIGHTING
Page 160

Pam Morris
Gate Five Road, Studio 100
Sausalito, CA 94965
Tel 415-332-0168
Fax 415-332-0169
E-mail lighting@sonic.net

As owner of EXCITING LIGHTING, I work with clients who encompass top restaurants, hotels and private collectors, including; Wolfgang Puck, Sugar Ray Leonard, Terry McMillan, Kelsey Grammar, Georgio Armani and the Hong Kong Regent Hotel.

In my work, I create highly original and evocative illuminated pieces. I use light, together with blown, slumped or cast glass and forged or cast metal, to create illuminated art pieces that reflect a special sense of place.

I love the custom design process, and have also found it interesting and rewarding to have lectured and been published internationally.

GUILD SOURCEBOOKS: *Architect's 12, 13, 15; Designer's 14; Architectural & Interior Art 17, 18; Artful Home 1*

NICOLA PAN
Page 118

125 Hollow Horn Road
Erwinna, PA 18920
Tel 610-294-9514
E-mail nicola@nicolapan.com
www.nicolapan.com

All of my creativity and energy is concentrated on where I see connections between art and nature. Monumentalism is written on all of my pieces, which vibrate with energy. My biggest inspiration is from Karl Clasfield, a German photographer who lived at the beginning of the 19th century. After finishing the Academy of Fine Art in Bulgaria and Beaux Art in Paris, I moved to New York and then to Bucks County in Pennsylvania, a big art community. I have worked out of my private casting studio there for 20 years. Some of my commissions are in France, Italy and Germany. I have had solo exhibitions in Paris, New York, New Jersey and Pennsylvania.

COLLECTIONS: N&R Plastics Corporation, Montreal; Universal Prints, Hamburg, Germany; Foundation Pagany, Milano, Italy; Bob Grosso & Co., New York City; Jean Mark Marty, Paris; private collection, Sofia, Bulgaria

SCOTT K. PARSONS
Page 95

802 Santa Fe Drive #4
Denver, CO 80204
Tel 303-902-0625
E-mail scottkparsons@yahoo.com
www.scottkparsons.com

I am an artist who creates metaphors that open the experience of the built environment to new understandings of history, siting, and the flow of people and their relationship to a site. I received an MFA from the University of Colorado at Boulder in 1990. My experience in public art includes percent-for-art and private commissions for museums, research facilities, university buildings and transportation centers. I work in precast concrete, light (solstice markers), glass, ceramic mosaic, terrazzo and stone in walls, floors, sidewalks and plazas. My design experience includes 3D pre-visualization, fabrication, design-team collaboration and early-integration public art planning.

AWARDS: National Terrazzo and Mosaic Association Honor Award for Floor of the Year, 2002

PUBLICATIONS: *Architectural Record,* 2003; *Art in America,* 2003; *Public Art Review,* 2003, 2001, 1998, 1997; *Sculpture* 1998; *Art Papers,* 1998

GUILD SOURCEBOOKS: *Architect's 14*

MALAY PATEL
Pages 156, 159

Inspired by Nature, Inc
353 East Bailey Road
Naperville, IL 60565
Tel 630-709-9511
E-mail malay@bymalay.com
www.bymalay.com

I'm inspired by nature to create exquisite, hand-carved and highly detailed natural stone furniture that is elegant, legendary—not only unique pieces of art but monuments in themselves. My creations are the outcome of over 10 years of constant creative experience and interaction between my sensibility, imagination and a unique hand-carving tradition. I rely on impeccable craftsmanship by using a strong sense of balanced design and uniquely colored and beautifully textured sandstone or marble to achieve a timeless look that will enhance any environment. Along with one-of-a-kind stone furniture, I have created truly remarkable outdoor stone projects. My natural leather and wool rugs blend different materials and elements of traditional to contemporary imagery with unique stitching techniques that offer luxuriant surfaces for floors and walls.

NANCY "STEVIE" PEACOCK
Page 178

Nancy Peacock Artworks
PO Box 47346
Seattle, WA 98146
Tel 206-242-8884
E-mail nancypeacock@comcast.net
www.nancypeacock.com

I grew up ballroom dancing to live jazz bands in New York and New Jersey. In jazz clubs and at dances, I sketch people playing music and dancing: 20-50 sketches an evening, gathering their range of motion and how the music comes through them. Later, in my studio, I use these sketches as reference, and employ sacred geometry to make visible their energetic, spiritual essence. Seeing who they are when they are at one with the music, the viewer may be awakened to experience, to feel his or her own fundamental divine beingness as a healing force.

RECENT PROJECTS: CD cover for National Public Radio's *Sweet and Soulful,* 2003; painted live onstage with The Buddy Catlett Quintet at the 2002 West Seattle Jazz Festival; painted live next to the main stage of the 2001 Big Sur Jazzfest, Big Sur, CA

G. BYRON PECK/CITY ARTS
Pages 164, 171

G. Byron Peck Studios
1857 Lamont Street NW
Washington, DC 20010
Tel/Fax 202-331-1966
E-mail byronpeck@earthlink.net
www.peckstudios.com
www.cityartsdc.org

Full-service studios for the production of public art, murals and mosaics for large-scale artwork or intimate private murals. Our studios have 25 years of experience working with architects, designers and organizations to create solutions for any environment.

RECENT PROJECTS: 1,500' mosaic on the Potomac River waterfront, Washington, DC; 100' mural for the City of Los Angeles, Cultural Affairs Department; two murals for the newly built visitors center at historic Mt. Vernon, VA; 60' mural for main subway station, Washington, DC

COLLECTIONS: The Kennedy Center for the Performing Arts; Chamber of Commerce, Washington, DC; U.S. Embassy, Santiago, Chile; U.S. Embassy, Georgetown Guyana; U.S. Nuclear Energy Commission; Marriott Corporation, Bethesda, MD

GUILD SOURCEBOOKS: *Architect's 6, 7, 8, 9, 10, 11, 12, 13, 14, 15; Architectural & Interior Art 16, 17, 18*

ARTIST STATEMENTS

MARTHA PETTIGREW
Page 129

201 West 21st Street
Kearney, NE 68845
Tel/Fax 308-233-5504
Tel 602-312-7979
E-mail dpettimar@aol.com
www.marthapettigrew.com

My goal is to create work that the viewer never tires of seeing. Solid composition and design are the hallmark of my work, regardless of subject matter.

RECENT PROJECTS: Recently completed and installed an eight-foot version of my work *Gossip*, for *Grounds for Sculpture*, Hamilton, NJ

COMMISSIONS: Eight-foot high buffalo, New Port Beach, CA; life-size running horse, Bedminster, NJ; nine major works installed at the Fairmont Princess Hotel, Scottsdale, AZ

COLLECTIONS: Fairmont Princess Hotel, Scottsdale, AZ; Hilton Hotel, Oak Creek Village, Sedona, AZ

EXHIBITIONS: City of Stamford, CT, June-August 2004,

PUBLICATIONS: Cover artist of *Southwest Art* magazine, July 1998

GUILD SOURCEBOOKS: *Designer's 13, 15; Architectural & Interior Art 17, 18* (cover)

MOANA PONDER
Page 134

4110 Hartford Street
Abilene, TX 79605
Tel 325-698-0866
E-mail moanaponder1@aol.com
www.pondersculpture.com

As a lifelong artist, I take my themes from a love of the environment—such as the four seasons or the wind and sea—and express them with the elegant, figurative forms of dancers. Working in full round and relief, I like a range of scale. Most of my work is classic figurative, but my newer projects include a more contemporary look. I am happy to consider commissions.

COLLECTIONS: Best Western Hotels, Port Lavaca, TX; Art Incorporated, San Antonio, TX; Borsini-Burr Galleries, Montara, CA; Bronze Coast Gallery, Cannon Beach, OR; Richard James Gallery, Charleston, SC; The Victorian Gallery, Dallas, TX

EXHIBITIONS: *Sculpture in the Park*, Loveland, CO; National Sculpture Society Awards Exhibition, 2002, Brookgreen Gardens, Pawley's Island, SC; International Exhibit, 1998, Chamizal National Monument, El Paso, TX

MARINA POPOVA
Pages 86, 173

Marina Popova and Associates Inc.
87 Angell Avenue
Montreal, QC H9W 4V6
Canada
Tel 514-630-9759
Fax 514-630-4009
E-mail info@marinapopova.com
www.marinapopova.com

My goal as a muralist is to create harmony between art and the surrounding architecture. I enjoy working in abstract, figurative and trompe l'oeil styles. In spite of such diversity, my works have a consistency in terms of personal vision and respect for the given architectural space. I work closely with the client, from concept through design to installation. I paint my murals on canvases and ship them to clients all over the world.

COMMISSIONS: Caesars Palace, Las Vegas, NV; Fairmont Queen Elizabeth Hotel, Montreal; Turning Stone Hotel & Casino, Verona, NY; Caprion Pharmaceuticals Inc. Montreal; Cineplex Odeon, Montreal; Swissotel, Dalian, China

COLLECTIONS: Department of Foreign Affairs, Government of Canada; Chase Manhattan Bank, New York, NY; State Tretiakov Gallery, Moscow, Russia; State Museum of Russian Art, St. Petersburg, Russia; Royal Bank of Canada, Toronto

LYNN POSHEPNY
Page 212

Horizons
5241 Downing Road
Baltimore, MD 21212
Tel 410-323-9428
E-mail lynn@horizonsart.com
www.horizonsart.com

During my first career as a landscape architect, I viewed space as something to be experienced—a series of happenings. Now, just as an architect translates three-dimensional space into two-dimensional drawings, I rephrase the experience of space in an intuitive style of painting. I allow my paintings to develop as a series of happenings and take as great a delight in the process as in the product. I begin each painting by reading poetry, essays or meditations and actually write onto the surface of coated watercolor paper those words that inspire me. This creates the textural base for my pieces. I then add many layers of acrylic paint and pieces of rice and tissue paper to achieve the desired depth of color and textural interest.

TERRY DAVITT POWELL
Page 213

1424 Mills Avenue
Redlands, CA 92373
Tel 909-793-8141
E-mail terry@tdpowell.com
www.tdpowell.com

My affinity for birds and animals has led me to an exploration of adaptability and coexistence. Though equilibriums are constantly upset, I find a strange beauty in the surprising new balances between the human and animal spheres that arise as humans continue to put their stamp on the physical world. Examining the conflicting forces of the natural and technological worlds through the use of representational shapes, color, movement and patterning, I introduce my own sense of balance. I build with ink and paint on unsized paper to develop foundation imagery for change and adaptation. The paper is affixed to primed wooden panels and then sealed before I continue adding and removing colors in layers. Upon completion, the entire surface is sealed and varnished.

PRECISION CUT TECHNOLOGIES, INC.
Page 53

Stevan R. Bronner
361 West Morley Drive
Saginaw, MI 48601
Tel 866-754-3555
Fax 989-752-3444
E-mail sbronner@precuttech.com
www.precuttech.com

Precision Cut Technologies, Inc. is a full-service design studio specializing in combining stone, metals and glass into a wide variety of custom architectural settings. Our unique business offers hand-crafted stone rugs, medallions, logos, borders, mosaics, inlays, donor walls, tabletops, custom hardware, decorative glass, decorative metals, garden features, wall art, furniture and accessories. Precision Cut Technologies, Inc. is an ASID Industry Partner member and an IFDA member. We are capable of fulfilling commissions for commercial, institutional and residential designs.

RECENT PROJECTS: New Anchor Bay High School, New Baltimore, MI; Northwood University, Midland, MI; Shepherd of The Lakes Lutheran Church, Brighton, MI; Saginaw Art Museum, Saginaw, MI; National Spy Museum, Washington, DC; Green Bay Packers Hall of Fame, Green Bay, WI; Chrysler Corporation, Detroit, MI

ARTIST STATEMENTS

JOHN PUGH
Page 170

PO Box 1332
Los Gatos, CA 95031
Tel 408-353-3370
Fax 408-353-1223
www.artofjohnpugh.com

My trompe l'oeil murals transform flat walls into other "spaces." I have been awarded an array of national public art projects, and articles about my work have appeared throughout the world. For all murals, indoor or outdoor, large or small, projects may be painted in my studio on canvas or non-woven media (outdoor material) and then site-specifically integrated. Prints are also available.

COMMISSIONS: Cities of Anchorage, Boise, Denver, Miami, Palm Desert, Sacramento, San Jose and San Francisco; University of Alaska; California State University, Chico; University of Northern Florida; Stanford University

PUBLICATIONS: *Time; Focus; Artweek; Via; Art Business News; Southwest Art; LA Times; New York Times; Tokyo Mainichi; San Francisco Examiner*

JANE RANKIN
Page 133

19335 Greenwood Drive
Monument, CO 80132
Tel 719-488-9223
Fax 719-488-1650
E-mail jrankin@magpiehill.com

I create limited-edition bronze sculpture and specialize in life-size and tabletop figures, mostly of children and child-related things.

COMMISSIONS: Cerritos Plaza, 2003, City of Cerritos, CA; Harvest Community, 2002, Ft. Collins, CO; Town Hall, 1999, Cary, NC; Morse Park, 1998, Lakewood, CO

COLLECTIONS: City of Cerritos, CA; Newton, IA; Pueblo Public Library, Pueblo, CO; Dogwood Festival Center, Jackson, MS; Waukegan Public Library, IL; Colorado Springs Fine Art Center, CO; Buell Children's Museum, Pueblo, CO; Lincoln Children's Museum, NE; Creative Artist Agency, Beverly Hills, CA

EXHIBITIONS: Pueblo Street Gallery, 2001-2004, Pueblo, CO; American Numismatic Association, 2000-2002, Colorado Springs, CO

GUILD SOURCEBOOKS: *Architect's 14, 15; Architectural & Interior Art 16, 17, 18*

PAUL REIBER
Page 146

PO Box 732
Mendocino, CA 95460
Tel/Fax 707-964-7151
E-mail preiber@mcn.org
www.mendocinofurniture.com

I have been making carved and sculpted furniture of the finest quality and craftsmanship for over 20 years. My work includes carved panels for cabinets, doors and other architectural uses, freestanding sculpture and relief-carved or sculpted furniture. I enjoy working with clients to identify images that speak to their own sense of beauty and spirit.

COMMISSIONS: St. Mary of the Angels Catholic Church, Ukiah, CA; Karuizawa Moriizume Golf Club, Japan; Angela Lansbury

EXHIBITIONS: 30th Anniversary Exhibition, Baulines Craft Guild, 2002, Bolinas, CA; *With the Grain: Mendocino Woodcraft,* 2002, Grace Hudson Museum, Ukiah, CA; Furniture and *Fiber Art: Contemporary California Designers,* 1992, UC Berkeley Museum, Danville, CA

PUBLICATIONS: *Woodwork Magazine, Paul Reiber: The Art and Spirit of a Chairmaker, 1998*

GUILD SOURCEBOOKS: *Designer's 9, 10*

DAN RIDER
Page 103

Dan Rider Sculpture
133 Bridge Street
Arroyo Grande, CA 93420
Tel 805-474-5959
E-mail dan@danridersculpture.com
www.danridersculpture.com

Over 20 years of sculpture design and mold making experience has culminated in my latest series of garden sculpture, *Spirit Markers.* These modern, abstract totems feature layers of varying materials such as rock, reinforced concrete, brass and copper. Each piece resonates with its own unique character. Since I have always favored large, bold statements for outdoor sculpture, my pieces begin at six feet high and head skyward from there. I begin with sketches, which allow me the freedom of unlimited imagination. Then I proceed to the fabrication, beginning with the top of the sculpture. Once I have the crowning element completed, I continue construction on the chosen site, utilizing molds, rock and concrete. The final touches may include patinas, staining or sealing. These organic pieces range from soaring and curving to jagged and angular.

ELLIE RILEY
Page 121

PO Box 491417
Los Angeles, CA 90049
Tel 310-560-5003
E-mail berty222@aol.com
www.ellieriley.com

The capture of light, form, space and time is my goal, using color, metals or wood with organic-abstract shapes. Exploring the harmony and balance we all strive for, against conflict and chaos, I try to reveal the human spirit as potential energy for change by giving a sense of motion and buoyancy to a combination of shapes. I also need to instill a sense of humor, surprise and vulnerability in my work because it reflects my personal belief in joy, love and the spontaneity of discovery.

RECENT PROJECTS: Recent projects include painted, polished and brushed aluminum and stainless steel wall reliefs, single and diptych, as well as free-standing sculptures and paintings

COLLECTIONS: My work is found in private collections throughout the United States.

KEVIN ROBB
Pages 98, 117

Kevin Robb Studios
7001 West 35th Avenue
Wheat Ridge, CO 80033-6373
Tel 303-431-4758
Fax 303-425-8802
E mail 3d@kevinrobb.com
www.kevinrobb.com

I create individual contemporary sculptures in stainless steel or bronze, as well as limited-edition cast bronze for intimate environments and large-scale public areas. I bring a natural curiosity to my work, combining it with the knowledge gained from an understanding of how positive and negative spaces, shadow and light work together.

RECENT PROJECTS: Deer Creek Development, Overland Park, KS; Healthpoint, Fort Worth, TX; Austin ranch, Austin, TX

COMMISSIONS: Rod Mitchell, Granite Bay, CA; Robinson & Shades Design Group, Tuscon, AZ; Keith and Sally Huzyak, yacht sculpture

GUILD SOURCEBOOKS: *Architect's 12, 13, 14, 15; Architectural & Interior Art 17; Artful Home 1*

ARTIST STATEMENTS

TALLI ROSNER-KOZUCH
Pages 190, 192

Pho-Tal, Inc.
15 North Summit Street
Tenafly, NJ 07670
Tel 201-569-3199
Fax 201-569-3392
E-mail tal@photal.com
www. photal.com

I work with professional 4x5 and 8x10 cameras at night, with candlelight, photographing black-and-white, sepia color and Polaroid films. From these I create platinum prints, etchings, lithographs and murals of all sizes. My images vary in style from architectural portraiture and documentary to landscapes and still life. I use my own signature techniques, achieving this unique blend of sepia and rough blue edge.

RECENT PROJECTS: Hotel design and corporation décor all over the world

COMMISSIONS: Commissions in law firm offices, corporations and hotels

COLLECTIONS: Collected by Polaroid and corporations; private collections

EXHIBITIONS: Exhibitions in the U.S., Europe and Israel

GUILD SOURCEBOOKS: Architect's 13, 14; Designer's 13, 14, 15; Architectural & Interior Art 16, 17, 18

ANDY SÁNCHEZ
Page 158

Custom Furniture by Andy Sánchez
4 Archibeque Drive
Algodones, NM 87001
Tel 505-385-1189
Fax 505-771-1223
www.andysanchez.com

Our unique juniper designs begin in the forests of New Mexico, where we find ancient juniper trees (sometimes over 1,000 years old) that have died from old age. I first determine how best to use the wood, employing its natural features as much as possible. If there is a natural hole in the wood, we often fill it with polished marble, turquoise or other semi-precious stones. After hours of sanding and polishing, we finally apply several coats of oil and wax to build an inviting finish. Rough edges create a rustic illusion, contrasting with the smooth finish and quality craftsmanship. My sons and I work together, and we have shown our work in art shows all over the U.S., including the Philadelphia Furniture and Furnishings Show, PA; The Western Design Conference, Cody, WY; and the Beaver Creek Art Festival. Recently, I was featured on the Home & Garden Network.

SAR FURNITURE, LLC
Page 65

Scott A. Reitman
1420 East 36th Street, 6th Floor
Cleveland, OH 44114
Tel 216-426-9990
Fax 216-426-9991
E-mail scott@sarfurniture.com
www.sarfurniture.com

With over 60 years of experience, ours is one of America's premier custom furniture companies featuring hand-carved, custom-crafted pieces created in the European tradition. We think of our studio as making not just custom furniture, but customized furniture: unique furnishings with character, utility and beauty, perfectly marrying function and form, and reflective of your tastes and individual style. From classic motifs and narrative scenes depicting wildlife in landscapes to original designs that speak to individual interests and passions, we carve it beautifully.

PUBLICATIONS: Log Home Design Ideas magazine, February 2004; Log Home Living, May 2004; Western Interiors and Design magazine, November/December 2003

263

NEIL SATER
Page 119

Water Wonders, Inc.
3042 Industrial Parkway
Santa Maria, CA 93455
Tel 805-549-1880
Fax 805-925-3485
E-mail sales@waterwonders.com
www.waterwonders.com

I specialize in engineering the elements of nature to harmonize with the simplicity of motion in water and wind. Each piece is assembled by hand in a variety of natural materials, including copper, slate, glass, mirror, rock, steel and state-of-the-art metals. My graceful sculptures are powered by wind in order to capture the ballet of metal in motion. My work is suitable for indoor and outdoor applications and may accommodate projects of any scale. Ideally utilized as artistic focal points, these pieces are suited for use as room dividers and atrium appointments or to punctuate lobbies, entrances and public spaces.

COMMISSIONS: Sony Pictures Corporate Headquarters; AAA Corporate Headquarters; Holiday Inn Express custom lobby installation; Santa Maria Country Club; assorted restaurant and hotel installations

COLLECTIONS: Various private collections, including Noah Wylie, Catherine Zeta-Jones, Shaquille O'Neal, and Brooks and Dunn

JOY SAVILLE
Page 154

244 Dodds Lane
Princeton, NJ 08540
Tel/Fax 609-924-6824
E-mail jsaville@patmedia.net
www.joysaville.com

Liturgical art should enhance the spirituality of the sanctuary, engage the congregation in the praise of God and contribute to the solemnity and mystery of the worship service. Using the language of color, abstract imagery and natural fabrics, I try to convey the essence and spirit of the liturgical season or the scriptures.

COMMISSIONS: Johnson & Johnson; Ortho Pharmaceutical; The Jewish Center, Princeton, NJ; Nassau Presbyterian Church, Princeton, NJ

COLLECTIONS: Museum of Arts & Design, New York, NY; The Newark Museum; Bristol-Myers Squibb; Time-Warner Inc.; Ropes & Gray, Boston, MA; Wilmington Trust, DE; H.J. Heinz; PepsiCo

EXHIBITIONS: Solo and group exhibitions throughout North America and internationally since 1976

GUILD SOURCEBOOKS: The GUILD 3, 4, 5; Architectural & Interior Art 17, 18; The Artful Home 2

SCHULTE STUDIOS
Page 116

Kai Schulte
41W020 Seavey Road
Sugar Grove, IL 60554-9573
Tel 630-406-0404
Fax 630-406-0505
E-mail kai@schultestudios.com
www.schultestudios.com

I forge dramatic art and unique metalwork from my studio in Sugar Grove, IL. My passion for metalwork developed as an artsmith apprentice in Germany under the guidance of K.T. Neumann. When Neumann retired five years ago, I brought his handmade tools to America. Specializing in diverse metals and subject matter, I use my unique vision to create powerful images designed to move the soul. I also choose materials to match my subject. By blending the traditional techniques of the artsmith with modern tools and materials, I use my work in stainless steel, carbon steel, brass, copper and bronze to create a distinctive aesthetic.

ARTIST STATEMENTS

MARSH SCOTT
Page 123

2795 Laguna Canyon Road #C
Laguna Beach, CA 92651
Tel 949-494-8672
E-mail marsh@marshscott.com
www.marshscott.com

Working in pierced metals allows me to present symbolic or abstract narratives in a sculptural context. My work is often a collaborative expression reflecting geographic and cultural diversity in a site-specific installation. The positive and negative piercing defines the design while creating dynamic shadows. The hand-brushed surface reflects the colors of the surrounding environment.

COMMISSIONS: Various public art commissions in California; Kaiser Permanente, 2003, Palmdale and Pasadena, CA; *Cascade Trilogy*, 2003, Redmond, OR; Hyatt Regency Hotel and Spa, 2003, Huntington Beach, CA; Associated Television, CA; Canal Plus U.S., CA; Discovery Museum, CA; Four Seasons, NV

EXHIBITIONS: Los Angeles County Museum of Art, 2003, CA; *Design for a Living*, Millard Sheets Gallery, a Smithsonian affiliate, Pomona, CA; *Affaire in the Gardens*, Beverly Hills, CA

GUILD SOURCEBOOKS: *Architectural & Interior Art 17, 18*

SUSAN SCULLEY
Page 174, 179

4731 North Paulina #3N
Chicago, IL 60640
Tel 773-728-6109
Fax 773-728-9305
E-mail susan.sculley@scdchicago.com

I work in both oil sticks and chalk pastels to create compositions of color and form, capturing the essence of peace and beauty found in the landscape. I work with interior designers, art consultants and galleries. My work is found in both corporate and private settings, and can be contemporary or traditional in style.

COLLECTIONS: Commonwealth Edison Corporate Headquarters, Chicago, IL; Amoco Corporation, Chicago, IL; Hartford Insurance Company, Chicago, IL; Loyola University Medical Center, Maywood, IL; numerous private collections

PUBLICATIONS: *Chicago Magazine*, May 2004; *Beautiful Things*, 2000; *Metropolitan Home*, November/December 2000

GUILD SOURCEBOOKS: *Designers' 15; Architectural & Interior Art 16, 18; Artful Home 1*

JOHN SEARLES
Page 202

Searles Sculpture
13462 Red Arrow Highway
Harbert, MI 49125
Tel 708-646-4161
E-mail johnsearles@searlesart.com
www.searlesart.com

My wall sculptures reflect my interests in mathematics, energy and freedom. Working with copper, brass, stainless steel or aluminum (sometimes melting one onto the other), I create sculptures that are puzzle pieces. I cut one piece of patinated metal into many pieces, then reassemble them into a more visually stimulating, higher level of order. Some of my sculptures are weavings, but all have some component of an under-over dimensional quality. I call my work "music for the eyes." Price range: $500-$10,000.

EXHIBITIONS: *Music for the Eyes*, 2003, National Wall Art Gallery, Tampa, FL

AWARDS: Best of Sculpture, 2003, Oconomowoc, WI

GUILD SOURCEBOOKS: *Designer's 15; Architectural & Interior Art 18; Artful Home 2*

PAMELA SHAWLEY-WEAVER
Page 136

Expressions in Sculpture
3597 East Valley Road
Loganton, PA 17747
Tel 570-725-2807
Fax 570-725-2211
E-mail pamela@expressions-in-sculpture.com
www.expressions-in-sculpture.com

I love to bring life to each sculpture—capturing that fleeting expression, evoking a tear or a chuckle, creating a sense of happiness and comfort, knowing that the artwork has spoken to the viewer. Whether the artwork is an interior decorative piece sculpted in terra cotta clay or a large garden sculpture cast in bronze, it provides the opportunity to feel, touch and maintain permanent relationships with our most cherished companions and fondest memories. A significant portion of my artwork is created by private commission and is representational in nature, with a strong emphasis on animal life, particularly the canine.

EXHIBITIONS: *Sculpture in the Park*, 2003, Benson Park, Loveland, CO

AWARDS: Dunwiddie Memorial Award for Sculpture, 2003, 2002, Catharine Lorillard Wolfe Art Club, New York, NY

JAMES SIMON
Page 141

James Simon Sculpture Studios
305 Gist Street
Pittsburgh, PA 15219
Tel/Fax 412-434-5629
E-mail mail@simonsculpture.com
www.simonsculpture.com

In the 20 years that I have been sculpting, my purpose has been to create work that is a celebration of people and contemporary life. My unique, figurative style lends itself to a variety of themes: music, dance, sports, literature, science, children, and animals. I collaborate well with developers and architects and can produce work in a broad range of mediums, including clay, bronze, aluminum, concrete, and sculptural relief panels. My work is engaging and accessible to diverse populations and is an innovative and vibrant addition to any project.

COMMISSIONS: *Raspberry Island Bronzes*, Saint Paul, MN; *Liberty Avenue Musicians*, Pittsburgh, PA; *Hillel Academy Bronze*, Fox Chapel, PA; Lee Violins, Chicago, IL; Rose Museum, Sao Paulo, Brazil; Flexible Systems, Eugene, OR

FRED SLAUTTERBACK
Page 215

652 Redwood Avenue
Sand City, CA 93955
Tel 831-394-5170
Fax 831-394-5346
E-mail fred@scfinearts.com
www.scfinearts.com

I am recognized for originating and developing a completely new form of abstract art. Using unique processes and materials, I heat and apply streams of molten plastics to paper or canvas. Watercolors and acrylics are often incorporated within the work. This original form of abstract art is colorful, upbeat and lyrical. The work is frequently assembled into three-dimensional panels and grid arrays. Designs can be scaled to fit small spaces or fill large wall surfaces.

RECENT PROJECTS: 8' x 10' five-panel wall art, Caddell Chapman Law Offices, Houston, TX

COMMISSIONS: Nordson Corporation, Westlake, OH; Stahl Motors, Monterey, CA; Mr. & Mrs. James Didion, Palm Desert, CA

EXHIBITIONS: Carl Cherry Foundation, 2004, Carmel, CA; ArtTech, 2003, Santa Cruz, CA; New York Art Expo, 2001, New York, NY

ARTIST STATEMENTS

JEFF G. SMITH
Pages 150-151

Architectural Stained Glass, Inc.
PO Box 1126
Fort Davis, TX 79734-1126
Tel 432-426-3311
Fax 432-426-3366
E-mail info@archstglassinc.com
www.archstglassinc.com

Unlike the easel painter, I must rediscover my "canvas" at the beginning of every stained glass commission. After first developing empathy for the needs and expectations of the users of a facility, I then closely examine the architectural concept and materials that comprise the building itself. When melded with my design sensibilities, this analysis leads to an innovative and thoughtful contribution to the overall architectural environment and a more fulfilling experience for those who work, worship or visit the site. By not limiting myself exclusively to the two-dimensional picture-plane within a window, my work is better able to explore the ever changing and fully three-dimensional experiences stained glass can produce within its architectural space.

GUILD SOURCEBOOKS: GUILD 4, 5; Architect's 7, 8, 9, 10, 11, 12, 13, 14, 15; Architectural & Interior Art 16, 17, 18

JEFF G. SMITH
Pages 150-151

Architectural Stained Glass, Inc.
PO Box 1126
Fort Davis, TX 79734-1126
Tel 432-426-3311
Fax 432-426-3366
E-mail info@archstglassinc.com
www.archstglassinc.com

Thanks to a wide range of site-specific installations during the past 26 years, I have developed strategies that anticipate and accommodate concerns about the fragility and maintenance of stained glass art. These strategies involve isolating stained glass from exposure using protective tempered glass on one or both sides. This protects the artwork and renders it as maintenance-free as conventional window glazing while exceeding UBC requirements. A carefully detailed *Maintenance & Conservation Manual* is prepared for each project.

RECENT PROJECTS: San Antonio International Airport Terminals, TX; Oncology Center, St. Vincent Hospital, Indianapolis, IN; St. Matthew Catholic Church, Windham, NH; Quentin N. Burdick Federal Courthouse, Fargo, ND; American Airlines Admirals Club, Dallas Fort Worth, TX; University of Alaska, Fairbanks, AK; Washington Hebrew Congregation, Washington, DC; Salt Lake Community College Library, UT

DENISE M. SNYDER
Page 220

3017 Alderwood Avenue
Bellingham, WA 98225
Tel/Fax 360-647-1152
E-mail dsnyder@artscan.com
www.artscan.com/dsnyder/

My work hints at the random chaos of nature and its patterns via vivid presentation and clean lines. The materials that I use are wood, metal, fiberous grasses and glass. I incorporate the concepts of light and dark to add depth and sophistication. Fields of tousled grasses in the fall or the rich silhouette of trees in the winter are aspects of nature captured in my sculptures.

COMMISSIONS: Wild Buffalo Blues Club, 1999, Bellingham, WA; Bellagio Casino, 1998, Las Vegas, NV

EXHIBITIONS: Teck Gallery, 2002, Vancouver, BC; International Fiber Art Symposium, 2001, Central Museum of Textiles, Lodz, Poland; Luther College Gallery, 2001, Decorah, IA; Miniartextil Como, 2000, Como, Italy

PUBLICATIONS: *Adobe*, Santa Fe, 2001-2002; *American Craft Magazine*, February 2002, August 2000; *FiberArts* magazine, September 1999

GUILD SOURCEBOOKS: *Designer's 12, 14*

265

JOSEPH SPANGLER
Page 176

Citybloques
2141 South Fairfield Avenue
Chicago, IL 60608
Tel 773-991-4537
joe@citybloques.com
www.citybloques.com

I create painted cityscapes that infuse highway overpasses, late-night CTA trains and platforms, well-used neighborhood intersections and urban municipal spaces with my own sense of their importance in our daily rituals. Rich colors, moody and delicate lighting, thoughtful solitary figures, heroic compositions of public interiors and exteriors on large canvases—all of these privilege the in-between moments of urban living when many of us retreat from our visual surroundings to our inner worlds. These renderings of such spaces frame this mental retreat to give these spaces a contemplative ethos.

COMMISSIONS: *Furtherance*, 2004, Stephen Huntley; *Fairy Tales*, 2002, Art Institute of Chicago; *Near West Triptych*, 2002, Phil & Lou's, Chicago, IL; *Canalport & Union*, 2001, Apple Naughton; *Van Gogh's Yellow House*, 2001, Art Institute of Chicago

CYNTHIA SPARRENBERGER
Page 132

Sparrenberger Studio
5975 East Otero Drive
Englewood, CO 80112
Tel 303-741-3031 (studio)
Tel 303-618-8974 (cell)
E-mail cynthia6@mac.com
www.sparrenbergerstudio.com

My work is figurative, with a loose, impressionistic quality. Because of my dance background, I am passionate about gesture, line and movement, for it is these very elements that bring a sculpture to life.

RECENT PROJECTS: Life-size sculpture for Mynelle Gardens, Jackson, MS

COMMISSIONS: Private portrait, 2003; canine portrait, 2002, Sedalia, CO; private portrait, 2000, Parker, CO

COLLECTIONS: Mynelle Gardens, Jackson, MS; The Washington Ballet, Washington, DC

EXHIBITIONS: Loveland Invitational, 2003, 2002; *Renaissance Sale*, 2001, Houston, TX; *American Art Classic*, 2001, Houston, TX; *Sculpture in the Park*, 2000, Loveland, CO

PUBLICATIONS: *Artists of Distinction*, 2003; *The Hilton Head Monthly*, 2001; *The Clarion Ledger*, 2001

JOHN SPEARS
Pages 186-187

2D-3D Inc.
441 Barbertown-Point Breeze Road
Flemington, NJ 08822
Tel 908-996-6086
Fax 908-996-7401
E-mail spears@blast.net
www.2D-3Dinc.com

I have been doing commissioned artwork for over 30 years, during which time I have elevated the silkscreen medium into a painting methodology. My artwork varies greatly in size and my subject matter includes everything from geometric patterns to cityscapes. My color palette ranges from subtle to vibrant, depending on the location and needs of the client. The paints I use are UV corrected so they will not fade. I welcome all inquiries and will provide estimates for both small and large projects.

RECENT PROJECTS: Astrazeneca, DE; Neustar Headquarters, VA; Fleet Bank, NJ; Nabisco Headquarters, NJ; Podolsky Northstar Realty Partners, IL; Merck Pharmaceutical, NJ; US Health Care, PA

COMMISSIONS: Citicorp, NY; Bally's Park Place, NJ; NationsBank, FL; Ortho Pharmaceutical, NJ; Johnson & Johnson, NJ; Price Waterhouse, CA; Texas Eye Institute, TX; Roche Biotech Center, NJ; Wyeth Labs, NJ; Post Perfect, NY; Bunzyl Corp, NJ

ARTIST STATEMENTS

SPOLAR STUDIO
Pages 17, 62, 167

Tony Spolar
126 East Mineral Street
Milwaukee, WI 53204
Tel 414-672-9847
Fax 414-831-2493
E-mail tony@spolarstudio.com
www.spolarstudio.com

Creating interiors that dazzle the eye and speak to the soul: this is what Spolar is all about. We bring a myriad of techniques to the task, including traditional and innovative design, fine art mural canvases, sculpted murals, hand-painted wallpaper, trompe l'oeil, faux and decorative finishes, Mac-driven computer-generated imagery, large-format museum-quality printing, reference library and three-dimensional/fabricating facilities. But more importantly we bring imagination and great passion. That, together with commitment to completing projects on time and on budget, has allowed us to thrive in the Milwaukee and Chicago areas since 1988. Thanks to 25-foot high ceilings and a modular design, our fully equipped 10,000 square-foot studio can be configured to meet the specific needs of any client, anytime, anywhere.

ARTHUR STERN
Page 23

Arthur Stern Studios
1075 Jackson Street
Benicia, CA 94510
Tel/Fax 707-745-8480
E-mail arthur@arthurstern.com
www.arthurstern.com

I create site-specific architectural glass installations, primarily in leaded glass, as well as other art glass techniques. Specializing in the collaboration with design professionals and clients, my studio currently has installations in 36 states, as well as Japan. Commissions range from residential work to large public art projects and churches. I have been widely published and have won numerous awards, including several American Institute of Architects design awards, as well as honors from the Interfaith Forum on Religion, Art & Architecture, The Construction Specifications Institute and *Ministry and Liturgy* magazine's BENE Awards. Each project receives the same thorough attention to detail and fine craftsmanship. I also work in other media, including wood and glass bas-relief sculpture, mixed-media works on canvas and works on paper.

STUART REID ARCHITECTURAL GLASS
Page 39

Stuart Reid
364 Annette Street
Toronto, ON M6P 1R5
Canada
Tel 416-762-7743
Fax 416-762-8875
E-mail stuartreid@sympatico.ca
www.stuartreid.net

I like works of art that engage you immediately but only reveal their richness to you slowly. Each work is designed to fit its specific environment and, like a fire in a hearth, can be a passive backdrop or can reward contemplation.

COMMISSIONS: Intercontinental Toronto Centre, Toronto, Canada, 2003; Salzburg Congress, Salzburg, Austria, 2001; Living Arts Centre Mississauga, Canada, 1998; St. James Cathedral, Toronto, Canada, 1997

EXHIBITIONS: Latitude 44, Toronto, Canada, 2003; Antiquo Monasterio de S. Maria, Valldigna, Spain, 2003; Augsburg Cathedral, Augsburg, Germany, 2001; Canadian Clay & Glass Gallery, Waterloo, 1999; Centre International du Vitrail, Chartres, France, 1997

PUBLICATIONS: *El Arte de las Vidrieras: Luz, Color, Espacio,* 2003; *Toronto Star,* 2003; OCAD Canvas, 2003; *Frankfurter Allgemeine,* 2001

MARTIN STURMAN
Page 200

Martin Sturman Sculptures
3201 Bayshore Drive
Westlake Village, CA 91361
Tel 818-707-8087
Fax 818-707-3079
E-mail mlsturman@sbcglobal.net
www.steelsculptures.com

I create original contemporary sculptures and furniture in carbon steel or stainless steel. My work is suitable for indoor or outdoor placement. Stainless steel surfaces are burnished to achieve a beautiful shimmering effect. Carbon steel sculptures are painted with acrylic and coated with polyurethane to preserve color vitality. I encourage site-specific and collaborative efforts.

COMMISSIONS: Hyatt Westlake Plaza Hotel, Westlake Village, CA; Tesoro Galleries, Beverly Hills, CA; Manhattan Beach Car Wash, Manhattan Beach, CA; McGraw-Hill Publishing Company, Columbus, OH

COLLECTIONS: McDonald's Corporate Art Collection, Oakbrook, IL

GUILD SOURCEBOOKS: *Architect's 12, 14; Designer's 7, 8, 9, 10, 11, 12, 13, 14, 15; Architectural & Interior Art 16, 17, 18; Artful Home 2*

ROBERT SUNDAY
Page 51

240 Lovesee Road
Roscoe, IL 61073
Tel 815-623-7487
E-mail robertsunday@aol.com

I have been a ceramic artist since 1973, professionally since 1980. My raku-firing techniques result in works of brilliant jewel-toned colors. I am best known for my geometric, art deco and prairie-style designs, which balance sharply with the free-form earth-and-fire nature of raku. I have installed site-specific wall murals ranging in size from 3 feet to 30 feet. I am also internationally recognized for my wheel-thrown vessels. I am able to create vessels as large as three feet in height with fluid shapes, as well as cutwork, inlay and double-wall features.

COLLECTIONS: Swedish-American Medical Center Executive Boardroom, Rockford, IL; The Burroughs Corporation, Chicago, IL and New York City; State of Hawaii Governor's Collection, Honolulu, HI

PROJECTS: Raku Ho'Olaulea, slide lecture, wet clay workshop and firing demonstration, 1996, HI

PUBLICATIONS: Feature artist, *Ceramics Monthly* magazine, 1994

TORK DESIGN GROUP
Page 131

Mark Lagergren
Anthony Ball
2505 Fairwood Avenue
Columbus, OH 43207
Tel 614-492-1810
Fax 614-492-1575
E-mail torkinfo@iwaynet.net
www.torkworks.com

Tork Design Group, based in Columbus, Ohio, is a team of experienced and versatile trained artists headed by Mark Lagergren and Anthony Ball. We create unique sculptural installations and functional works for commercial and individual clients. Adept at working on both large-scale public installations (both interior and exterior) and small detailed objects, Tork collaborates with architects and art consultants to meet site-specific goals. We specialize in metal and resin design, fabrication, sculpting and casting in unique combinations of materials.

COMMISSIONS: Columbus Conservatory, Columbus, OH; *Sisters Garden,* Columbus Metro Parks/Inniswood, Westerville, OH; COSI Space Exhibit, Columbus, OH; Stride Rite Corporation, nationwide; Cameron Mitchell Restaurants, nationwide; Darden Restaurants/Red Lobster, nationwide; Bethesda Hospital, Cincinnati, OH

ARTIST STATEMENTS

LUIS TORRUELLA
Page 81

Tenerife Building, Apartment 1201
1507 Ashford Avenue
San Juan, PR 00911
Tel/Fax 787-722-8728
Tel 787-268-4977
E-mail luistorruella@aol.com
www.luistorruella.com

I design in a contemporary, abstract context. My Caribbean heritage is reflected in my work's color, rhythm and movement. I collaborate with architects, designers and developers in public and private commissions.

COLLECTIONS: Museo de Arte de Puerto Rico, San Juan; Mead Art Museum, Amherst, MA; Performing Arts Center, San Juan, PR; Skokie Sculpture Park, IL

EXHIBITIONS: Palma de Mallorca, 2001, Spain; Galeria Botello, 2002, 1997, 1994, 1992, San Juan, PR; Theatrical Institute, 1992, Moscow; World Expo, 1992, Seville, Spain; numerous private collections

GUILD SOURCEBOOKS: *Architect's 14, 15; Architectural & Interior Art 16, 17, 18; Artful Home 1*

TRIO DESIGN GLASSWARE
Page 163

Renato Foti
253 Queen Street South
Kitchener, ON N2G 1W4
Canada
Tel 519-749-2814
Fax 519-749-6319
E-mail renato@triodesignglassware.com
www.triodesignglassware.com

Contemporary design and bold colors exemplify the styles of my works in fused and slumped glass. The main focus of these works is to add structure, balance, color and simplicity to the home and working environments. Balance is of critical importance to the designed pieces; It is a reflection of my personal philosophy in life.

EXHIBITIONS: *Material Matters,* 2003, Toronto, ON

AWARDS: NICHE award, 2004

GUILD SOURCEBOOKS: *Architectural & Interior Art 17, 18; Artful Home 1*

KAREN URBANEK
Pages 222, 224

314 Blair Avenue
Piedmont, CA 94611-4004
Tel 510-654-0685
Fax 510-654-2790
E-mail krnurbanek@aol.com

I build painterly images and sculptural forms—both abstract and representational—in luminous layers of complex color and texture. My extensive palette comes from natural sources and working methodologies that adhere to principles of environmental responsibility. Constructed primarily of compacted tussah silk fiber, I apply a penetrating coating that adds crispness and strength. Surfaces range from smooth and translucent to dense, high relief. Works may be double-sided and hang freely or may be composed of separate layers and elements. Light in weight and easy to ship, mount, maintain and clean. Framing is optional. Commissions are accepted. Visuals and pricing are available upon request.

COLLECTIONS: Lockheed Martin Corporation; Aspect Communications; Kaiser Hospital; McGraw Hill Publishing Co.; Grace Cathedral, San Francisco

GUILD SOURCEBOOKS: *Designer's 13, 14, 15; Architectural & Interior Art 16, 17, 18*

SUSAN VENABLE
Pages 7, 211

Venable Studio
2323 Foothill Lane
Santa Barbara, CA 93105
Tel 805-884-4963
Fax 805-884-4983
E-mail susan@venablestudio.com
www.venablestudio.com

My work is an exploration of structure and surface and the relationship between the two. The constructions are bas-reliefs of stacked steel grids woven with copper wire juxtaposed with encaustic paintings. I want to maximize the physicality of the materials, seeking a presence and energy field through the structure and the surface. My exploration is on a perceptual and tactile level to elicit an abstract response. I want to create a transcendent reality, not recall a specific place or object. My work has been installed in public spaces, homes and museums. The commissions have involved collaboration with collectors, architects, and designers and have included installations throughout the world. The materials are durable, low maintenance and suitable for installation in public areas.

ROBERT VOGLAND
Page 57

Vogland.com
PO Box 6288
Kaneohe, HI 96744
Tel 808-262-8479
E-mail voglandr001@hawaii.rr.com
www.vogland.com

I try to bring life to my ceramic tile murals by giving each image a three-dimensional sculptural look. My work can be installed anywhere ceramic tile is suitable. In swimming pools my work creates a new dimensional element that is very entertaining to the eye.

COLLECTIONS: My works are included in over a thousand private collections in Hawaii, Florida, Virginia, Texas, California, Washington, Illinois, Indiana, Arizona, Hungary and French Polynesia

PUBLICATIONS: "Modern Masters," HGTV, 2002

LOIS WALKER
Page 182

149 Harbor South
Amityville, NY 11701
Tel 631-691-2376
Fax 631-691-1920
E-mail loiswalker@aol.com
www.artfulstyle.com/walker

My work is always an exploration of the visual seeking to communicate the inexplicable. I work in many mediums, creating two- and three-dimensional pieces with prices from $400 to $6,000 utilizing oils, acrylics, found objects, cloth, hardware, antiques and words. I try to allow each material its own unique voice. My art is never passive.

EXHIBITIONS: *Revelations,* 2002, Port Washington Library Gallery, Port Washington, NY; *Adam and Eve,* 2002, South Huntington Library Gallery, South Huntington, NY; *Inner Exiles: Shadow Poets, Paintings and Poetry,* 2000, Sylvia White Gallery, Santa Monica, CA

AWARDS: Third award, 1998, Palm Springs Desert Museum; Award of Excellence, 1995, Tri-county Art League of Long Island; Award of Excellence, 1994, Heckscher Museum

PUBLICATIONS: *Northport Journal,* March 2002; *Xanadu 20,* 1998; *Xanadu 21/22,* 2000; *Artspeak,* November 1997

ARTIST STATEMENTS

SCOTT WALLACE
Page 97

PO Box 8
Hendricks, MN 56136
Tel 507-275-3300
Fax 507-275-3304
E-mail swallace@itctel.com
www.wallacesculpture.com

Past public art projects include large-scale free-standing sculptures, hanging sculptures and wall reliefs produced in bronze, stainless steel and painted aluminum. Given the sometimes whimsical and optimistic nature of my work, I am especially interested in developing artwork for spaces where the public will welcome interaction with forms that evoke positive emotions. I recognize the special concerns involved with integrating durable artwork into public spaces and am open to working with architects, landscape designers and interior designers.

COMMISSIONS: City of Minneapolis, MN; Center for the Arts, Whitewater, WI; University of Central Florida, Orlando, FL; Arizona Cancer Center, Tucson, AZ; Bay Colony Technology Center, Tucson, AZ; McCormick Place Convention Center, Chicago, IL; Student Recreation Center at the University of Arizona, Tucson, AZ

MYRON WASSERMAN
Pages 66, 68

Wasserman Studios
1817 North Fifth Street
Philadelphia, PA 19122
Tel 215-739-5558
Fax 215-739-5448
E-mail myronwasserman@earthlink.net
www.wassermanstudios.com

My work focuses on harmony and balance. We work with a myriad of metals and an array of natural and chemical patinas, which are suitable for both interior and exterior applications. Kinetic mobiles and stabiles comprise most of our work. For more than 30 years, I've enjoyed collaborating with clients and design professionals, primarily for site-specific commissions, working together to establish a specific design direction. Once this direction is determined, I begin final designs and specifications for approval. Then we begin fabricating finished elements. I invite clients to the studio to inspect all elements before assembly. Then preparations for installation begin; cleaning, wrapping, crating, shipping, etc. We create wall sculptures, panels, hardware, design elements, lighting, accessories and other artworks requested. Call me for a quote. Complete listings of clients, exhibits, awards and honors, along with additional images and information, are available upon request.

BARBARA WEBSTER
Pages 208, 210

Starforest Quilts
1610 Lickskillet Road
Burnsville, NC 28714
Tel 828-682-7331
Fax 828-682-7987
E-mail barbara@starforestquilts.com
www.starforestquilts.com

My dramatic quilts spring from my digital photographs of my farm, the Blue Ridge Mountains, or my client's favorite scenes. My exclusive custom-printed fabrics are rich in color and detail. Commissions welcomed.

COMMISSIONS: Holy Cross Hospital, Silver Spring, MD; Mountain Air Country Club, Burnsville, NC; Biltmore Swim Club, Asheville, NC

EXHIBITIONS: *Art Quilts at the Sedgwick*, 2004, Philadelphia, PA; NC Crafts Gallery, 2004, Carrboro, NC; New Morning Gallery, 2003, Asheville, NC; Blue Spiral Gallery, 2003, Asheville, NC; U.S. Embassy, 2003, Guatemala; Mint Museum of Craft and Design, 2002

AWARDS: First place group, American Quilters Society Show, Paducah, KY; first place, Cleveland Metroparks Quilt Show, Cleveland, OH; first place, Burnsville Quilt Show, Burnsville, NC

PUBLICATIONS: *American Quilter, FiberArts Magazine, Bobbin, LDB Interior Textiles, Quilts Japan*

STEWART WHITE
Page 166

Stewart White Studios
1121 Tyler Avenue
Annapolis, MD 21403
Tel 410-263-7465
E-mail stewhite30@earthlink.net
www.stewartwhitestudios.com

My paintings are done in acrylic and/or oil, sometimes at actual size but more recently at 20% actual size and then digitally enlarged and printed on wall covering or canvas. My commercial work is well researched and is often a collaboration with committee members. I pride myself on my ability to translate and express my clients' intentions in a fresh and creative way. Prices start at $3,000.

RECENT PROJECTS: The National Museum of American History, Washington, DC; City of Annapolis, MD; City of Baltimore, MD

COMMISSIONS: Massage Associates Building, 2001, Warrenton, VA; Marriott Inner Harbor, Baltimore, MD

COLLECTIONS: murals in countless homes, hotels and restaurants nationwide

PUBLICATIONS: *Baltimore City Paper*, 1996; *Architectural Rendering*, 1991

GUILD SOURCEBOOKS: *Artful Home 2*

ANDREA WILKINSON
Page 137

3502 Shady Village
Kingwood, TX 77345
Tel 281-358-4094
Fax 281-359-0033
E-mail aclayworks@yahoo.com

A lifelong love of animals inspires me to capture their forms and spirits in clay for bronze casting. My goal is to reach beyond a mere physical representation and catch the light in their eyes. As I work I am guided by my awe and respect for each species' unique and integral place in the diversity and balance of life on our planet.

COMMISSIONS: Numerous private commissions; Houston Zoological Gardens, 2000

EXHIBITIONS: *Art Show at the Dog Show*, 2004, 2000, Wichita, KS; *Sculpture in the South*, 2003, 2002, Summerville, SC; Loveland Invitational, 2003, 2002; Archway Gallery, 2002, 2000, Houston, TX

AWARDS: Gilroy Roberts Scholarship Award, 2000, 1999, American Numismatic Association; special exhibit, 2000, AKC Museum of the Dog; First Place and People's Choice Award, 1999, Kingwood Art Society; First Place, 1999, Lone Star Art Guild

BRUCE WOLFE
Pages 124, 126-127

Bruce Wolfe Ltd.
206 El Cerrito Avenue
Piedmont, CA 94611
Tel 510-655-7871
Fax 510-601-7200
www.brucewolfe.com

Most of the subjects of my portraits are imposing, dynamic personalities. I hope to portray that energy and presence, putting my ego aside to make a likeness that reflects the spirit of the subject—not just a mask and body. Projects include a monumental bronze of Barbara Jordan at the Austin-Bergstrom Airport, TX. I was selected to complete this portrait after a comprehensive artist selection process. I installed two large bronze figures at the Old Mission in Santa Barbara, CA, and unveiled two additional figures there, *Christ* and *Mary Magdalene*, on Easter day 2003. I also created a bronze bust of Chong-Moon Lee, a major donor to the New Asian Art Museum in San Francisco, CA.

268

ARTIST STATEMENTS

ANDREW CARY YOUNG
Page 32

Pearl River Glass Studio, Inc.
142 Millsaps Avenue
Jackson, MS 39202
Tel 601-353-2497
Fax 601-969-9315
E-mail prgs@netdoor.com
www.prgs.com

Pearl River Glass Studio is committed to pursuing the craft of stained glass as an art form. We work in a broad range of styles and employ a wide variety of methods. Central to our mission is the principle of applying creative solutions to complex problems where thoroughness and quality count.

RECENT PROJECTS: Lobby window, St. Dominic's Hospital, Jackson, MS; church windows, Christ United Methodist Church, Jackson, MS

EXHIBITIONS: *Made in USA: Contemporary Crafts*, 2003, Peoria Art Guild

AWARDS: Governor's Award for Excellence in the arts, 2002, MS

PUBLICATIONS: *The Stained Glass Association of America Sourcebook 1998, 1999, 2000, 2001, 2002, 2003, 2004; Stained Glass Quaterly*, winter 2002

GUILD SOURCEBOOKS: *Designer's 15; Architectural & Interior Art 16, 17, 18*

LARRY ZGODA
Pages 25, 230, 238

Larry Zgoda Studio
2117 West Irving Park Road
Chicago, IL 60618
Tel 773-463-3970
lz@larryzgodastudio.com
www.larryzgodastudio.com

Having come into stained glass and the architectural crafts in the 1970s, much of my work has paralleled the renaissance in ornamental architecture. Original design, meticulous craftsmanship and innovation in material and architectural application have been my hallmarks. Often the works reference the past or period architecture, but never anything like what may have once been made. Today I work in various media in the assembly and ornamentation of an environment. These include glass, metals, wood and mosaic. I'm especially interested in how a work of ornament beneficially changes the nature of an environment.

GUILD SOURCEBOOKS: *THE GUILD 1, 2, 3, 4, 5; Architect's 6, 7, 8, 9, 10, 11, 12, 13, 14, 15; Architectural & Interior Art 17, 18; Artful Home 1, 2*

RAY ZOVAR
Page 217

Silk Purse Enterprises, Inc.
2499 Keenan Road
McFarland, WI 53558
Tel 608-345-2991
Fax 608-838-6617
E-mail ray@zovar.com
www.zovar.com

My current work in mosaics is an exciting and relatively new medium for me. Previously, the majority of my work was acrylic and oil painting, resulting in wall art with strong three-dimensional sculpture and elements. I think this background is obvious in my mosaics, which are made largely of porcelain (on which I blend color) with the addition of granite, slate and marble. Added glass, metal and wood give the pieces life, depth and tactile interest. Some of my work is luminous and/or kinetic, but all of it demands to be touched. Commission inquiries for both abstract and representational pieces are welcome.

EXHIBITIONS: *Art Fair on the Square*, 2003, Madison, WI

GUILD SOURCEBOOKS: *Architectural & Interior Art 18*

Location Index

LOCATION INDEX

LOCATION INDEX

273

Index of Artists & Companies

INDEX OF ARTISTS & COMPANIES

INDEX OF ARTISTS & COMPANIES

INDEX OF ARTISTS & COMPANIES

278

Celebrating Our 20th Anniversary

For 20 years, GUILD Sourcebooks have connected artists to their best markets, generated significant commissions, helped launch careers and build national reputations.

Each volume in the Sourcebook collection showcases an exhilarating compilation of commissioned projects by some of the finest artists at work today, and our 20th Anniversary Edition will be no exception.

Publication date: August 2005

Sourcebook 20 will feature:

- Artwork from hundreds of GUILD Sourcebook artists past and present

- Interviews with architects, designers and art consultants

- Favorite projects resulting from GUILD Sourcebooks

- In-depth artist profiles

- Tips for commissioning artwork

We have exciting plans for 2005!

Contact us today to learn how you can participate in this very special edition of *The Sourcebook of Architectural & Interior Art.*

toll free: 800-930-1856 ■ e-mail: sourcebookinfo@guild.com